The Secret Teachings of the Tao Te Ching

The Secret Teachings of the Tao Te Ching

Mantak Chia and Tao Huang

Destiny Books
Rochester, Vermont

Destiny Books
One Park Street
Rochester, Vermont 05767
www.InnerTraditions.com

Destiny Books is a division of Inner Traditions International

Originally published in Thailand in 2002 by Universal Tao Publications under the title *Door to All Wonders*

Library of Congress Cataloging-in-Publication Data

Chia, Mantak, 1944-
The secret teachings of the Tao te ching : Mantak Chia and Tao Huang.
p. cm.
Includes bibliographical references and index.
ISBN 978-0-89281-191-5
1. Laozi. Dao de jing. 2. Laozi. 3. Taoism. I. Huang, Tao. II. Title.
BL1900.L35C556 2005
299.5'1482—dc22

2004023388

Printed and bound in the United States

10

Text design and layout by Jonathan Edward Desautels
This book was typeset in Jansen Text, with Present as the display typeface

Contents

Acknowledgments

The Universal Tao Publications staff involved in the preparation and production of *The Secrets of the Tao Te Ching* extends our gratitude to the many generations of Taoist masters who have passed on their special lineage, in the form of an unbroken oral transmission, over thousands of years. We wish to thank the thousands of unknown men and women of the Chinese healing arts who developed many of the methods and ideas presented in this book.

We thank Taoist master I Yun (Yi Eng) for his openness in transmitting the formulas of Taoist inner alchemy. We offer our gratitude to master Lao Kang Wen for sharing his healing techniques.

We offer our eternal gratitude and love to our parents and teachers for their many gifts to us. Remembering them brings joy and satisfaction to our continued efforts in presenting the Universal Tao System. Their contribution has been crucial in presenting the concepts and techniques of the Universal Tao.

We wish to thank Susan Bridle and Vickie Trihy for editing the new edition of this book, and the following people who worked on the first edition: Dennis Huntington for his editorial work and writing contributions; Colin Campbell and senior instructors Rene J. Narvarro and Annette Derksen for their insightful contributions; and Marion Knabe for her editorial assistance with early drafts of the book.

Thanks to Juan Li for the use of his beautiful and visionary paintings, illustrating Taoist esoteric practices. Special thanks also to Raruen Kaewapadung, computer graphics; Saysunee Yongyod, photographer; and Udon Jandee, illustrator.

Putting the Teachings into Practice

Chinese medicine and Chi Kung emphasize balancing and strengthening the body so that it can heal itself. The meditations, internal exercises, and martial arts of the Universal Tao are basic approaches to this end. This book contains descriptions of physical and spiritual practices that have been used successfully for thousands of years by Taoists trained by personal instruction. Readers should not undertake these practices without receiving personal instruction from a certified instructor of the Universal Tao because some of these practices, if done improperly, may cause injury or result in health problems. This book is intended to supplement individual training with a Universal Tao instructor. Anyone who undertakes these practices on the basis of this book alone does so entirely at his or her own risk. Follow the instructions for each exercise carefully. The Universal Tao and its staff and instructors cannot be responsible for the consequences of any practice or misuse of the information in this book.

Introduction: Conveying the Heart of Lao Tzu's Teaching

Based on the ancient Chinese sage Lao Tzu's Tao Te Ching, *The Secret Teachings of the Tao Te Ching* is the result of collaboration between contemporary Taoist masters Mantak Chia and Tao Huang. The authors bring their deep knowledge and experience of Taoist philosophy and practice to this mystical scripture and illuminate its meaning for Western readers.

Tao Huang, with assistance from Edward Brennan, offers a new translation of the Tao Te Ching, and Mantak Chia and Tao Huang together offer penetrating discussion and meditation on the text. *The Secret Teachings of the Tao Te Ching* also provides a number of practices and meditations to enable the reader to vitalize the body and mind and open oneself further to the inner meaning of Taoist teachings. The authors at times bolster traditional Taoist perspectives with corroborating contemporary scientific knowledge. They also periodically draw on the wisdom of the ancient Chinese *I Ching*, or *Book of Changes*. Above all, they seek to bring the inner essence of the Tao Te Ching to life through transmitting the heart of Lao Tzu's teaching.

LAO TZU AND THE TAO TE CHING

For over 2,500 years, the five thousand pictographs of the Tao Te Ching have been regarded as among the greatest treasures in the world. The scripture is the basis of Laoism (the Chinese philosophy expressed in the writings attributed to Lao Tzu) and Taoism (the religious tradition based on this philosophy that has developed over the centuries).

The Tao Te Ching, roughly meaning "Classic of the Way and Virtue," is popularly attributed to Lao Tzu, who, according to tradition, was an older contemporary of Confucius born in the sixth century B.C.E. Lao Tzu was born Li Er. His legendary name, Lao Tzu—meaning the "old philosopher" or the "ancient child"—rose from his mother's lips as she delivered him under a plum tree. His white hair gave him the countenance of an aged man, which elicited his mother's cry of joy upon seeing him emerge into this world.

During his lifetime Lao Tzu worked in the capital as an archivist in the Imperial Library of the Zhou Dynasty court. This enabled him to reconstruct the spiritual paths of many enlightened sages and holy men who came before his time. After having meditated for three years in a cave in northwest China (now known as Lao Tzu's Cave), he achieved his enlightenment.

According to legend, Confucius met Lao Tzu in Zhou, where Confucius was going to study the library scrolls. Confucius, over the following months, discussed ritual and propriety, the central tenets of Confucianism, with Lao Tzu. Lao Tzu criticized what he felt to be hollow practices. Taoist legend holds that these discussions proved far more fruitful for Confucius than all of his academic studies.

Lao Tzu eventually resigned from his post at the Imperial Library and retired to the mythical K'un-lun mountains. He transmitted his teachings to a border guard who convinced him to write down his wisdom before disappearing from society. The result was the Tao Te Ching.

This short and poetic work is one of the most influential of all Chinese philosophic and religious texts. Its influence has also spread widely outside the Far East and is probably the most translated Chinese book. The Tao Te Ching is divided into two parts, the *Tao Ching* and the *Te Ching*, and into eighty-one chapters. Each chapter is succinct, using few characters to poetically express subtle ideas. Many chapters lend themselves to multiple levels of interpretation, from guidance on political leadership to instruction on higher spiritual development.

ESSENCE ILLUMINATED

Tao Huang, during a powerful spiritual experience that took place on the winter solstice in 1988, experienced a direct mind-to-mind transmission from the old master Lao Tzu himself. Tao Huang explains, "He came to me through meditation. It was the beginning of the heart-sealed teaching of my life, or direct spiritual initiation."

In *The Secret Teachings of the Tao Te Ching*, Tao Huang and Mantak Chia shed light on the essence of the Tao Te Ching through their in-depth and personal knowledge of Taoist philosophy and practice. It is the first book to integrate meditation, interpretation, and illustration in its illumination of the text. "The essence of this project is more experiential than conceptual in nature," explains Tao Huang, "even though it is laced with all sorts of Taoist concepts. Taoism is all about experience."

The Secret Teachings of the Tao Te Ching particularly deals with the nature, meaning, and practical ramifications of Tao and Te, two principles of utmost importance in Taoism. The word *Tao* does not have an English equivalent; it can be translated as God, creation, nature, universal essence and its manifestation, or the Way of all life. *Te* is similarly difficult to translate; it refers to action, virtue, morality, beauty, and gracious behavior. *The Secret Teachings of the Tao Te Ching* examines the text of the Tao Te Ching in a different sequence than is typical. The authors discuss the text in an organic, flowing manner that presents the true meaning of the integration of heavenly power and human power in the mystic field within us.

This book is neither a strict translation of nor a commentary on the Tao Te Ching. While the teachings of Lao Tzu have been passed down for many centuries in literary form, their inner essence has to be transmitted through faithful devotion and practice, and illuminated through heart awakening. Faith opens the door to the wisdom mind, allowing the power of the teaching to be illuminated within the golden chamber of the heart.

The authors, as ethnic Chinese, have witnessed how the real meaning of the original text of the Tao Te Ching has become altered through personal, cultural, or literary filters. As Taoist masters destined to present the teachings of the Tao in the West, Mantak Chia and Tao Huang have the rare ability to transmit the true meaning of the Tao Te Ching to their Western students and readers.

Whatever the inherent limitations of words, they nonetheless can serve to convey the insights of enlightened life experience—just like our physical bodies are vessels that can glorify God through their destined journeys. To this end, the authors have digested all the words of Lao Tzu's teaching, knowing how they should be registered in the mind and echoed in the heart. Lao Tzu's teaching opens the heart and charges the will. Its universal power transcends cultural distinctions.

A FRESH TRANSLATION

The Tao Te Ching was written in classical Chinese, which is difficult even for modern native speakers of Chinese to understand completely. Additionally, many of the terms used in the Tao Te Ching are deliberately ambiguous, and numerous important Chinese words and concepts have no equivalents in English. These factors have contributed to editors' and translators' enormous difficulty in preserving and conveying the original meaning of the text.

As noted above, *The Secret Teachings of the Tao Te Ching* relies on a new translation by Tao Huang and Edward Brennan. The translators have sought to bring the essence of Lao Tzu's text to life, with immediacy and authenticity, for contemporary English readers. The entirety of the new translation is presented at the end of the book, and throughout the chapters that follow, sections of the verse of the Tao Te Ching are presented in italic type. Chapter and verse numbers appear in abbreviated form. For example, chapter 3, verses 2–5 would be designated as (3:2–5).

James Legge, in his translator's preface to his 1882 translation of *I Ching, Book of Changes,* elucidates a special challenge of translating Chinese: "The written characters of the Chinese are not representations of words, but symbols of ideas, and the combination of them in a composition is not a representation of what the writer would say, but what he thinks." The characters of the Chinese language are pictographs or ideographs; they are graphical representations of abstract ideas. Legge explains that when the symbolic characters have brought the translator's mind "en rapport" with that of the author, the translator is free to render the ideas in another form of speech, in the best manner that he or she is able. "In the study of a Chinese classical book," he writes, "there is not so much an interpretation of the characters employed by the writer as a participation in his thoughts—there is the seeing of mind to mind." This seeing of mind to mind is the key to the power of the fresh translation presented here.

Further, the new translation avoids the distortions that have accrued over the centuries to the "standard version" established by Wang Bi in the third century C.E. The new translation relies directly on the Mawangdui manuscript, unearthed by Chinese archeologists in 1973. Tao Huang has great confidence in the originality and simplicity of the Mawangdui manuscript, and used the "standard version" only to fill in the blanks in cases where there are words or phrases missing in the Mawangdui text.

Throughout its history, the Tao Te Ching has been altered through a myriad of translations and commentaries. This process of translation, interpretation, and speculation has often defeated the illumination and application of wisdom and mystical truth offered by the text. Yet, regardless of how philosophers rationalize, leaders manipulate, military strategists deploy, scholars garble, meditators chant, and religious people worship, the essence of the text remains untouched and unscathed by time.

When comparing the Mawangdui text with other sources, Tao Huang found numerous problems. Throughout the centuries, the philosophical Laoists have tended to standardize the text as their own philosophy and dismiss its practical application, central to its essential meaning. Some, who have been influenced by Buddhism, have dismissed the Tao Te Ching as rife with tricks and sophistries. These configurations of the text reflect various biases and subsequently distort its meaning. Tao Huang of course discovered similar difficulties with the numerous English translations available.

In order to avoid these abundant distortions, English readers must endeavor to connect to Lao Tzu's original mind, not to others' mindless minding of Lao Tzu. They need the energetic vibration generated through Lao Tzu, not the linguistic interpretation. They need a direct spiritual sensation passed down by Lao Tzu. The authors respond to this deep societal need with *The Secrets of the Tao Te Ching.* They wish to capture the original state of Lao Tzu's conscious flow and to sense the vibration of the wordless uttering of the Tao.

A Note on the Transliteration

There are several different systems for transliterating Chinese words into English (representing or spelling Chinese characters in the English alphabet). For this book, the authors have opted to use the Wade-Giles system, used in Mantak Chia's previous books, for most words. Thus, they use the spelling *Tao*, *Lao Tzu*, *Chi*, and *Ching*. (In the Pinyin system, these words would be spelled *Dao*, *Lao Zi*, *Qi*, and *Jing*.) Some Chinese words may appear in the Pinyin system.

COSMIC BRIDGE

The Secret Teachings of the Tao Te Ching serves as a bridge or door, a conscious connection between oneself and the wonders of the universe, or

God's creation. The "door" functions as a middle point between the internal world and the external world, between the information within and without—or between those who have been initiated and those who have the gifts of God but have not yet established a cosmic bridge within themselves. The cosmic bridge or door becomes a necessary vehicle for people's communication on both sides—such as the teachers, who are always inside the door, and the students, if not initiated, who are wondering (or wandering) outside the door.

In order to open the door, one's heart must be ready, and one must have completed a purification process. Otherwise, the heart-sealed transmission of teachings between teacher and student cannot begin. Ultimately, the door refers to a specific realm of consciousness of God, a line connecting two sides, or a flowing river touching both sides of the riverbed.

As you go through the book, read the words as if you were listening to a storyteller. Hear your inner conscious dialogue talking back and forth dreamingly between your true self and God; the messages in the teaching will shine upon you.

The Taoist exercises presented throughout the book emphasize emptying the mind, vitalizing the stomach, softening the will, and strengthening the character—important physical/emotional/spiritual skills that will help you to open to the inner meaning of the Lao Tzu's teaching. "Emptying the mind" enables the mind to become tranquil and return to its childlike state. Only when the mind is empty will the body be full with love and the spirit be able to present itself. "Vitalizing the stomach" is filling the stomach with purified Chi. "Softening the will" discusses the process of fully accepting the body/mind and world by diminishing ego expectations and the will of self-deception/punishment. And finally, "strengthening the character" is standing up with one's authentic character—the true self—and allowing the mind to shine.

In *The Secret Teachings of the Tao Te Ching* the authors present their transmission of Lao Tzu's message. His words are now their words. You cannot read Lao Tzu here; he has died into their hearts. The transmission you will receive depends on how your own heart is driven by your faith. The Tao is always present, the Tao Te Ching is always alive, and Lao Tzu is always smiling upon us. The Tao is always open to those who wish to step into the mystery of life and beyond.

AN EXTRAORDINARY COLLABORATION

The following chapters are the result of the collaborative efforts of two distinct Taoist masters who have different backgrounds and orientations in their practice of the Tao. In Taoist literature, there are eight famous "immortals," legendary Taoist masters, each of whom has a unique style of life and approach to the Tao. Yet they all share a commonality of experience as they evolved into the oneness of the eternal, universal void of the all-encompassing Tao. While masters Chia and Huang may have attained different realms of expertise in their approach to the Tao, their ultimate destination is the same. We are fortunate to be the beneficiaries of their combined offerings.

Master Chia is like an older brother, a more experienced teacher of the Tao in Western cultures. He teaches an ascending range of practices designed to culminate in the Wu Chi (the origin or source of all things, the undifferentiated, primordial void) and spiritual immortality and physical/spiritual immortality. He is popularly known for teaching Taoist fundamentals for health and inner peace, which include understanding, cultivating, and gaining mastery of sexual energy. Working with physical and spiritual energies is the main focus of Master Chia's approach to the Taoist path: Sense the Chi (vital energy or life force) and Jing (generative energy/sexual essence) and cultivate these energies; conserve them and refine them into Shen (spiritual energy). Use the Shen to enter the Wu Chi, to return to the Tao, and to attain immortality. His focus is on practical cultivation: "You do it; you get it!"

Tao Huang, the younger Taoist, has a more introspective approach to the Tao and emotional/psychological liberation. After his spiritual initiation through experiencing in meditation the direct transmission of Lao Tzu's teaching, he "received the Tao and was sealed internally with the power of the inner alchemy tradition." From that day forward he was surrounded by twenty-five hundred years of Taoist tradition and connected to the sacred teachings through the power of Lao Tzu. He was then initiated into the Dragon Gate school of Taoism, which emphasizes *neidan*, or inner alchemy practice. As a result of his particular path in Taoism, Tao Huang focuses more on the inner dimension of Taoist practice through dream yoga, *neidan*, and other meditation practices.

Tao Huang lays the foundation of *The Secret Teachings of the Tao Te Ching* with his commentary and practical information related to Lao Tzu's Tao Te Ching. Mantak Chia provides complementary perspectives and practices refined from his extensive experience of teaching people from all over the world. The thrust of the book is directed to the practical significance and ramifications of cultivating the Tao (the Way of all life) and Te (Virtue). Mindfulness of the Tao and Te in our lives and in our cultivation practices transforms all that we are and all that we do.

NOTE TO WOMEN READERS

The Tao Te Ching and the Taoist practices discussed in this book originated in a society vastly different from most modern societies. Ancient China was an overwhelmingly male-dominated society in which men possessed the political, civil, and monetary power and women had little or no opportunity for independent action or existence. While evidence of this imbalance may remain in some of the language of the ancient Taoist literature and discussion presented here, it is intended that the contents of this book be used to provide equal and mutual benefits for women and men.

Wordless Uttering of the Tao

The Tao that is voiced is no longer that of eternal Tao.
The name that has been written is no longer that of eternal name.
The nameless is the beginning of the cosmic universe.
The named is the mother of the myriad creatures.
Being at peace, one can see into the subtle.
Engaging with passion, one can see into the manifest.
They both arise from a common source but have different names.
Both are called the mystery within the mystery.
They are the door to all wonders. (1:1–4)

DEFINING THE TAO

The word *Tao* (pronounced "dow") is no longer a strange term in Western society; it is used with increasing frequency in English language and literature. However, the word *Tao* represents something that is profoundly subtle and impossible to grasp with the conceptual mind. For Lao Tzu, the Tao is a mysterious, numinous unity underlying and sustaining all things. It is inaccessible to normal thought, language, or perception.

Understanding its meaning is paramount to viewing the magnificence of the cosmos, tapping into the mystery of the universe, and searching for the origin of nature. It encompasses the vast, outer reaches of the universe; it is invisible, unfathomable, and unreachable; it is remote, ancient, and untraceable. It is beyond conception; it is too abstract to convey literally; it is mystical beyond comprehension. It remains forever silent, unmoved, and sublimely peaceful. Before the reality of the Tao, the voice can no longer utter sound, the eyes can no longer express their curiosity, and movement is halted in its forward journey. The veil of its mystery cannot be pierced. Philosophy cannot define its elusive meaning. Science cannot calculate its potential.

To define the Tao is to listen to silence, observe nakedness, and activate stillness. It can be likened to communicating with your inner voice, awakening your innate talent, finding a home with eternal beauty, and releasing your full potential. There can then be no alienation nor intimidation of your ultimate power.

To define the Tao is to catch your breath, focus your attention, calculate and refine your action, move with care, and make friends with the enemy. The breath is life's inspiration; attention forms concentration, and action results. Stepping forward is the reward. As the enemy recedes in the shadow, the Tao permeates your aura.

To define the Tao is to stand on the highest mountain peak, swim in an ocean of love, and soar with the dove in the valley of death. It is to connect with power. To sense the Tao is to stand in a cool spring shower; to view the Tao is to observe from a high tower; to smell the Tao is to breathe in a fragrant flower. It is to sleep peacefully behind a closed door, to peer through a window no more; to observe first the natural law, and to judge only the mind's intractable flaw.

To define the Tao can be anyone's individual response, but is no one else's business. To attempt to describe the Tao is a meaningless pursuit yet boundless in scope. To rationalize the Tao is futile. To reject the Tao is to render yourself powerless. To know the Tao is to leave one breathless; to understand the Tao is to be deathless; to walk the Tao is to be weightless; to ignore the Tao is senseless.

To define the Tao is to chant with Lao Tzu, to laugh with Chuang Tzu, to interpret Confucius, to understand Buddha, to love Christ, to listen to Muhammad, to follow Moses, to view the cosmos, and to embrace the ultimate.

COMMUNICABLE TAO AND INCOMMUNICABLE TAO

Communicable Tao

At the same time, the Tao is expressed in many ways through our gifted power of communication. Oral communication is primary, resulting from the power of the voice: the manifestation of inner consciousness and our spiritual trumpet. Verbalization is our first approach to living an independent life, finding the gateway to the Tao through the breath of life and vibration of sound. At the time that oral communication no longer served our human needs and expectations, letters and numbers were employed symbolically, marking the beginning of civilization as a cultural process.

The voice is a powerful force that can reach from one person (dead or alive) to the multitudes. The voice can express the will and permit the self to be expressed, to touch hearts, to justify morality, and verify deeds accomplished. Our inner justice is profoundly different from the legal practice of justice for the sake of justice. It is a direct spiritual communication that goes beyond ego-anticipation and social culture; it is an actualization process of human willpower.

Lao Tzu states: *The Tao that is voiced is no longer that of eternal Tao. The name that has been written is no longer that of eternal name.* The Tao that is voiced defines the origin of the universe through subjective expression. This is, in essence, the communicable Tao of inner self that connects deeply to both our microbiological and psychological self as well as our macrocosmic and celestial self. The name that has been written extensively objectifies any subjective expression of this inner voice. Anyone who has reached her or his prime can verbalize and name. Upon dying, the voice and name are extinguished by the will, enabling the person to enter into immortal and eternal life.

Inner Voice

The inner voice is the most sacred spiritual vessel. Without this inner voice, God is not alive, the Tao is not present, and the self is not active. This inner voice expresses and characterizes the beauty, meaning, and strength of life. It is sometimes silent; at other times it is immeasurably powerful. We often turn a deaf ear to this inner voice, refusing to abide by it or give it credence. We choose instead to rely on the external world, on external authority and discipline, to define our life as something meaningful, leaving us with confusion and distortion of our life's true meaning.

In order to establish a clear relationship with the sacred vessel of our inner voice, the first set of meditation practices in this book begins with finding, restoring, and listening to our inner voice in any given circumstance or crisis.

To develop your attunement to your inner voice:

1. Sit upright with your spine straight. Be simultaneously relaxed and alert. Place one hand on top of the other, and place both hands over your heart.
2. Listen intently to the sound of silence. You will begin to recognize a combination of spiritual voice and personal voice.
3. Pay attention to the most immediate direction and clear message. This is the manifestation of your inner voice.
4. Verbalize it inwardly, whether or not it makes sense to you.
5. Name it with no preconceived notion.
6. Meditate upon it as a part of the visualized journey of your life before it actually takes place.
7. Connect your own name with it. See how it conforms to you and your personality.

8. Make it work for you. It is the divine plan and your decision must be made now.

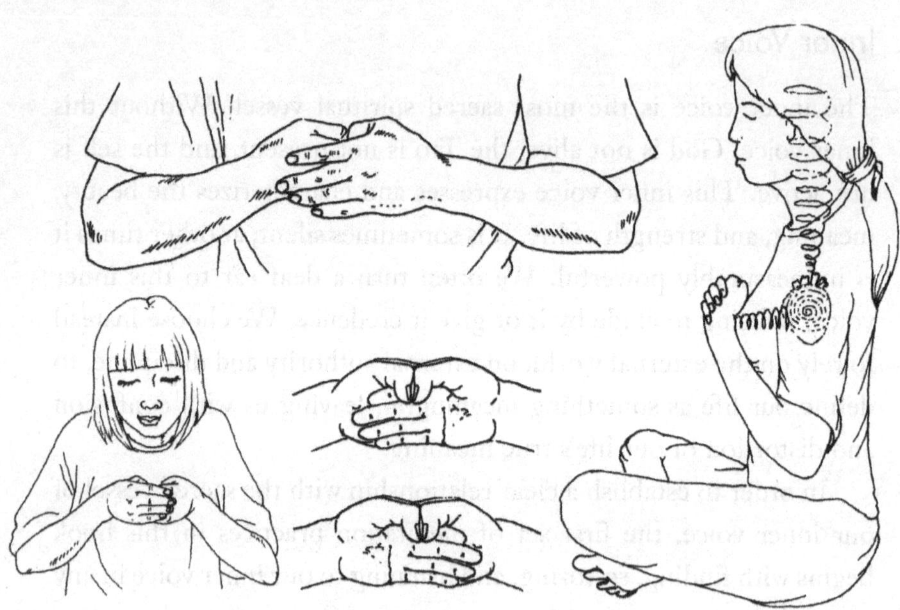

WHEN THE HANDS, HEART, AND MIND ARE UNIFIED, THE INNER VOICE SPEAKS

Incommunicable Tao

We have discussed the first part of Lao Tzu's first two sentences: the Tao that is voiced and the name that has been written. The second part of the two sentences warns us that the eternal Tao cannot be voiced and the eternal name cannot be written. This demonstrates to us also that what has been voiced can never be the eternal Tao, and what has been written can never be the eternal name. The eternal Tao can never be expressed completely and comprehensibly; in attempting to do so, the Tao becomes lost. The mouth cannot express an image, a colorful vision, or an awareness of the total environment while simultaneously penetrating the subtlety of the Tao. It is for this reason that voicing the Tao will automatically and instantly disconnect the utterance from the eternal Tao. When an inner message is verbalized, the speaker's true communication is lost and the listener will interpret the received message according to whatever she or he may desire, fear, or wish. The eternal name is thus lost.

Before something is named, it is subjected to how the observer regards it. Before Lao Tzu used the word *Tao*, many other words may possibly have been chosen. When something is named, changes occur due to the nature of the act of naming. Thus, the word *Tao* has become a fixed word with fixed meaning, far and away from Lao Tzu's initial vision, and it is forever changing. This is why the Tao has had many names, God has many names, and we have had many names. What has been expressed is not that which can be described. No matter how hard we try, we are bound to fail.

Bridging the Communicable Tao and the Incommunicable Tao

In the world,
Everyone recognizes beauty as beauty,
Since the ugly is also there.
Everyone recognizes goodness as goodness,
Since evil is also there.
Since being and nonbeing give birth to each other,
Difficulty and ease complete each other,
Long and short measure each other,
High and low overflow into each other,
Voice and sound harmonize with each other,
And before and after follow each other,
Therefore the sage
Lives in actionless engagement,
And preaches wordless doctrine. (2:1–3)

Between the communicable Tao and incommunicable Tao, the mind and the heart, and the voice and the hand, there are three bridges we must navigate: the bridge of the inner voice, the bridge of mutual understanding between speaker and listener, and the bridge of language itself.

The first bridge is the inner voice, which is exemplified by the baby's voice. There is no thinking or reasoning involved, only the sound of the voice. It is the soul of the Tao, the true innermost spirit of that person at that moment in that particular place and in that state of mind.

The second bridge is the mutual connection, empathy, and understanding between the speaker and the listener. This link can be either verbal or nonverbal. At times, when two people hold an international phone conversation it is not the content that matters but the continuous connection between them.

The third bridge is the use of language. When the meaning is conveyed with clear and definitive language, there will be no misunderstanding. When the information communicated is clear and the listener understands the words, the purpose of language has been successfully served.

Throughout the history of human civilization—the course of mental objectification—we have evolved from the use of a single voice to the many-faceted forms of oral, written, and digital audiovisual communication. We have shortened vast spatial distances by means of global telecommunication. In communicating spiritual teachings, the methods have changed dramatically, but not the source. We remain as we are. Each momentary flash of an idea differs from other moments, and each individual idea differs from others, yet all the ideas are but the manifestation of mind through the expression of soul being guided by spirit. The eternal, invariable, unwavering, enduring, and unchanging Tao is beyond expression.

How then can we know the Tao? Only through our own peace and desire can we open ourselves to its ever-present presence. When we have peace and serenity, we capture its subtlety. When we are attracted and seduced by the passion of desire, we limit it within our own boundaries and experience it as individual or personal. When we are relaxed and free from passion and excitement, we see beyond the futile pursuit of games being played. To be lost in the passion and excitement of the game is a deviation from our connection with our center and inner balance. We are divided when we enact our little scenarios. We become as two: being and nonbeing, birth and death, beauty and ugliness, good and bad. *Being and nonbeing give birth to each other, difficulty and ease complete each other, long and short measure each other, high and low overflow into each other, voice and sound harmonize with each other, and before and after follow each other.* This is how the world is harmonized in great accord. This ancient teaching enables us to become nonjudgmental, nonprejudicial, and equanimous.

Between the pairs of opposites lies the hidden mystery. *The mystery within the mystery is the door to all wonders.* The mystery is where the unmoving center and the striving outward reach embrace, balance, and unify. The mystery is where perfection and competition face their opposites in a peaceful manner. The mystery is where beauty and ugliness no longer appear attractive or repulsive, where good and bad are no longer distinct.

THE NATURE OF THE TAO

Look for it and it can not be seen, it is called invisible;
Listen to it and it can not be heard, it is called inaudible;
Reach for it and it can not be touched, it is called intangible.
(14:1)

Look, but that is not sufficient for seeing.
Listen, but that is not sufficient for hearing.
Use it, but it is not exhausted. (35:4)

Tao functions in empty harmony.
When used, it remains full.
For sure, this source is the very ancestor of the myriad things.
Blunting the sharp edges,
Unraveling the tangles,
Husbanding into the light,
Being as ordinary as the dust.
Ah! Limpid, it seems to exist forever. (4:1–4)

In order to understand the nature of the Tao we must first understand nature itself, since the Tao takes its origin from nature. Taoists approach nature with openness and not-knowing: "I don't know why it is so, and I don't know why it is not so; I cannot make it such, and I cannot make it not such." The first part speaks of human comprehension and understanding, while the second encompasses human ability and capacity.

We can neither change a mountain into a river nor a river into a mountain. We cannot prevent the plate convergence that causes mountains to rise, nor can we reverse the eroding effects of wind and water on their surface. Our knowledge of nature must admit our inability to control it; we cannot change its true nature. Neither can we know nor name the ineffable Tao. Lao Tzu has explained succinctly that Tao is eternally nameless, is praised but is unnamable.

The Tao is formless and functions in empty harmony. This empty harmony cannot be grasped by the senses. Our human eyes and ears and hands are rendered helpless in this endeavor. *Look for it and it can not be seen, it is called invisible; listen to it and it can not be heard, it is called inaudible; reach for it and it can not be touched, it is called intangible.* Use it, but its use is inexhaustible. The Tao inexhaustibly creates all things in their beginning; it is the ancestor of all the myriad things in the world. When the Tao is spoken, it is very plain, with no excitement and no stimulation. It is close to silence and has no flavor at all. How can we become excited about silence or sense that which is beyond the senses?

We can be aware of the Tao when we are aware of self and universe. We can be aware of the Tao when we are one with the creative force. We can be aware of the Tao when we blunt sharp edges, unravel what is tangled, and become as ordinary as dust. We must see through that which is limpid; this is analogous to entering into the realm of the kingdom of light. *Blunting the sharp edges* means diminishing all the desires of the heart. *Unraveling the tangles* is dissolving and clarifying the constant puzzles generated by mind.

When the body returns to its infantile stage and the mind is completely cultivated, one is permeated with the limpid light. In the Taoist tradition this light embraces both universal light and bodily light through the transformation and purification within the trinity of Chi, Jing (sexual essence/energy), and Shen (spiritual energy). According to modern quantum theory, photons or particles of light have the ability to share their existence mutually. Electrons, on the other hand, have the ability to exclude each other from occupying the same space. When sexual electrons and light photons are joined, their union is transformed into a golden elixir. This is the meaning of *husbanding into the light.* As the spirit enters its limpid state, the body returns to its original quality: dust.

The substance of Tao is boundless and unfathomable.
Unfathomable and boundless,
In its center there is form;
Boundless and unfathomable,
In its center there is an object;
Embryonic and dark,
In its center there is essence;
The essence is very pure,
In its center there is trust.
From now to the days of old,
Its name never dies,
Because it creates all things in their beginning. (21:1–2)

The substance of Tao is boundless and unfathomable. Since the substance of Tao is not a concrete form, it cannot be perceived other than in the symbolic sense. Yet as unfathomable and boundless as it seems, there is form in it. It can be said that its form is the form of the world: the image appears but is not yet apparent. The form is the matter at its center that looks embryonic and dark; there is essence (Jing) within. The essence is very pure and complete, and there is trust in it. Because of this trust, from now to the days of old, its name never dies even though its name cannot be defined in human terms.

From substance to form, from form to matter, from matter to Jing, and from Jing to trust, we encounter the various manifestations of the Tao. It is macrocosmically large and microcosmically small. Being as large as it is and as small as it is, it remains pure and limpid, and ineffable and immutable. What more do we need other than trust in the Tao?

How do I know how the world is such?
Thus. (55:4)

It is this very trust in the Tao that connects Lao Tzu with the all-pervading sustenance of the Tao. Lao Tzu denies himself the comfortable life that can inevitably hold but one future: death. He gives up his mind—the identity of ego and its illusions. What he ultimately receives is *thus*—the thusness or suchness of pure being that is ever present and does not arise from, and is not affected by, conditions. Nothing more than thus and nothing other than thus. What an enormous, powerful, all-consuming, and all-sustaining thus this is!

Tao moves by returning.
Tao functions by weakness.
All things under heaven are born of being.
Being is born of nonbeing. (41:1)

Tao gives rise to one.
One gives rise to two.
Two gives rise to three.
Three gives rise to all things. (42:1)

Humankind takes its origin from earth.
Earth takes her origin from heaven.
Heaven takes its origin from Tao.
Tao takes its origin from Nature. (25:4)

The Tao functions as empty harmony. Harmony is where and how the matter of the Tao produces, promotes, regenerates, and renews itself in its constantly full state. Since the action of the Tao is in its nonformed state, or emptiness, its best harmony is within itself where nothing is yet produced and nothing can be lost. It also remains in its constant fullness, wholeness, and completion by preserving its unused and potential perfection. *When used, it remains full.* Even as the Tao is producing, promoting, preserving, and regenerating at the same time, it utilizes both heaven and earth in order to conceive its formless state of oneness: nothingness. It functions in its weakness and emptiness by preserving its fullness and perfection. This source is undoubtedly *the very ancestor of the myriad things.*

Because *all things under heaven are born of being* and *being is born of nonbeing*, being forms the creatures that result from the process of the Tao: from the Tao to one, one to two, two to three, and three to all things. The Tao of oneness is the Tao of all things. This is why we have the Tao of heaven, the Tao of earth, the Tao of human beings, the Tao of plants and animals, and the Tao of sand and rocks. All things are perfectly as they are. This is why competition of any sort has no value or reality; it is meaningless in the great scheme of things.

In our modern society, we have evolved from animal-eating predators into self-striving competitors. The gains and losses conceal each other; master and slave depend on each other; wandering souls and hungry ghosts abound between heaven and earth. Stress is the consequence of our society, and anxiety and loss of self-esteem is the price we pay. Unless the awakened mind is recentered, the soul restored, kindness and virtue (Te) enriched, the self and society will never be whole and healthy.

Tao moves by returning points to the many actions of "returning": body to its destiny, mind to its creativity, and spirit to its oneness. Humankind returns to earth since *humanity takes its origin from earth.* Earth returns to heaven *since earth takes her origin from heaven.* Heaven returns to the Tao since *heaven takes its origin from Tao.* The Tao returns to Nature since *Tao takes its origin from Nature.* This is the ultimate reality: returning is the foundation of being Taoist. Only through this practice can we find the way, the one direction, the means to return to our source, to become one with the Tao. This is the unwavering path leading to the door of mystery.

Nothing in the world is softer and more supple than water.
When confronting strength and hardness nothing can overcome it.
Using nothing simplifies.
Using water overcomes hardness.
Using weakness overcomes strength.
There is no one in the world who does not know it, but no one can apply it.
So it is a saying of sages that:
Whoever can bear the disgrace of the country is the ruler of the country.
Whoever can bear the misfortune of the world is the ruler of the world.

(80:1–3)

What is the model of being one with oneself? How does one lose one's selfishness? Water is the answer. Water provides the life force for all creatures. It nurtures them, satisfies them, sacrifices itself, and once again purifies itself. Water, on earth, is life. Nothing can live nor complete its journey without water. This is the power and virtue of water. This is the material that resembles most closely the nature of the Tao.

Water is soft and gentle; nothing can compete with it. It occupies more area than anything on the face of the earth does. Water is weak and pliable, yet nothing can fight against its power. Water is clean and pure; nothing can contaminate it since it purifies other matter by purifying itself. Water is at peace with nature; nothing can surpass it as a tranquilizer, since its murky states are stilled by its inner tranquility. Water is inactive, yet nothing can be more active than water itself; it is everywhere, ceaseless in its wanderings. Water is noncompetitive, yet conquers all.

Water is always happy in its present dwelling place. Pouring as rain and drifting as snow, water travels endlessly through the seasons. Forming dews, storms, and glaciers, existing as solid, fluid, and steam, it continues its endless forms. It washes away all toxic materials that harm living creatures. Being noncompetitive enables water to remain at peace at all times. Water joyfully speaks its true faith, but our poisonous understanding of it dispels its tranquil state. Water acts in its own right time; we manipulate our affairs with an imaginary clock that destroys the natural rhythms of our bodies.

Water dwells within earthly creatures, and reveals itself as the largest substance on earth. There is no need to prove itself. The yielding strategy it employs enables it to be flexible, adaptable, and unattached. Water trickles or races on, returning to its destination with no need for strategy.

Lao Tzu concludes that *nothing in the world is softer and more supple than water. When confronting strength and hardness nothing can overcome it. Using nothing simplifies. Using water overcomes strength. Using weakness overcomes strength.* Everyone knows it, yet none can apply it. Following this, the sages' wisdom tells us: *Whoever can bear the disgrace of the country is the ruler of the country. Whoever can bear the misfortune of the world is the ruler of the world.*

Matter is formed from chaos.
It was born before heaven and earth.
Silent and void.
Standing alone, without territory,
Able to be mother to the world.

I do not yet know its name,
I call it Tao.
With reluctance I deem it to be Great.
Great refers to the symbol.
The symbol refers to what is remote.
What is remote refers to returning.
Tao is great.
Heaven is great.
Earth is great.
Kingship is great.
These are the four great things in the world,
Kingship is one of them. (25:1–3)

Through the process of regaining his youth by transforming his life force into spirit, Lao Tzu expresses that *matter is formed from chaos*, which precedes heaven and earth. Silently and formlessly, it stands alone, never changing. It is eternal, penetrating every area of the universe, never growing, never changing, and never dying. It is the mother of heaven and earth. Lao Tzu said to himself, "I don't know what name it has. With reluctance, I pronounce it Tao and deem it to be great." Yet it remains well beyond our mind's comprehension. Symbolically far-reaching, it penetrates the mind's spirit. We cannot grasp it, but it forever returns to us, like sky or ocean or earth. This Tao is truly great. Heaven is also great. Earth is equally great. Kingship is realistically great.

Knowing that you don't know (everything) is superior.
Not knowing that you don't know (everything) is a sickness.
So the sage's being without sickness is that he knows sickness as sickness;
Thus, he is without sickness. (73:1–2)

Lao Tzu expresses the word *Tao* with great caution and meticulous care. The Tao is wordless, nameless, formless, and motionless. No one, not even Lao Tzu, can have a clear, concrete, precise, and absolute definition of the Tao. He is unable to summon up a portrayal because he understands that *knowing that you don't know (everything) is superior. Not knowing that you don't know (everything) is a sickness.* He rationally states that the best he can do is to call it *Tao.* The word Tao is simply a sound uttered through Lao Tzu's mouth. He doesn't create it; he states it arbitrarily. Clearly, Lao Tzu must employ a sound or a word. When the right understanding appears, words disappear; they are no longer necessary. When the right spirit appears, understanding disappears. Which would you choose?

Chi and Taoist Inner Alchemy

Chi means "energy" or "life force"; *kung* means "work." Traditionally, Chi Kung is the cultivation of the ability to conduct Chi for the purposes of healing and spiritual transformation. According to the Taoist view, there are three sources of Chi: cosmic Chi, universal Chi, and earth Chi. Cosmic Chi is born out of the original Chi of the Tao and literally carries the intelligence and essence of life. Guided by this intelligence, it spreads out into the universe and manifests in different densities and forms defined by the cosmic laws. This is how stars, planets, human cells, subatomic particles, and all other forms of life take form and are nourished.

Universal and earth Chi also have their genesis in the original energy of the Tao. The universal Chi is the radiating force of all galaxies, stars, and planets throughout the whole universe. It is the all-pervasive force that nourishes the life energy in all the forms of nature. The earth Chi is the third force of nature, which includes all the energies of mother earth. This force is activated by the electromagnetic field originating in the rotation of the earth. It is also integrated into all aspects of nature on our planet. The earth energy is accessed through the soles of the feet, the perineum, and the sexual organs. Earth energy nourishes the physical body. It supplies our daily life force and is one of the principal forces used to heal ourselves.

For the past five thousand years, practitioners of Chi Kung have used time-tested methods to tap into these unlimited reservoirs of Chi, greatly expanding the amount of energy available to them.

The Universal Tao system also speaks of two types of Chi operating in the human being: prenatal Chi and postnatal Chi. Prenatal Chi, which is a combination of universal Chi and Jing (generative energy/sexual essence), is inherited from the parents, and is visible as innate vitality. Postnatal Chi, which is the life force an individual cultivates in his or her lifetime, is visible as the light shining behind personality and self-awareness. To build their postnatal Chi, humans normally access Chi through food and air. Plants take the universal energies of the sun and the magnetic energies of the earth and digest and transform them, thereby making these energies available to all living beings.

Rather than connecting to this universal Chi only after it is processed through plants, however, Taoist practitioners of Chi Kung learn to go directly to the source of this primordial energy. The Taoist recognizes that human beings have a limited capacity for Chi. However, if we are able to connect with the sources of Chi within the universe, we gain an infinite capacity for Chi, and we constantly fill ourselves, within the limitations of our human nature, with the unlimited abundance of energy around us.

Taoist inner alchemy involves the three Tan Tiens, or energy centers in the body. It particularly focuses on the lower Tan Tien, which is the primary energy center of the body. It is the major generator and storage place for Chi energy in the body as well as the seat of awareness. The other two Tan Tiens, or energy centers, are the middle Tan Tien (the center of consciousness) and the upper Tan Tien (the center of observation). The three Tan Tiens each have specific energetic functions.

The lower Tan Tien is the center of the physical body and of physical strength. It is located behind and below the navel—in the triangle between the navel, the "kidney center point" (in the spine between the second and third lumbar, also called the "gate of life"), and the sexual center. For men, the sexual center is the prostate gland and for women it lies in the top of the cervix between the ovaries.

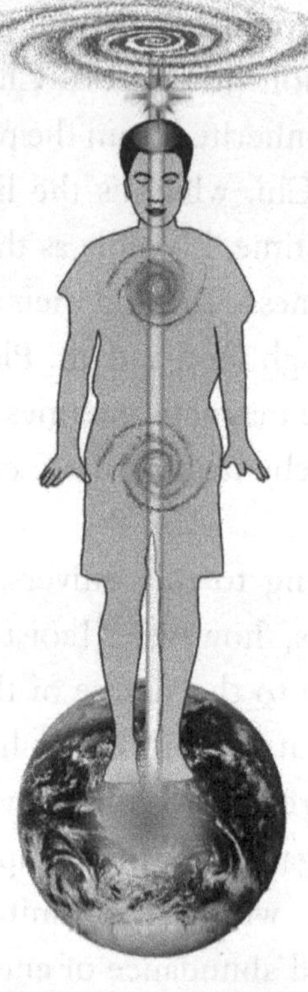

THREE TAN TIENS

Because the lower Tan Tien is the place where our prenatal Chi is stored, where all the energy that we absorb and collect during the Chi Kung exercises is stored, and where denser energies are transformed into more subtle energies, Taoist inner alchemy places a great deal of attention on this area. The lower Tan Tien is also called the "medicine field" or "elixir field," as it gathers and contains the healing power of Chi. Other names for it are the "cauldron" and the "navel center." The expression "cauldron" refers to the function of the lower Tan Tien as the center of internal alchemy that transforms energy.

The lower Tan Tien serves as the source of the life force or vital force. This then becomes transformed into the more subtle Shen Chi, or spirit power/energy. Thus, throughout all Universal Tao practices, the lower Tan Tien remains the key to supplying the body and the mind with a free, uninterrupted flow of energy. Taoist Chi Kung is above all a practice by which the unity of what is above and below is acknowledged and honored. Through its service as a reservoir and transformer of Chi, the lower Tan Tien confirms the unity between earth and heaven in the body.

THE THREE MINDS

As illustrated on page 28, Taoist masters discovered that human beings have three minds: the upper mind, which is the observing mind; the middle mind, which is the consciousness mind; and the lower mind, which is the awareness mind. The upper mind is valuable for analytic activity and planning, but negative emotions can cause the upper mind to be agitated with excessive thinking and worrying, which drains energy. The upper mind works practically all the time, stirring up the emotions and using up to 80 percent of our body energy. We should train the upper mind to be relaxed and to just observe when we do not need to be involved in specific mental activity. The key is to "seek the released mind" by relaxing, emptying, and sinking the upper mind down into the lower mind/lower Tan Tien. Western science has recently discovered that there are nerve endings in the stomach and intestines that are related to emotional responses. By smiling into the lower Tan Tien, we can activate the lower mind. We can then use the upper mind (observing mind), middle mind (consciousness mind), and lower mind (awareness mind) together, grounded in the abdomen.

If we can use the lower mind more, the upper mind can rest and listen (observe) from the abdomen. The upper mind, or, as the Taoists refer to it, the "monkey mind," can, when agitated, suppress consciousness or awareness. Once the upper mind rests, we can be conscious and aware of much that we were never conscious or aware of before. We can be at ease, save energy, and build up strength for any tasks.

We need to use the brain in the head in order to perform complex functions such as reasoning, making plans, and making calculations. These are typical left-brain functions. However, for our daily life of consciousness, awareness, and feeling, which is typically governed by the right brain, we can use either the brain in the head or the brain in the gut (the lower Tan Tien). We should train the upper mind to be relaxed and to just observe when we do not need to be involved in specific mental activity. When we use the upper brain less, it becomes charged with energy and its power increases, and as a result more power is available to the body. When the upper brain is resting, brain repair and maintenance occur, and new brain cells can grow. This is the reason Taoism insists that we train the feeling and awareness in the lower Tan Tien/lower brain so that we can use it when the upper brain is resting. With more charging of the upper brain, we have more power for creativity or whatever we want to use it for.

When you are not using the upper brain, allow it to rest by sending consciousness down to the lower Tan Tien, and send a warm, relaxed inner smile down to the abdominal area. Maintaining an awareness of the relaxed, smiling sensation in the lower Tan Tien is the first step in training the lower brain. The key is to "seek the released mind" by relaxing, emptying, and sinking the upper mind down into the lower mind.

RETURNING TO THE SOURCE

Emptying the mind in this way is returning to the source. This is also the meaning of *Tao moves by returning*. To take this one step further, emptying the mind and returning to source means not following any outward or worldly direction.

This applies as well to sexual urges, common to us all. We need to practice returning sexual energy to the chest as selfless love, and to the brain as spiritual wisdom. Control of sexual energy and its transformation into life force is essential in Taoist inner alchemy. For men this implies preserving the life essence of the sperm during intercourse or self-stimulation. Through controlling ejaculation they can transform the sexual essence/generative energy (Jing) of the sperm into Chi. For women, controlling and transforming sexual energy means learning to regulate and control menstruation, thereby transforming the generative essence in the blood into Chi. (The practices for cultivating the ability to control and transform sexual energy are presented in the first two chapters of *Taoist Cosmic Healing*, by Mantak Chia.) In the Universal Tao System, it is very important to learn how to transform sexual energy into spiritual energy. The original balance between love and sex, or water and fire, contains in itself the essence of healing and creation.

Taoist inner alchemy involves many exercises for cultivating, conserving, and transforming energy. These practices enrich the quality of one's life and fuel the process of spiritual "returning." Many of these practices involve working with the energy pathways, or meridians, in the body. There are twelve main meridians in the body, six yin and six yang, and each relates to one of the organs.

To better visualize the concept of how Chi circulates through the meridians, think of the meridians as a riverbed over which water flows and irrigates the land, nourishing and sustaining all that it touches. (In Western medicine, the concept would be likened to the blood flowing through the circulatory system.) If a dam were placed at any point along the river, the nourishing effect that the water had on the whole river would be constricted at the point the dam was placed.

The same is true in relation to Chi and the meridians. When the Chi becomes blocked, the rest of the body that was being nourished by the continuous flow of Chi now suffers. Illness and disease can result if the flow is not restored.

The following exercise is a simple energy circulation practice that can help facilitate the smooth flow of Chi throughout the entire body:

1. Sit with spine straight. Be relaxed and alert.
2. Cover the navel with the palms—left hand over right for men, right hand over left for women.
3. Smile into the mid-eyebrow and feel it relax. Smile and relax the upper mind, and allow it to sink, moving slowing down to the neck, down to the chest, and gradually down to the lower Tan Tien.
4. Feel the navel area starting to get warm. Visualize a ball of energy in this area, and then visualize this energy spiraling like the yin/yang spiral.
5. Feel the Chi in the navel area getting warmer and warmer and starting to rise up through the spine to the brain.
6. Keep five percent of your awareness on the spiral of energy in your lower abdomen. At the same time, visualize the energy that has risen up to the brain begin to form a spiral in the head. Continue to spiral that energy, feeling the Chi pressure in the brain begin to grow.
7. Feel the Chi pressure pushing outward as it grows stronger. Gradually guide the Chi into the sinuses and allow it to build until you feel the Chi pressure push down into the nose and open the sinuses. Feel the nose open and your breathing improved. Moving Chi down into the sinuses in this way may help prevent colds and flu.
8. Touch your tongue to the roof of your month. In this way, you will link the Governor Channel (the line of energy that runs up the spine) to the Functional Channel (the line of energy that runs down the front of the torso), thus connecting the Microcosmic Orbit. Feel the Chi circulating through the Microcosmic Orbit.
9. After a few minutes, slowly let the Chi drop down into the navel area. Smile down into the navel a while and feel the energy being condensed and safely stored in the lower Tan Tien. Remember to always bring the energy back to the lower Tan Tien as this is the best place to store it. It is unsafe to leave excess Chi in your organs, as this may cause the organs to accumulate too much energy and overheat from the process.

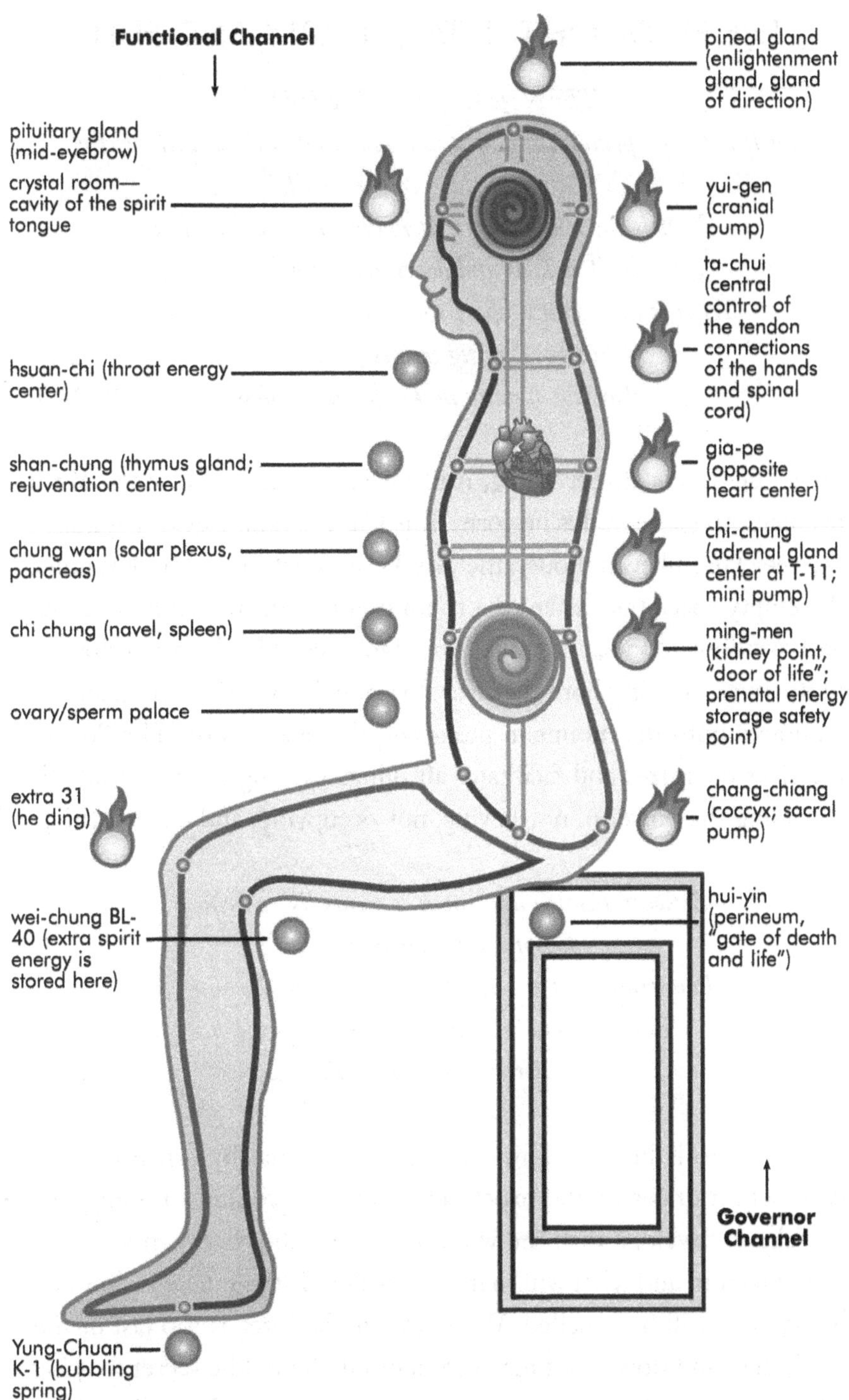

LEARN TO CIRCULATE YOUR CHI IN THE MICROCOSMIC ORBIT

THE FLOW OF THE TAO: EMPTY AND FULL

Thirty spokes join at one hub,
Yet it is the emptiness inside the hub that makes the vehicle useful;
Clay is molded into a vessel,
Yet it is the hollowness that makes the vessel useful;
Windows and doors are cut out,
Yet it is their empty space that makes the room usable.
So, any having makes for excess,
Any not-having makes for usefulness. (11:1–2)

Since the Tao is all-pervading, it fills every corner at all times. Yet it occupies no space, holds no form. It is like the hollowness that makes the vessel useful even though the vessel is molded and colored. It is like the empty space that makes the room useful even though it is framed with windows, doors, and walls. This Tao is also like the water flowing in the river, creating both the river flow and carving the river banks. It embraces both the mountain peaks and the ocean floor. The flow of the river energizes and facilitates all things existing on either side by providing the power of not-having, not-occupying, and not-attaching.

Between heaven and earth it seems like a bellows:
Empty, yet inexhaustible,
The stronger it is activated, the greater the output.
Being overly informed leads to exhaustion,
Better to be centered. (5:2)

The Tao is like a bellows, an instrument that by expansion and contraction draws in and expels air. A bellows contains nothing. Its usefulness develops with the working relationship between what has been taken in and what will then be expelled. If the intake is slow and weak, little will be expelled. When the intake force is too fast or too hard, the wind flow is not maximized or efficient. The secret to using a bellows is gentleness, steadiness, and consistency. The bellows rep-

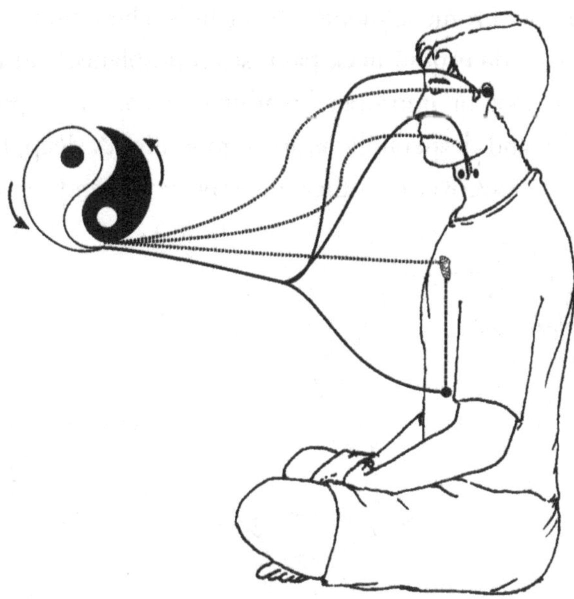

WE INHALE THE POWER OF TAO INTO OUR LIFE AND RETURN IT WITH THE VIRTUE OF TE

resent the flow of life: the input is the Tao of life and its masculinity, the output is the Te of love and its femininity. The two sides are constantly merging yet standing alone to generate their harmonious flow.

We can practice the flow of the Tao and Te with the bellows of our lungs. We can practice breathing consciously, deeply, gently, and steadily, inhaling the power of Tao into our life and exhaling the virtue of Te.

We can practice three forms of energy "breathing" in our bodies. The first bellows is the function of lungs, the working breath of life. The second bellows is the perineum, known as the "gate of life and death." It constitutes the lowest point of the yin or descending energy channels, and is the lower meeting point of the Governor (ascending) Channel and the Functional (descending) Channel (see illustration on page 33). Through the legs and feet, it is the main link with the earth Chi. The third bellows is the third eye, the opening gate to the reality of mystery. We can practice conscious breathing with each of these three bellows.

An array of chronic ailments—bronchitis, chest pain, tightness of shoulders, poor digestion, neck pain, sleep problems, and more—are the result of poor or improper breathing. If you are experiencing a sleep disorder and desperately desire a good night's sleep, lie on your back, place one foot over the other, and cross your hands on your chest.

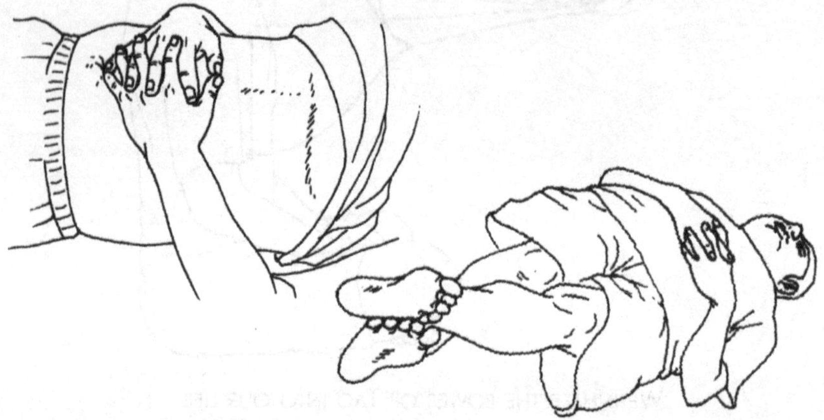

BREATHE AND DRIFT INTO A DEEP SLEEP (THE POSITION OF HANDS AND FEET ARE OPPOSITE TO EACH OTHER. IF YOU ARE RIGHT-HANDED, PLACE THE LEFT FOOT ON THE TOP OF RIGHT ONE, AND VICE VERSA)

Close your eyes and concentrate on your breath. As you listen to your breathing, you will soon drift into a deep and restful sleep. Before you realize it, it will be morning. You will generate more productivity within this creative environment with less time and effort.

If you have lower back problems, constipation, frequent urination, poor or irregular menstruation and urination, and other related problems, you should pay attention to the perineum pressure point. It is the key to a happy, healthy, and energetic life. Kneel down with toes pointing toward the head. Bow the forehead to the floor and place the hands together flat on the floor in front of the brain. Take a deep breath and contract the perineum and anus muscles firmly. Hold the breath while contracting the muscles for as long as possible. Then release quickly. Relax for a few seconds, breathing naturally. Then take in another deep breath and contract the muscles again, holding the breath and muscle contraction. Repeat for several minutes. When you inhale and

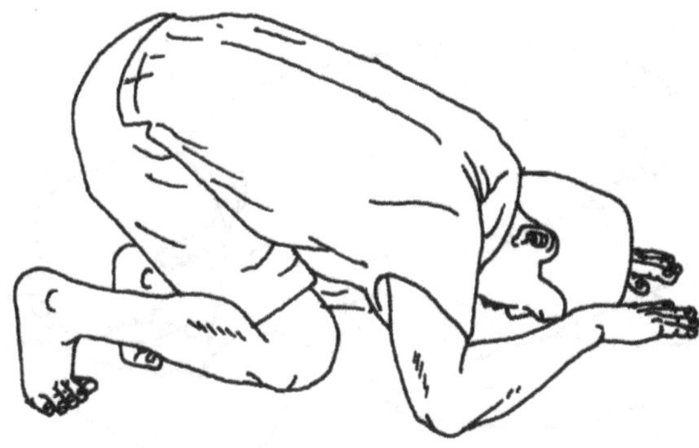

TAKE A DEEP BREATH AND CONTRACT THE PERINEUM AND ANUS MUSCLES

contract the muscles, you are drawing Chi into the body. This exercise can also be done while standing, sitting, or lying down.

You may experience pain in all the related muscles, joints, or organs. Pain is often the first step in healing. When the lower part

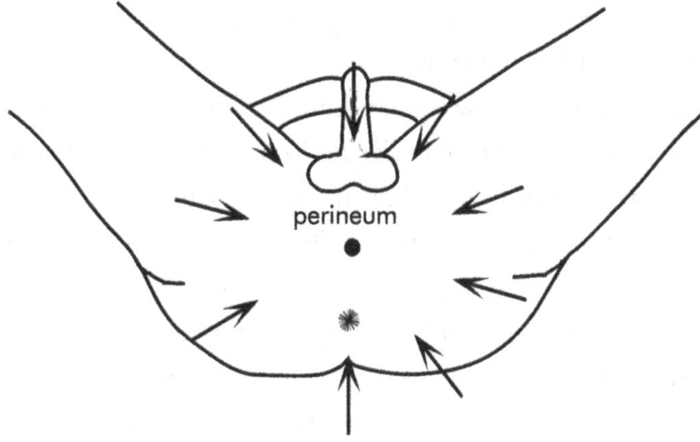

BREATHING CHI IN THROUGH THE PERINEUM

of the body is fully open and relaxed, the entire back, neck, and brain will become open and relaxed. The benefit of this exercise is beyond measure. Your appreciation of yourself and your life will expand as you continue this practice.

In order to open your third eye and expand your consciousness in both waking and dreaming states, practice "breathing" through the third eye, or mid-eyebrow area. Kneel, bow your head forward,

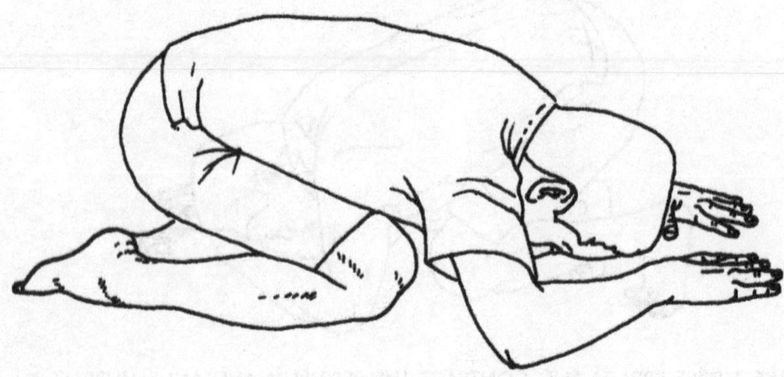

DRAW CHI IN THROUGH THE THIRD EYE

and place your hands flat on the floor just above your head. Gently tap the forehead on the floor in rapid momentum. You may experience temporary dizziness. Then focus on the pituitary gland. Inhale and mentally gather the cosmic light through the third eye, in the middle of the forehead. As you exhale, visualize the energy being condensed in the third eye area.

Meditation is, in a sense, expanding our mental space into the vastness of the universe. Human life and its existence on this planet depend on creating and discovering the most useful space to occupy, then utilizing it fully and gratefully. When a person finds a suitable space, they will survive and live a long life. This space can be both physical and mental: a good physical space implies a good location and good living conditions, while a good mental space must have the capacity for flexibility and acceptance. These two "spaces" are equally important and often difficult to occupy, expand, and preserve.

During our lifetime we are all granted a natural space in which to dwell and make our life meaningful, enabling us to realize a dream to make the heart joyful and delight the spirit. Living in this environment, we can exercise our kingship within our own precious kingdom.

Sensation, the Brain, and Taoist Practice

To perceive is to be aware of our surroundings by means of receiving and interpreting sensory stimuli. All living things from plants to insects to animals possess sensory abilities. Plants have the most simple form of perception, as they detect and grow toward the light. Animals and humans depend on their five sensory receptors to perceive, identify, and utilize objects in their environment to meet their needs.

Humanity has developed abilities through evolution to distinguish the differences among colors, sounds, and smells with the aid of the five senses. We also experience more subtle sensations, such as pressure, temperature, weight, resistance, tension, pain, position, sexual sensations, equilibrium, hunger, and thirst. All these sensations arise from the interaction between internal organs and the external world. The primary role of the senses—to ensure our survival and avoid any dangerous and disastrous situation—enables us to discriminate what is good from what is harmful, and what is valuable from what is useless. Upon optimizing these sensory abilities, we gradually become more effective in various areas, as well as more aesthetic. We continually strive to improve those abilities to discern or perceive the natural forms, to make life simpler and more peaceful, and ever more meaningful and wonderful.

In spiritual practice two things are required. The first is to perceive something exactly as it is. This is the precision of accuracy. The other is selflessness. When the self is absent, the discrimination and judgment will be absent as well. There can be no space for duality when the true value of perception is apparent. Passing judgment is the real poison to our life, our health, and our spiritual environment. True spiritual judgment is selfless: perceiving things as they are and responding accordingly. In life, all good things are transformative gifts and all bad things are valuable learning and transforming materials. Understanding this reality—the meaning of perception—is the beginning of Taoist awareness practice. It is being consciously aware that the perception of eyes, nose, and ears functions to form the greatest portion of information. When we reach the point where what we perceive is ideal to what our consciousness is perceiving, life then presents its true meaning to us. At this point, the sensory organs are not only reliable tools but also valuable conscious and spiritual vehicles. Through this organic awareness, our deeper emotional and spiritual nature will be awakened and comprehended.

With the aid of light, all things can be seen. To know the Tao, no special talent or knowledge is required. All things on earth are sacred. To know this is to know your true self and how to apply the skill of spiritual perception. With this device, we can know not only the worldly appearances we observe but also their hidden messages. Then oneness is achieved, making human perception a joint venture between our biological, emotional, and spiritual sensitivity as well as the external world negotiated by the mind and heart. The perception of the world, of the Tao, and of God is then achieved as life flows on of its own accord.

Taoist practice provides us with the resources to extend beyond the realm of our senses. By tapping into our internal resources and channeling the energy around us, we can perceive much more than the senses normally report to the mind. We extend our perception from the limited perspective of the sociologically conditioned senses to the unlimited awareness of the universe. For example, our senses tell us that the earth is flat, that we are stationary, and that heaven is above us. In reality, the earth is a sphere hurtling through space at thousands of miles per hour and the heavens are above, below, and beyond the earth in every direction.

Along with the five senses, all animals possess souls or animal spirits. Taoists call this form of spirit *po,* which is instinctive, selfish, and egoistic. Just as plant lives range from seasonal to perennial, animal spirits exist from cyclical to eternal. All animal spirits are cyclical, but the human spirits, being the most highly evolved, can reach the eternal. All animal spirits are self-protective since they must safeguard their own existence. Only human beings are consciously aware of their traits of selfishness and are willing to, at times, transcend these traits. All animals are realistically selfish; only humans can sacrifice today for the benefit of tomorrow.

When a spirit/soul is regenerated into a physical body, it unifies its organic ability with the conscious ability to form ego: the master of the five senses. In the Taoist interpretation, the ego is the powerful coordinator of sensory perception and response. The human conscious awareness perceives both the present reality (natural or cultural) and the projected reality (wished or planned), and anticipates and acts accordingly.

With spiritual discipline we become fully aware of the reality we perceive through the senses, the plans and intentions we consciously create, and the transcendence of spiritually awakening. This is the presence of spirit and its wisdom force. The perceived world is the realistic world we now inhabit. Yet there is also a more subtle, mystical dimension that is always present. In spiritual cultivation practice, the senses are organic and biological, but also psychological and intuitive. Our sensory powers represent the power of nature, mind, force, and matter.

THE BRAIN: PERCEPTION, EMOTION, AND RESPONSE

Sensory impulses are interpreted through the cerebral cortex, the layer of gray matter encasing the cerebrum. In addition to interpreting sensory impulses, the cerebrum and cerebral cortex determine personality, motor functions, and planning and organization. The cerebrum is the largest part of the brain; it is the seat of consciousness and the center of the higher mental faculties such as memory, learning, reasoning, and emotions. It consists of two hemispheres separated by a deep longitudinal fissure and four lobes. The occipital lobe is involved in interpreting visual stimuli, the parietal lobe is involved in interpreting the stimuli of touch and taste, the temporal lobe is involved in interpreting the stimuli of smell and hearing, and the frontal lobe is involved in motor function, problem solving, spontaneity, memory, language, initiation, judgment, impulse control, and social and sexual behavior.

All sensory activities governed by the cerebral cortex are centralized through the thalamus glands and executed through the limbic system—the name being derived from *limbus*, the Latin word for "ring." This system enables us to learn and to memorize. Prior to development of the limbic system, all species possessed a brainstem that encircled the top of the spinal cord and was poorly developed, particularly among fish and insects. The brainstem regulates the functions of breathing and metabolism. It controls our instinctual reactions as well. It is vital in maintaining our conscious wakefulness and alertness. The primary functions of life—heart rate, blood pressure, swallowing, coughing, and breathing—are directed by the brainstem. The alarm system in the brain, the reticulating activating system (RAS), consists of a reticular formation, subthalamus, hypothalamus, and medial thalamus—with the hypothalamus serving the highest purpose of all. It contains many tiny clusters of nerve cells called nuclei monitors that regulate body temperature, food intake, water balance, blood flow, sleep-wake cycle, and the activity of the hormones secreted by the pituitary glands.

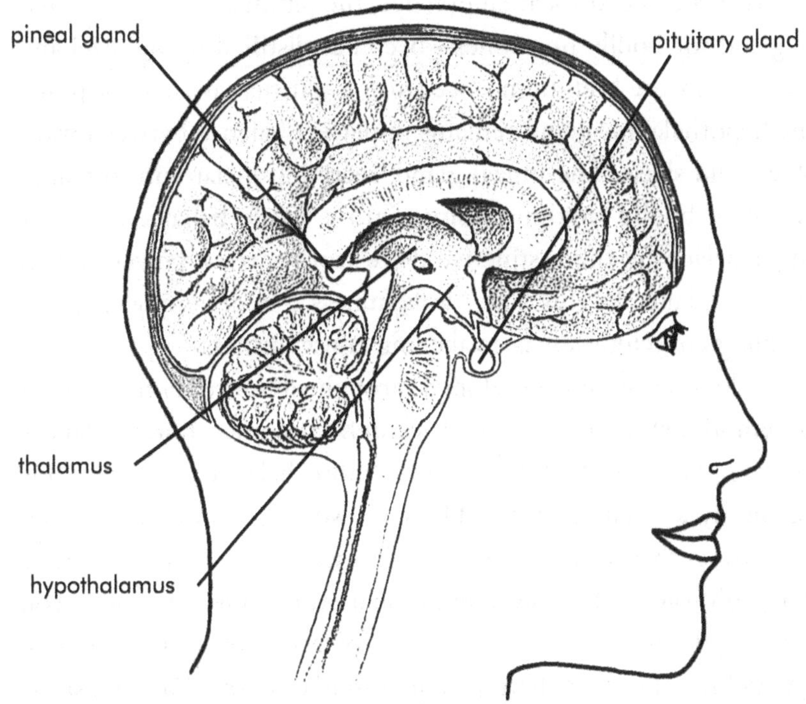

THE HUMAN BRAIN

The brainstem, in Taoist practice, is the storeroom of sexual energy as it rises through the spinal cord. It then further nourishes the pituitary gland and pineal gland in meditation practice at the second level. This is the practice of transforming Chi into Shen, then Shen into emptiness, and finally emptiness into the Tao.

By keeping the adrenal hormones at their lowest levels, inner peace will remain undisturbed. In such a state, the sensory receptors that are controlled by the thalamus gland, with the exception of the olfactory, will consciously withdraw. In complete darkness, as is found within caves where meditators engage in the highest forms of practice, the visual and auditory abilities become ever more sensitive. By withdrawing ordinary light energy from the adrenal glands and charging them with primordial sexual energy, the mind sees the subtle light and the inner ear hears the cosmic vibration within both the body/mind and mother earth.

With continued spiritual practice, the pituitary gland—the master gland for bodily hormones—becomes distilled by the exchange of energy in the body/mind needed for spiritual awakening power. The hypothalamus gland remains in perfect balance between wakefulness and sleep. The pineal gland, secreting melatonin to control the subtle bodily rhythms, comes into a subtle balance and is no longer driven by the instinctive drive from adrenal power and the thalamus gland. In this state, wakefulness is a dreaming state and dreaming consciousness is awakening consciousness.

As the brainstem is developed through advanced Taoist practice, the emotional and instinctual centers become more balanced, enabling the body to function in a more balanced manner, both organically and emotionally. The root word for emotion is *motere*, the Latin verb "to move." The Taoists view emotional activities as energy diffusions. The seven emotional expressions are closely connected with the seven openings in the face expressing happiness, rage, sadness, joy, love, hatred, and desirable action. The first six are the organic expressions of heart, liver, and spleen.

The amygdala, an almond-shaped mass of gray matter in the brain's medial temporal lobe, plays a central role in the emotions. It forms part of the limbic system and is linked to both fear responses and pleasure. The amygdala receives input from the sensory systems

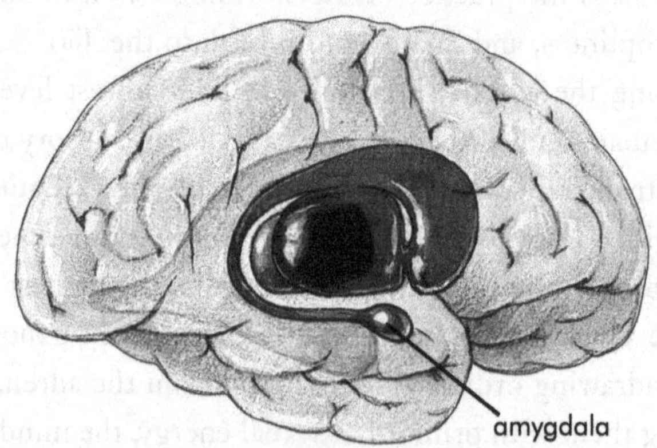

THE AMYGDALA PLAYS A KEY ROLE IN THE EMOTIONS

and is necessary for fear conditioning and emotional arousal. It sends outputs to the hypothalamus for activation of the sympathetic nervous system, the reticular nucleus for increased reflexes, and the trigeminal nerve and facial nerve for facial expressions of fear.

In Taoist tradition, as sexual energy merges with the light above the brain, the light in the pituitary becomes gray-white. This activates the amygdala, and Chi then circulates on either side of the head above the ears and around the temples. As the light moves forward, the third eye will be opened.

The overall functioning of the amygdala is related to the energy of the kidney Chi (which includes the adrenal glands, kidneys, bladder, and ovarian/prostate glands), particularly the activation of the will and the expression of fear. Fear is the oldest negative emotion. It is felt by all animals, and is even stronger among humans since they have so little power to protect themselves, especially the newborn. The longer time required for human development into adulthood makes fear the basis of the entire civilization process. Emotional fear and negativity can freeze or numb the body/mind in its confrontation with danger. Yet, humans are also capable of swiftness and fearlessness in response to challenging situations. The kidneys have their corresponding facial locations within the temples and ears. When your kidney Chi is vibrant and flows freely to the brain, there is no blockage in either temporal lobe or around the umbilical cord. The energy flows freely to create pure emotional vibration: compassion.

FIVE COLORS BLIND THE EYES

Five colors blind the eyes.
Racing and hunting madden the heart.
Pursuing what is rare makes action deceitful.
Five flavors dull the palate.
Five tones deafen the ears.
So, the sage's method is for the belly, not for the eyes.
He abandons the latter and chooses the former. (12:1–2)

Here Lao Tzu speaks about the organic interaction of self with the world. *Five colors blind the eyes* reveals the eyes as one of the primary sensory receptors. Colors are the first visible objects in the universe and the most powerful natural stimuli. Their significance is so important to our life, both biological and artistic, that we dye our fabrics with colors, stain utensils with color, paint our rooms and houses with colors, and express ourselves through colors. We are the consumers of colors. When colors, as the spectrums of light, enter the heart through eyes, the heart is fired and maddened, and the body is driven by the "go for it" message. Racing and hunting commence.

The more rare an object is, the more intensely the body/mind pursues it. *Pursuing what is rare makes action deceitful.* This is the beginning of human grasping, greed, and sinfulness. The word "rare" is used in reference to the most sought after stimuli since that which is rare satisfies the ego. Cheating, fighting, disguising, lying, envying, admiring, appraising, degrading, denying, hiding, exaggerating, labeling, disregarding, abusing, humiliating, killing . . . on and on, endlessly. All for the purpose of pursuing five flavors and enjoying the five tones: the rewards of racing and hunting.

All the pleasures of the senses may be experienced and enjoyed, but excessive indulgence leads to a negative or even destructive influence on taste, the physical body, and the soul. This is a warning to those who wallow in sensuous enjoyment or a hedonistic way of life. As the eyes are blinded, the palate dulled, and the ears deafened through overindulgence, the body becomes toxic and the mind numb.

We are exposed to the stimulation of the forms of this world, and their invitations can seem inescapable. Colors, sounds, smells, tastes, and textures from all the forms of nature constantly beckon us. It is this invitation from nature that allows us to go with the flow of the outside world. We can mindfully engage this experience.

In Chinese philosophy, the universe is composed of the five elements—water, metal, earth, fire, and wood—each of which has a yin and a yang mode. All natural forms are expressions of these elements. Traditionally, the five seasonal changes (spring, summer, late summer, fall, and winter) produce five colors (green, red, yellow, white, and black) and five flavors (sour, bitter, sweet, tart, and salty). They activate the five tones (call, laugh, sing, cry, and moan), the five facial organs (eyes, ears, nose, mouth, and tongue), and the five primary internal organs (liver, heart, spleen, lungs, and kidneys). All these fives are conceived within the bodily five elements (a body with two arms and two legs), expressed with five emotions (anger, joy, worry, sorrow, and fear); and manifested with five fingers. Lao Tzu acknowledges the interaction with the fives of the universe: *five colors blind the eyes, five flavors dull the palate, five tones deafen the ears.* The Taoist approach is to mindfully find the middle way as we navigate the stimulation of our encounters with all the forms of the world.

Savoring Non-Flavor

> *Do nondoing.*
> *Engage in non-affairs. Savor non-flavor.*
> *Large or small, many or few, reward or punishment, are all being done through Action.* (63:1–2)

Our life cycle is determined by the interaction of eternal and external stimuli. The initial excitement of external stimuli then emerges as competitive action to reap the rewards of food, drink, sex, and being surrounded by possessions and values. These material satisfactions and objects become our status symbols. Our life energy is further consumed in dealing with dual reactions such as happiness and anger, joy and frustration. An inner war ensues and life grinds on to the end.

The sensory organs are driven constantly by internal demands and external pressure. Eventually, the five receptors tend to become jammed, the sixth sense (the bodily sense) is overwhelmed, and the seventh sense (conscious awareness) is cluttered by words and beliefs.

When in touch with the Tao, the senses do not become overly stimulated. We do not become slaves to experiences or to objects. We practice nondoing, engaging in non-affairs, and savoring non-flavor. This action is the real product of the mind and heart. The mind pursues and the heart rewards. There is no need to hasten our own demise by driving ourselves to defeat.

In following this practice of nondoing, we must give attention to each and every stimulating agent, whether internal or external. According to Taoist inner alchemy and Chinese medicine, colors, flavors, and tones may cause an organic imbalance, which could then lead to emotional turmoil and spiritual distortion. The five colors, flavors, and tones impart corresponding internal organic reactions on biological, emotional, and intellectual levels. When the pressures exerted by these stimuli become overwhelming, there will be a blockage to the sensory receptors of eyes, ears, and mouth. The inner organs will then be harmed: anger frustrates the liver; hate causes rage in the heart; worry eats away at the spleen; sadness depresses the lungs; and fear distills itself in the kidneys. In like manner the high frequency brought on by shouting or blatant noise can inflict damage to the heart; drinking can poison the liver, pornography leeches away at the kidney Chi. Then much energy is required to detoxify and restore the body/mind to its normal state.

In the sense of Tao,
This is said to be eating too much and acting too much.
It results in disgust.
Those who desire will not endure. (22:2-3)

Not constraining the living environment.
They do not get bored by life.
Because we do not get bored, there is no boredom. (74:2)

Our sensory organs are vulnerable. Rather than honoring and respecting them, we burden them mercilessly. When the eyes become tired, we continue to look. When the ears are jammed with excessive sound, we continue listening. When the stomach is full, we continue to eat. The eyes become shortsighted and the ears deafened. The body loses its sense of balance and our health is at stake. *This is said to be eating too much and acting too much.* How do we find the right balance?

We are easily bored and grow tired of our routine and surroundings. This motivates us to seek more stimulation. This is the wrong form of seeking.

Searching for answers to the purpose of our life journey is the highest form of motivation to be cultivated. We are what we are. Living through what we are is the answer, but we sometimes refuse to accept it. When we refuse to accept the truism that we are what we are, we are compelled to add colors, labels, and meanings. We then empower our ego to demand and direct our actions instead of listening to the warning signals and devoting ourselves to virtuous action. Artificial practices retard and destroy our sacred sensitivity, our going with flow. This is the exorbitant price exacted by our egoistic demands. If our minds are *not constraining the living environment, we do not get bored by life. Because we do not get bored, there is no boredom.* If we can wholeheartedly accept that we are what we are, we can *savor non-flavor* and consistently and spontaneously manifest virtuous action.

For the Ego, There's Never Enough

During the course of humanity's forward march toward civilization, we have become emotionally entrapped. We are intellectually encouraged to believe that being productive is of value and the reason to live. Our productivity must be measured according to given standards: social, economic, academic, political, religious, or other positions, usually within rigid social organizations. Upon achieving these strived-for positions, we feel justified for having paid such a high price. The need to "be productive" requires that we make a good impression, and be young, smart, creative, hardworking, and most importantly, obedient and pliable. Social organizations are anxious to "hire" these qualities and make full use of them. Their expectations are that we will improve and become more efficient and productive in order to set an even higher standard of success for others to follow. Those that follow us proceed to compete with us and eventually take over our own hard-won positions. What is happening? We have sold ourselves to the highest bidder.

In the realm of ego life, there is never enough of anything. Ego uses a great deal of physical and mental space to fill and store its ambitions and to preserve and expand its possessions. Consider the physical space: there is no way to measure how big is big enough. An apartment is not as good as a house, a house not as good as a mansion, a mansion not as good as a country.

When a person owns a decent house, they proudly announce ownership. The papers are signed and legally approved. This person never realizes that the first and only true owner of the house is the earth mother *herself.* From the earliest times, humans have demonstrated the pride of ownership, believing that owning land means owning all the resources, such as food and water, on it. All creatures living on earth will fight for food, sex, and shelter.

Which is more cherished, the name or the body?
Which is worth more, the body or possessions?
Which is more beneficial, to gain or to lose?
Extreme fondness is necessarily very costly.
The more you cling to, the more you lose.
So knowing what is sufficient averts disgrace.
Knowing when to stop averts danger.
This can lead to a longer life. (44:1–3)

Once ownership is established, business deals are made to enhance the growth of the property and maintain its ownership. The possessive ego never wants to stop, since ego serves only its possessiveness. Therefore ego cannot distinguish when enough is enough. *Extreme fondness is necessarily very costly.*

Since the body will necessarily die, what is the value of it? If the ego can be completely abandoned, how can it be possessed? Since gain and loss complement each other, how can we have one without the other? We come from nothing and we have nothing. We gather nothing on our journey to death other than our own energized deeds. What we gain is what we will lose. The more we gain, the more we will lose. *The more you cling to, the more you lose.* The hope and the loss are equally important and mutually proportional; each hope generates a loss and each loss is a loss of energy driven by hope.

BEYOND EGO CONFLICT

Our ego attempts to play its game in the domains of body and mind. During our lifespan we experience three kinds of memory: biological, psychological, and spiritual. Biological memory is our instinctive behavior. Sensory perception is, mostly if not entirely, biologically determined. How to breathe, see, listen, sustain our bodies, and procreate is all built into our biological memory. Psychological memory is the master game of ego. It stands between mind and heart, soul and spirit, gliding back and forth, up and down. Ego occupies the largest space in our world, much larger than our biological self, and larger than our human soul can encompass. When something extraordinary occurs and the ego can neither control it nor let it go, it will cause psychic conflict leading to a physical, defensive reaction. Many chronic problems, some organic ailments, and all the psychosomatic symptoms are caused by this conflict.

When the psychic conflict becomes more intense, ego will go to any extreme to retain control. However, if the ego's grip is released, it will create a valuable spiritual journey, a deep realization, a total internal cleansing, and a new freedom of life. Love, compassion, kindness, and faith are the greatest assets in spiritual practice and in going beyond ego grasping and conflict. Many traumatizing events become transformed to bliss for those who have mastered them. The mechanism is our conscience, love, compassion, kindness, and faith. The conscience is one of the highest forms of activity that the soul can conduct. When ego relaxes, there is a connection between soul and spirit at the level of conscience, enabling stillness of spirit, clarity of insight, and swiftness of action. In this way, all realms of conflicts can be dissolved through virtuous acts, acceptance, forgiveness, and inner trust.

Walking the Way: Energy Transformation

The art of walking the spiritual path does not apply to the physical act of walking, but centers on our drive to follow our dreams and achieve our goals. It is the journey of our soul. On this journey, although each step forward may prove difficult, it leads necessarily and naturally to the next step, geared always toward eternity.

Taoism has accumulated only a handful of documented teachings but provides endless practical advice. Taoist teachings contain few rules to be followed but offer rich and invaluable direction. There are no commandments to obey, only revelations to be explored. Many enlightened teachers are here, ready to guide our pilgrimage. They can help us to understand the body and teach us how to distill the mind. We will then awaken to the harmonious flow of universe.

The Taoist teachings focus essentially on the transformation of Jing and Chi into Shen. Chi is vital energy or life force. Jing is the generative energy or sexual essence. We cultivate these energies, conserve them, and refine them into Shen, the spiritual energy. We then use the Shen to enter the Wu Chi (the origin or source of all things, the undifferentiated, primoridal void) and return to the Tao.

Chi manifests as psychophysical energy between body and spirit. Shen represents the cosmic/wisdom spirit. Our spiritual pilgrimage is a Chi-gathering practice. *Cai Chi* means to collect or gather Chi. The spiritual pilgrimage becomes the practice of gathering the Chi of dews, flowers, mountains, spirits, and stars into the Jing-body, the vessel of spirit.

The complete Taoist pilgrimage consists of planting the seed of *zhenren*, the pure or authentic person, in the fields of body and soul, and then cultivating that seed to its fruition. This is accomplished through the practice of gathering, circulating, and transforming the Chi of the universe in our various energy centers. This involves calming the desires of the heart, abandoning the minding mind, stilling the confused spirit, and unifying these three conscious realms into one spirit within the cosmic void.

In order to merge three into one, we must be in harmony with two. Just as the Tao Te Ching has two distinct sections, Tao and Te, our spiritual practice concerns harmonizing the seed of Tao (the Way) with the deed of Te (Virtuous Action). As the Tao and Te become one, we awaken and manifest our true spirit. This chapter is devoted to presenting some of the practices that can assist us in our spiritual pilgrimage of gathering, conserving, refining, and transmuting Chi, and to exploring some of the ways that the ancient Taoist *I Ching*, or *Book of Changes*, and the principles of energy alchemy can assist us on our pilgrimage.

THE WISDOM OF THE I CHING

A major role in the discovery of Taoism's practical way to work with the energy of the universe was played by the legendary Chinese emperor Fu Hsi, who has been credited in Chinese history with the discovery of the symbols that are the foundation of the *I Ching*, the most ancient scripture of Taoist philosophy.

The *I Ching* is a book of prophecy and wisdom centering around the ideas of balance through opposites (yin and yang) and acceptance of change. The oldest parts of its text are thought to have attained their present form in the century before Confucius. Its images and concepts were taken partly from oracles and partly from the mythology, history, and poetry of earlier ages. The *I Ching* consists of eight trigrams (simple patterns composed of a series of lines), corresponding to the powers of nature, which, according to legend, were copied by Fu Hsi from the back of a turtle. The various combinations of the eight trigrams give us the sixty-four hexagrams used in the *I Ching*.

The hexagrams that embody the *I Ching* symbolism are each composed of six horizontal lines; each line is either yang (masculine, creative, associated with the sun) or yin (feminine, receptive, associated with the moon). The yang lines are solid and unbroken; the yin lines are broken lines with a gap in the center. These six yin or yang lines are stacked from bottom to top in each hexagram. There are 2^6 or sixty-four possible combinations and thus sixty-four hexagrams.

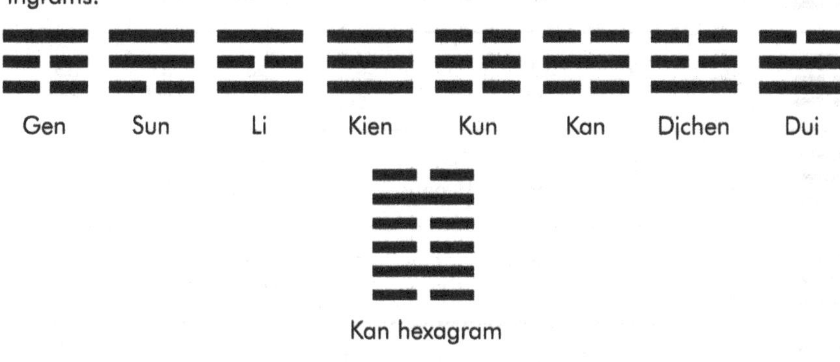

THE EIGHT TRIGRAMS AND THE KAN HEXAGRAM

As noted previously, each hexagram is made of two trigrams. The lower trigram is regarded as the earth trigram and the upper trigram is the heaven trigram. Alternatively, the lower trigram is seen as the inner aspect of a change that is occurring. The upper trigram is the outer aspect. The change described is thus the dynamic of the inner (personal) aspect relating to the outer (external) situation.

The figure on page 55 illustrates the eight trigrams and the hexagram known as *Kan.* Eight of the hexagrams pair the same two trigrams, and these hexagrams retain the same name as the individual trigrams, as in this example.

Each hexagram represents a state, a process, or a change that is happening at the present moment. The process of consulting the *I Ching* for wisdom or prophecy involves determining the hexagram that reflects the situation by some random method—such as casting yarrow stalks or coins—and then reading the *I Ching* text associated with that hexagram. The sixty-four possible hexagrams symbolize all states of being or tendencies of energy orientation. Energy transformations occur in the unending flow of changes in life from the

FU-HSI'S TABLE OF THE I CHING

upper Trigram Lower								
	2 Kun	23 Bo	8 Bi	20 Guan	16 Yü	35 Dsin	45 Tsui	12 Pi
	15 Kiën	52 Gen	39 Giën	53 Dsiën	62 Siau Go	56 Lü	31 Hiën	33 Dun
	7 Schï	4 Mong	29 Kan	59 Huan	40 Hië	64 We dsi	47 Kun	6 Sung
	46 Schong	18 Gu	48 Dsing	57 Sun	32 Hong	50 Ding	28 Da Go	44 Gou
	24 Fu	27 I	3 Dschun	42 I(Yi)	51 Dschen	21 Schï Ho	17 Sui	25 Wu Wang
	36 Ming	22 Bi	63 Gi dsi	37 Gia Jen	55 Fong	30 Li	49 Go	13 Tung Jen
	19 Lin	41 Sun	60 Dsië	61 Dschung Fu	54 Gui Me	38 Kui	58 Dui	10 Lü
	11 Tai	26 Da Tschu	5 Sü	9 Siau Tschu	34 Da Dschuang	14 Da Yu	43 Guai	1 Kiën

microcosmic through the macrocosmic levels of existence. Likely possibilities and probabilities of the outcomes of change may be ascertained based on relevant variables present in a "snapshot" of experience at a given moment in time. These possibilities and probabilities can be perceived through the use of the *I Ching* hexagrams and traditional interpretive texts.

Once a hexagram is determined, each line is determined as either changing (old) or unchanging (young). Since each changing line is seen as being in the process of becoming its opposite, a new hexagram can be formed by transposing each changing yin line with a yang line, and vice versa. Thus, further insight into the process of change is gained by reading the text of this new hexagram and viewing it as the result of the current change. In this way, the *I Ching* can be a powerful tool for guidance on the Taoist path.

Tao Huang: My Discovery of the I Ching

At the beginning of the Chinese Revolution, the *I Ching* was forbidden reading. It was considered by the government to be a reflection of a pernicious feudal culture and a poisonous, conservative Confucian heritage. But I had an unwavering desire to gain a thorough understanding of the *I Ching*, which was considered by many to be one of the great treasures of China. It had always been valued as the foundation of Taoist cosmology and the origin of Chinese traditional wisdom.

To my disappointment, my initial study of the *I Ching* left me feeling very confused. I was unaware at the time that throughout Chinese history, the interpretation of this work had provided an ideological battleground for commentators. It had been the subject of a deep-seated conflict between Taoist practitioners and Confucian scholars. The Confucian interpretation focused largely upon linguistic explanation and analytical understanding. The Taoist version centered on practicality, on understanding natural events, and deepening one's conscious process. I was becoming aware of the fact that the Taoist view of the universe and of nature, as well as of human relations and Chinese science, was at the very root of Chinese civilization. Conversely, Confucian ideology had served, since very early times, as a principal instrument of the feudal order.

I realized that as Confucian culture had become dominant, the Taoist worldview and its theory on nature-related practices had often been viewed by rulers as dangerous, weird, and obscure, despite its contributions to science, medicine, and other areas of Chinese culture. I had been quite unaware of the extent to which the Taoist worldview had been systematically repressed by the establishment, nationally as well as locally.

I began to understand that in the Taoist tradition, the *I Ching* was considered a sacred book. It was understood to contain a secret code that would awaken human consciousness. It served to reveal one's true destiny, and provided a key for transforming and enriching the life force we inherited from our ancestors and our parents, as well as the energies of heaven and earth. This view of life as a process of self-transformation—an inner journey—was rooted in the view that human beings are a microcosm that reflects the energies of the macrocosm. In the Taoist view there is no limit to the self-cultivation of one's intrinsic creative and spiritual potential.

I have been thrilled to discover the *I Ching*'s wisdom about the Taoist path of spiritual cultivation. Throughout this book, we will incorporate elements from the *I Ching* to illuminate our discussion. For example, in this chapter we will be exploring some of the practices that can assist us in our spiritual pilgrimage of gathering, conserving, refining, and transmuting Chi on the path of transformation. The *I Ching* hexagrams Xiaochu and Dachu convey much wisdom about this process.

Small mystical field (Xiaochu) of the 9th hexagram

LARGER MYSTICAL FIELD (DACHU) OF THE 26TH HEXAGRAM

In the *I Ching* there are two mystical energy fields, the small mystical field (Xiaochu) of the ninth hexagram and the larger mystical field (Dachu) of the twenty-sixth hexagram. Xiaochu deals with the animal body and its spirit, while Dachu refers specifically to the human body and its spirit. How to integrate within ourselves these two fields into oneness of spirit is the essence of Taoist inner alchemy. We need to be in harmony with the energy field of mother earth, and be able to transform the energies of fruits, vegetables, nuts, and seeds. Yet we also need to be in harmony with the energy field of the human realm, so we can walk the way of beauty, values, justice, and spiritual immortality.

PRACTICES FOR ENERGY ALCHEMY

Intuitive sensitivity has always played an important role in traditional Chinese culture, philosophy, and medicine. Traditional Chinese cultural innovators were grounded in meditative awareness, and the intuitive and meditative dimension came forth in early cultural formations, such as prehistoric shamanistic Taoism, the *I Ching*, alchemy, and Chinese medicine. These visionaries drew the energies of the earth, sun, moon, mountains, lakes, and plants into their bodily awareness. They also gathered the energies of the wind, storms, and rain into the body's energetic channels, or meridians.

Traditional Chinese medicine builds on the foundation laid by early Chinese alchemy, which aimed to understand the principles underlying the formation and functioning of the cosmos. Alchemists sought to utilize the energies and properties of various substances, ascend to higher states of being, and become a *zhenren*, a true or authentic person, a Taoist sage.

Throughout its history, Chinese alchemy evolved two distinct traditions: *waidan* ("external alchemy") and *neidan* or ("internal alchemy"). The former, which arose earlier, is based on compounding elixirs through manipulating natural substances. Its texts include recipes that include rituals and descriptions of the cosmic properties of various organic and inorganic elements. Internal alchemy developed as an independent discipline around the beginning of the Tang period. It relies substantially on the *waidan* tradition, but aims to produce a spiritual "elixir" within the body/mind of the alchemist.

The Chinese have an insightful theory about all natural elements and beings on the face of the earth. This theory advocates that water and fire have Chi but no being. Plants have Chi and being but no consciousness. Animals have Chi, being, and consciousness but no righteousness. Human beings have Chi, being, consciousness, and righteousness. Sages can rise beyond the limits of human freedom.

Nonbeings (water and fire) are the invisible substances used to construct beings. Living beings are the biomechanical formations of earth and heaven. Human beings stand firmly on two legs with feet planted on the ground, facing the sky. The body/mind is itself a cosmic body, a cosmic tree, and a mystic field. The five fingers on each hand represent the five elements of the universe (wood, fire, earth, metal, and water). The five fingers also connect the human being to the earthly kingdom of five (monera, protista, fungi, plantae, and animalia).

In the five elements theory of traditional Chinese philosophy, wood, fire, earth, metal, and water are the basic elements of the material world. These elements are in constant movement and change. In traditional Chinese medicine, the five elements theory is used to interpret the relationship between the physiology and pathology of the human body and the natural environment. The five elements represent the processes that are fundamental to the cycles of nature, and therefore correspond to the human body.

The five elements philosophy assigns each of the five elements a series of qualities and then applies them to the classification of all phenomena. Wood, for example, is characterized by the qualities of germination, extension, softness, and harmony. It is then inferred that anything with those characteristics should be included in the category of the wood element. Fire involves the aspects of heat and flaring; earth involves the aspects of growing, nourishing, and changing; metal is associated with cleaning up, killing, strength, and firmness; and water is associated with cold, moisture, and downward flowing.

Fire descends from heaven. Water rises from earth. Earth stands on top of water. Wood represents the soft, watery, and murky element of evergreen. Metal forms a hard, dry crystal. All plants are devoid of the metal element, whereas animals have all five elements. All plants and most sea creatures are devoid of blood. Their bones, if any, are very soft. Only animals possess all five elements: bodily water, conscious fire, the governing element of muscles and glands (earth), the constructive element of blood (wood), and the skeletal element of proteins and mineral (metal).

The Beauty of the Body

Life is challenging; we inevitably meet a variety of physical, emotional, and spiritual difficulties during our lifetime. But the body doesn't understand the meaning of suffering. It is the conscious mind that discriminates and gets involved with all feelings and sensations, and with the meaning of suffering and sin. The egoistic mind identifies with these experiences as concepts and categories, as good and bad. This explains the reason that many religious followers actively blind-side their true selves by misinterpreting the nature of life. They are unable to cast off their negative memories, experiences, and attitudes; they choose to be attached to them through fear of the unknown. They fail to understand the ultimate oneness of all things.

The body is the structure of human physical existence, the foundation of mind and spirit. Without the bodily form, there can be no growth of mind, spirit, and culture. Without the body, the beauty of human life would cease to exist. The body is the foundation for the personality and emotional qualities that reflect the inner self. The human body is the most beautiful object in the world: the source of attraction for love and longing, both biological and spiritual. The human body is our most precious human gift. It is the vehicle and alchemical vessel whereby extraordinary and limitless physical-emotional-spiritual transformation can take place.

Three Mystical Energy Fields

In the human body there are three mystical energy fields or "cauldrons" where energy transformation takes place: the lower Tan Tien, the middle Tan Tien, and the upper Tan Tien, in the abdominal, chest, and brain regions, respectively. (See the discussion about the three Tan Tiens in Chapter Two.) All three fields are fueled by the energy pathways (meridians) than run throughout the body. Taoist practitioners work with the three Tan Tiens in three stages.

In the first stage, one works with the lower Tan Tien, and focuses on gathering and concentrating Chi in the lower Tan Tien. Taoist practitioners learn to increase the flow of Chi in the body and strengthen the Chi pressure in the lower Tan Tien, organs, and fascia (connective tissue). Chi "pressure" refers to the result of condensing a large amount of energy into a small space. This is not unlike the effect of packing air into a tire until the tire becomes strong enough to safely support the weight of a heavy vehicle. "Strengthening Chi pressure" means to increase the level of Chi and to increase the internal pressure of the body so that we will be healthier and live longer. Much like a living battery, we may build up and store energy (Chi). If we store enough of this energy, then we are able to use it to accomplish greater things, including the healing of our bodies.

Developing the Chi pressure is one of the best practices we can use to reverse the downward spiraling movement of the quantity and quality of our life force into an upward spiraling movement. The increase of the Chi pressure in our lower Tan Tien will enhance our healing, meditation abilities, and the art of daily living. It will also nourish our original force.

Chi pressure in the lower Tan Tien roots our body and mind. When you want to become a big tree, you need deep roots, which require a high Chi pressure in the lower Tan Tien. The inner power in the Tan Tien helps us to regain our inner peace and stillness and our connection with the mind of the Tao.

The lower Tan Tien is the energy reservoir in the body. It is the place where we store the energy we generate, gather, and absorb in Chi Kung practices and meditation. If the energy is stored in the lower Tan Tien it can be accessed later, but if it is not stored, the Chi dissipates and cannot be used.

The lower Tan Tien is also called the "ocean of Chi." According to Chinese medical theory, once the ocean is full, it will overflow into the eight extraordinary meridians, the eight principle energy channels of the body. Once these are full, the Chi flows into the twelve ordinary meridians, each of which is associated with a particular organ. The lower Tan Tien is therefore the foundation of the entire energetic system of the body.

We usually refer to the lower abdominal area as the lower Tan Tien; this is the area that Chi Kung practitioners particularly work with. However, as noted previously, we have three Tan Tiens: the lower Tan Tien (in the abdomen, the seat of awareness), the middle Tan Tien (the heart, the seat of consciousness), and the upper Tan Tien (behind the mid-eyebrow point, the seat of Shen, or spirit). All three Tan Tiens are used in Taoist inner alchemy. Because of their capacity to deal with a large amount of Chi, the Tan Tiens are used as a "laboratory" for inner alchemical work. Translated from the Chinese, the word *Tan* means "elixir." *Tien* means "field or place." It is the place where all the energies of our body, the earth, the universe, and nature come together to form the "pearl," the elixir of immortality, and the nourishment for our soul and spirit.

The second stage works with the middle Tan Tien and involves a practice known as "fusion of the five elements," in which we gain control over the energies of our inner universe so that a connection can be made to the tremendous energy of the universe beyond the body. This energy becomes useful for self-healing, day-to-day living, and reaching spiritual goals.

In this practice, we learn to control the generation and flow of emotional, mental, and physical energies within our body. The practice involves locating and dissolving the negative energies hidden inside our body. Using the five elements theory, a connection is made between the five outer senses—eyes, tongue, mouth, nose, ears—and the five major emotions—anger, hate, worry, sadness, and fear. Once the negative emotion is identified with the organ it is stored in, it can be controlled.

In this practice, negative emotions are neither suppressed nor expressed. Instead, their negative energy is brought to specific points in the body where it is easily neutralized, purified, and then transformed back into our original positive, creative energy. Our original positive energy is crystallized and stored in the middle Tan Tien and harmonized with the Chi we have cultivated and stored in the lower Tan Tien. The Microcosmic Orbit and Six Healing Sounds practices are particularly useful at this stage.

The challenge at this stage is transforming the emotions, transforming the personal into the impersonal, and purifying selfish love into selfless love. Ultimately there is an inner marriage of masculine and feminine, negativity no longer exists, all karma has been met, and only the selflessness and oneness of the *zhenren* (pure, authentic person) is apparent.

In the third stage, which is an advanced stage, we work with the upper Tan Tien. The upper Tan Tien is also known as the "crystal palace." It is a precious energy center or mystical cauldron at the center of the brain. Through a process of purification, Chi is transformed into spirit and lower-energy substances are transformed into higher-energy substances. Once the energy in the lower and middle Tan Tiens has become pure and strong through the transformation of sexual energy and negative emotions, it will then naturally ascend to the upper Tan Tien and be transformed into Shen, or spiritual energy. At every stage, as one comes closer to unity with the Tao, the energies take on a more refined and subtle form.

The brain, of itself, does not produce energy. The subtle psychospiritual energy activated in the upper Tan Tien is supplied through the biomechanical energy from the lower center, the psychosomatic energy from the middle center, and the light from above.

The upper Tan Tien is associated with the pineal gland. When this gland is activated, it is said to become illuminated like thousands of shining crystals, able to receive light (as energy and knowledge) from the universe. When a meditator reaches this state, he or she will see the three different flowers at the three energy centers: Guatama Buddha is seated on the lotus flower; Jesus Christ adorns the snowflake flower; and Lao Tzu embraces the star flower.

The Taoist way of life is to direct the treasured life force downward and outward only for the purpose of procreation. At all other times we preserve it and direct it upward and inward to nourish and rejuvenate the body and brain, and transmute its energy for spiritual transformation and cultivation of the *zhenren*.

Closing the Gate of Life and Death

Taoist energy transformation practices involve locking the energy gate located at the perineum pressure point, known as the "gate of life and death." This opening is locked before the pubic stage begins, and closed after menopause or with the absence of sperm, but opens fully in the productive stage and when sickness manifests.

In order to create and maintain the correct pressure in the lower Tan Tien, we must be able to tighten and seal the sexual organ, the perineum, and the anus. In order to do this, we must be able to contract the pelvic floor and be able to tighten the sexual organ, perineum, and anus in a controlled and coordinated manner. This ability prevents leakage of sexual essence/generative energy (Jing) and preserves it so that it may be transformed into vital life force energy and

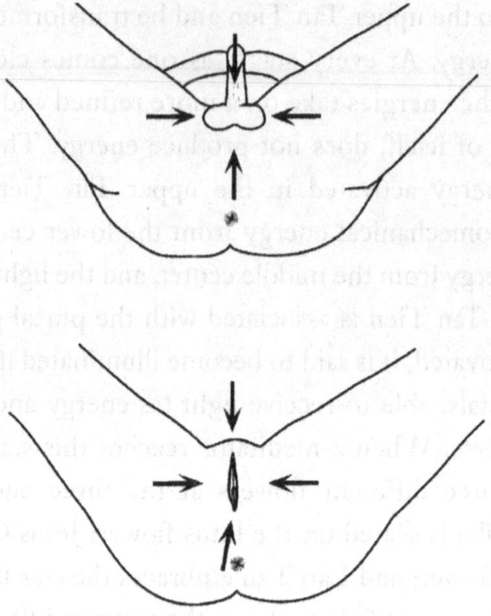

THE GATE OF LIFE AND DEATH

spirit energy. Tightening and sealing the sexual organ, the perineum, and the anus is called "closing the gate of life and death."

The perineum is known as the gate of life and death as it plays such a crucial role both in preventing degeneration and in activating all the organs, glands, and other body functions. The perineum—called the *hui yin*—is located between the genitals and the anus. It constitutes the lowest point of the yin or descending energy channels, and is the lower meeting point of the Governor (ascending) Channel and the Functional (descending) Channel. Through the legs and feet, it is the main link with the earth Chi. When the perineum is strong, the organs remain firm and healthy; when it is weak the organs lose cohesiveness and Chi energy drains away.

The ability to achieve control over the perineum gate and to lead the energy up and inward rather than allowing it to flow down and outward is very important. The dense form of Chi (Jing) produced in the sexual organ is brought into the loop of the Governor and the Functional Channels and thence upward into the brain. On its upward journey, the Chi undergoes several transformations and

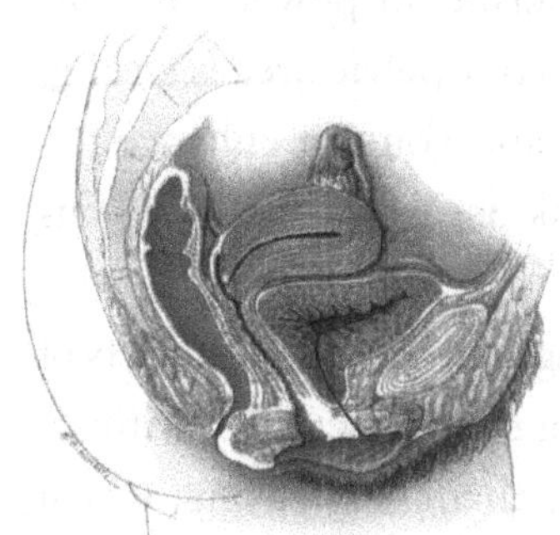
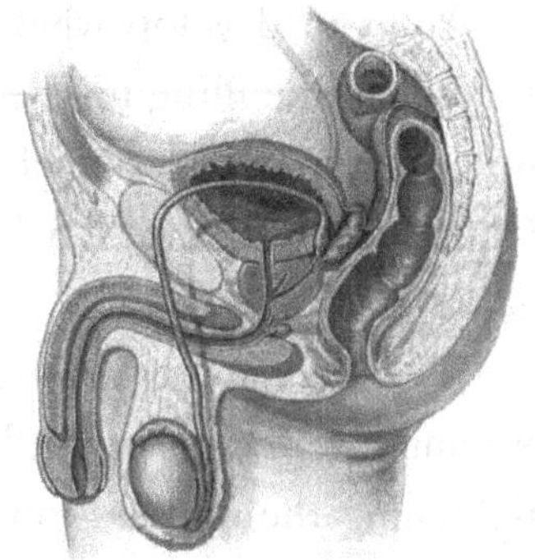

Perineum in the Female and Male Bodies

nourishes and activates all the organs before it finally brings fresh energy and hormones to the brain.

A good beginning practice as we learn to control the perineum gate is massaging the perineum. Massaging the perineum vitalizes the sexual organs and strengthens the pelvic floor. It also contributes to activating the pineal gland, to which it has a direct connection through the Thrusting Channel, the energy channel that is located in the center of the body between the perineum and the crown. Perineum massage also helps one to become aware of the unity of high and low in one's body. It acknowledges the most honorable function of what are often called "the lower organs."

Contracting the muscles of the perineum, sexual organs, and anus activates our connection with the earth energy. By pulling up these areas and drawing in energy through the soles of the feet, we immediately become grounded and energized. Holding a very gentle contraction in the muscles of the perineum, sexual organs, and anus will keep you grounded during Chi Kung or other Taoist practices.

As we practice contracting the perineum, sexual organs, and anus, Chi is pressed inward from all sides, and Chi pressure in the lower Tan Tien rises. The more the Chi is concentrated, the higher its expansive potential becomes. This practice has been called the creation of a "Chi ball." Scattered Chi is concentrated and compressed in the lower Tan Tien, which raises the inner power needed to activate the whole body and all its flows and networks.

You can develop what is known as "perineum power" by contracting and pulling up these areas. When your pelvic area is strong, no energy will leak out of the lower gate, and you can enhance the Chi pressure in your Tan Tien. With a weak perineum and anus, this is not possible.

There are good Taoist exercises to strengthen the different parts of the anus (perineum/pelvic floor) and to learn to contract them without tightening the muscles too much. To make them very strong, which means giving the muscles a strong tonicity, you must do these exercises many times a day. The pleasant thing about them is that you can do these exercises everywhere; good times and places to practice are while waiting at the post office, the bus station, the shop, when you watch a movie or TV, or work on the computer. When you are creative, you will find many occasions during the day to practice these exercises.

The best way to do these exercises is in the standing position. However, you also can practice them sitting or laying on the ground, in bed, or even in the bathtub.

1. First, stand with the feet parallel and shoulder width apart. Root the feet firmly to the earth.
2. Keep part of the awareness on the anus, perineum, and sexual organs.
3. Put your hands below the navel on the lower abdomen, very gently and softly. Smile and do a few deep, abdominal breaths.
4. Exhale and flatten and contract the abdominal area. Follow this action with the fingers of both hands.
5. Next, inhale with a half breath, using the dragon sound. The dragon sound is a high-pitched *Hummmmm*. Feel a pressure, like that of a vacuum cleaner, in the abdominal area and the throat. This vacuum/sucking sensation is a sucking in of Chi pressure.
6. Lightly pull up the anus, perineum, and sexual organs. At the same time, expand the abdomen, while holding the breath and Chi pressure in the abdomen. Always keep the chest diaphragm down and the chest relaxed.

7. Now, exhale with the tiger sound. The tiger sound, *Hummmmm*, is a low-pitched, growling sound. Push the energy pressure down to the lower abdominal area.
8. Next, hold the breath out and laugh softly inside. Feel the vibration in the abdomen. Hold the breath out as long as is comfortable, then inhale and slowly regulate the breath.
9. Repeat the whole process with the dragon and tiger breath three to six times. Feel the pressure becoming stronger with every breath. When you inhale and exhale consciously, you draw in and hold Chi. When you inhale and exhale unconsciously, you lose Chi.
10. When you are ready to conclude the exercise, collect the energy at your navel.

Microcosmic Orbit Energy Circulation

The Chinese discovered the energetic channels or meridians through the practice of meditation, acupuncture, massage, and spiritual healing. These meridians can be charged and recharged through practicing the Microcosmic Orbit internal energy circulation exercise (discussed briefly in Chapter Two).

The Microcosmic Orbit circulates Chi between the Governor Channel, which ascends from the base of the spine up to the head, and the Functional Channel, which runs from the tip of the tongue down the middle of the torso to the perineum.

The practice of Microcosmic Orbit meditation will help you to feel Chi more easily inside, outside, and around the body. It awakens, circulates, and directs Chi through the two most important energy routes in the body. The Microcosmic Orbit also strengthens Original Chi and teaches you the basics of circulating Chi. It allows the palms, the soles of the feet, the mid-eyebrow point, and the crown to open. These specific locations are the major points where energy can be absorbed, condensed, and transformed into fresh new life force. Dedicated practice of this ancient esoteric method eliminates stress and nervous tension, energizes the internal organs, restores health to damaged tissue, and builds a strong sense of personal well-being.

The following are the steps involved in the Microcosmic Orbit meditation:

1. Focus on the lower Tan Tien (the area between the navel, kidneys, and sexual organs). Feel the pulsing in this area, and observe whether this area feels tense or relaxed, cool or warm, expansive or contracting. Notice any sensations of Chi: tingling, heat, expansiveness, pulsations, electric or magnetic sensations. Allow these to grow and expand. Let the Chi of the lower Tan Tien flow out to the navel.
2. Use your mind/heart power to spiral the Chi in the navel point, guiding and moving it. Let the energy flow down to the sexual center (the ovaries for women, or the testicles for men).
3. Move the energy from the sexual center to the perineum and then down to the soles of the feet.
4. Draw the energy up from the soles of the feet to the perineum and then to the sacrum.
5. Draw the energy up from the sacrum to the Door of Life (the point in the spine opposite the navel).
6. Draw the energy up to the mid-spine point (the T-11 vertebrae).
7. Draw the energy up to the base of the skull (also known as the "jade pillow").
8. Draw the energy up to the crown.
9. Move the energy down from the crown to the mid-eyebrow point.
10. Touch the tip of your tongue to your upper palate; press and release a few times. Then lightly touch the palate with the tongue and leave it there, sensing the electric or tingling feeling in the tip of the tongue. Move the energy down from the mid-eyebrow to where the tip of your tongue and the palate meet.
11. Move the energy down from the palate through your tongue to the throat center.

12. Move the energy down from the throat to the heart center.
13. Bring the energy down from the heart to the solar plexus. Feel a small sun shining out.
14. Bring the energy back down to the navel.
15. Continue to circulate your energy through this sequence of points, making at least nine cycles. Once the pathways are open, you can let your energy flow continuously like a river, without needing to stop at each point.
16. When you are ready to conclude the exercise, collect the energy at your navel.

    Men: Cover your navel with both palms, left hand over right. Collect and mentally spiral the energy outward from the navel thirty-six times clockwise and then inward twenty-four times counterclockwise.

    Women: Cover your navel with both palms, right hand over left. Collect and mentally spiral the energy outward from the navel thirty-six times counterclockwise and then inward twenty-four times clockwise.

The Six Healing Sounds

The Six Healing Sounds exercise is a simple yet powerful Taoist practice that uses natural sounds to stimulate, energize, and heal our inner organs and their corresponding energy centers. This practice promotes physical, energetic, and emotional healing and balance. Regular daily practice of the Six Healing Sounds will help you keep in touch with the energetic and emotional state of your internal organs. Practice this exercise in the evening before you go to sleep. By clearing out negative emotions before sleeping, you allow the night's rest to recharge your energy positively. It will help sensitize you to the varieties and differing qualities of Chi.

The sounds are used to generate certain frequencies for specific healing. Each sound can generate different energy for the healing of different organs. Cultivating the positive qualities associated with each organ is essential so that the negative or sick energy has less room to grow.

When practicing the Six Healing Sounds, keep your eyes open only while making each sound. Close your eyes, take a deep breath, and smile to appropriate the organ between each healing sound exhalation. For more details of this practice, see the book *Taoist Ways to Transform Stress into Vitality* by Mantak Chia.

LUNGS ARE THE CHI OF DUI (LAKE) HEXAGRAM

Lung Sound

Element: metal
Associated organ: large intestine
Sound: *ssssss* (tongue behind the teeth)
Emotions: negative—grief, sadness, depression
positive—courage, righteousness, high self-esteem
Color: white, clear, metallic
Season: fall
Direction: west

Position: Sit in a chair with your back straight and your hands resting palms up on your thighs. Have your feet flat on the floor about hips' width apart. Smile down to your lungs and be aware of any sadness, grief, or excess heat in your lungs. Slowly inhale, and raise your hands up your upper chest, with your fingers pointing toward each other. Continue raising your hands past shoulder level, and begin to rotate the palms out as you raise your hands in front of you and above your head, with the palms up. Point your fingers toward the fingers of the opposite hand and keep your elbows slightly bent.

Sound: Part your lips slightly, holding your jaw gently closed. Look up through the space between your two hands and push your palms slightly upward as you slowly exhale and make the sound *ssssss*.

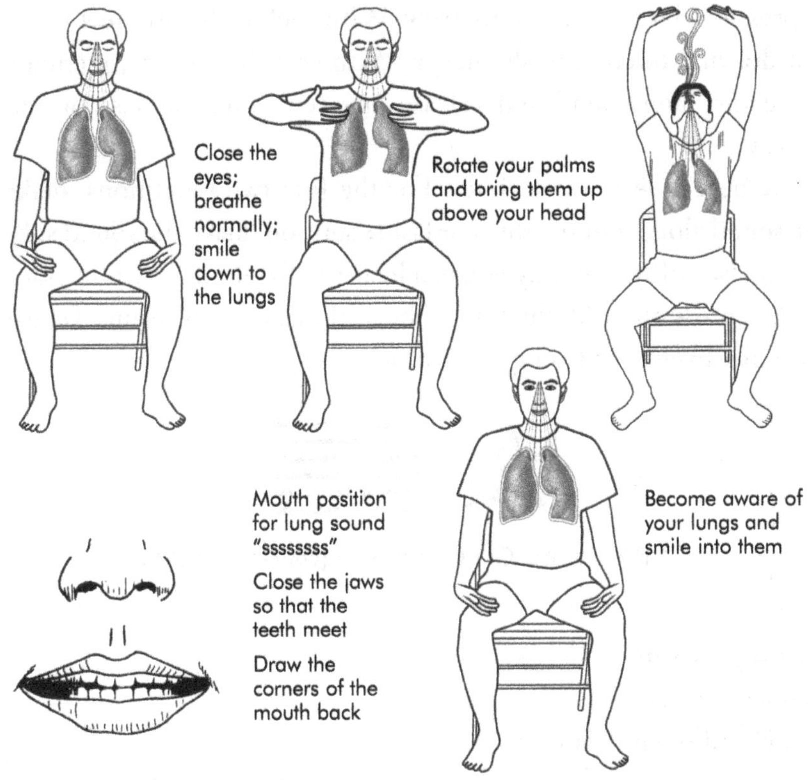

LUNG SOUND AND EXERCISE

Picture and feel any excess heat, sadness, grief, depression, sickness, or dingy white color expelled and released as you exhale slowly and fully.

Resting posture: When you have completely exhaled, rotate the palms to face downward with the fingers still pointing toward each other. Slowly lower the palms and bring them just in front of the chest, feeling the lungs' aura.

Close your eyes and be aware of your lungs. Smile into your lungs, and as you inhale, imagine that you are breathing in a bright white mist of light. Breathe this light into your lungs and feel it cooling, cleansing, invigorating, healing, and refreshing your lungs. Feel it flowing down to the large intestine to balance the energy of the yin lungs and yang large intestine, allowing the courage quality of your lungs to emerge. Grow more courage so that sadness and depression have less room to grow. With each in-breath, feel yourself drawing in cool, fresh energy. With each out-breath, mentally make the lung sound and release any remaining sadness or hot energy.

Repeat at least three times. For the first two repetitions, make the sound aloud. On the third or last repetition, make the sound subvocally (so softly that only you can hear it). To alleviate extreme sadness, depression, cold, flu, toothache, asthma, or emphysema, repeat six, nine, twelve, or twenty-four times.

KIDNEYS ARE THE CHI OF THE KAN (WATER) HEXAGRAM

Kidney Sound

Element: water

Associated organ: bladder

Sound: *chooooo* (with your lips forming an "O" as if blowing out a candle)

Emotions: negative—fear, shock

Positive—gentleness, wisdom

Color: dark blue or black

Season: winter

Direction: north

Position: Begin with you hands facing upward on your opened thighs. Smile to your kidneys, and be aware of any excess cold or heat in the kidney region. Then bring your legs together, ankles and knees touching. Lean forward and clasp the fingers of both hands together around your knees. Inhale, and pull your arms straight from the lower back while bending the torso forward (this allows your back to protrude in the area of the kidneys). Tilt your head upward as you look straight ahead, still pulling on your arms from the lower back. Feel your spine pulling against your knees.

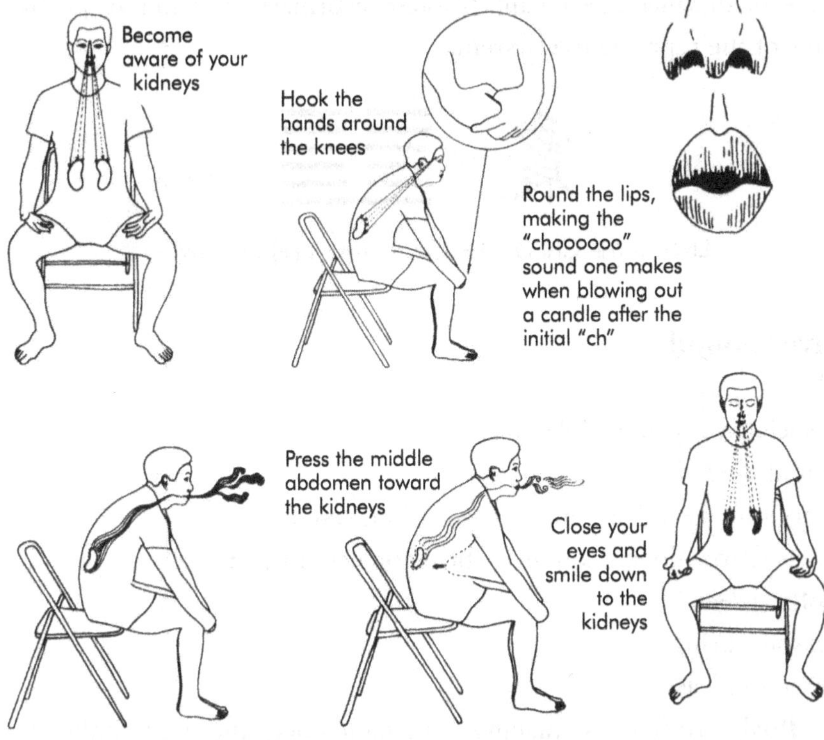

KIDNEY SOUND AND EXERCISE

Sound: Round the lips slightly and slowly exhale while making the sound *chooooo*. Simultaneously contract your abdomen, pulling it in toward your kidneys. Imagine any fear, sickness, imbalances, excess cold, or excess heat energy being released and squeezed out of the fascia surrounding the kidneys.

Resting posture: After you have fully exhaled, slowly straighten until you are erect and return your hands to touch the aura of the kidneys. Close your eyes and again be aware of your kidneys. Smile to your kidneys, and on the in-breath, imagine you are breathing a brilliant luminous blue light mist into them. Feel this mist healing, balancing, and refreshing your kidneys and bladder, and picture them glowing a bright blue color. On the out-breath, imagine you are still making the kidney sound.

Repeat at least three times. Repeat six, nine, twelve, or twenty-four times to alleviate extreme fear, fatigue, low-pitched ringing in the ears, dizziness, back pain, bladder or urinary infection, or problems of the reproductive system.

LIVER IS THE CHI OF THE CHEN (THUNDER) HEXAGRAM

Liver Sound

Element: wood
Associated organ: gallbladder
Sound: *shhhhh*
Emotions: negative—anger, frustration, resentment
positive—loving kindness, benevolence, forgiveness
Color: green
Season: spring
Direction: east

Position: Start by placing your hands over the liver. Smile to your liver, and be aware of any anger, frustration, resentment, or excess heat in the liver region. Slowly begin to inhale a deep breath as you extend your arms up from the sides with your palms up. Raise your palms over your head. Interlace your fingers together and turn your joined hands over to face the sky, palms up. Push out through the heels of the palms and extend the arms up, keeping the shoulders relaxed. Bend a little to the left and stretch your right arm slightly to gently open the area of your liver.

Sound: Open your eyes wide (the eyes are the sensory opening of the liver). Slowly exhale, making the sound *shhhhh* subvocally. Feel that you are releasing any trapped excess heat, anger, illness, or negativity from your liver and that these are riding out of your body on your breath.

Resting posture: Once you have fully exhaled, close your eyes, separate your hands, turn the palms down, and slowly lower your arms to the sides, leading with the heels of the hands. Smile, and inhale a

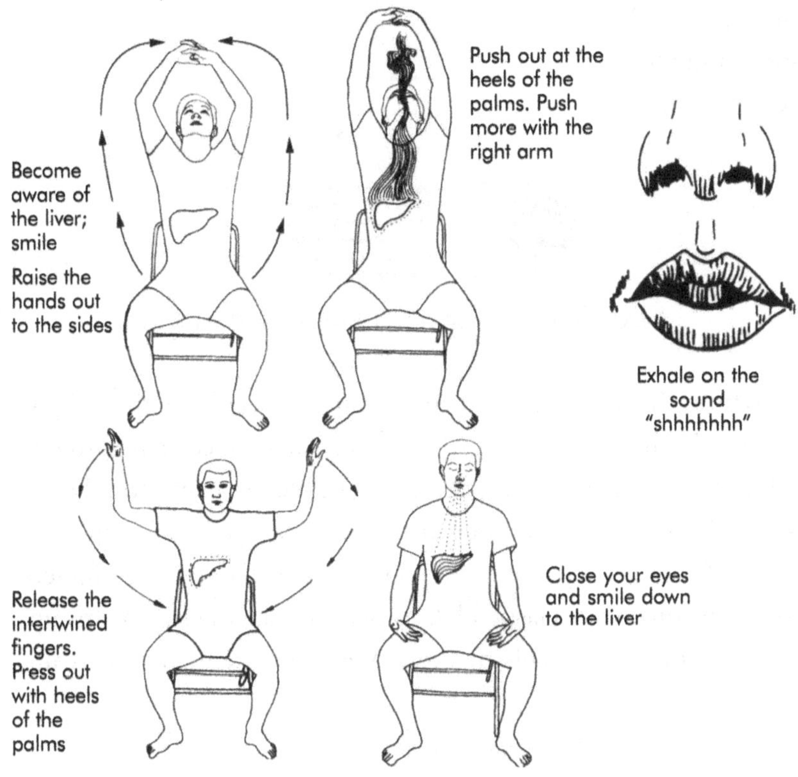

LIVER SOUND AND EXERCISE

shiny spring green mist, illuminating the liver and gallbladder. Bring your hands back to rest on the liver's aura. Close your eyes and smile into your liver. With each in-breath, breathe fresh Chi into your liver and gallbladder. With each out-breath, mentally make the liver sound.

Repeat at least three times. Repeat six, nine, twelve, or twenty-four times to alleviate extreme anger, to relieve red or watery eyes, to remove a sour or bitter taste in the mouth, or to detoxify the liver.

Heart Sound

Element: fire

Associated organ: small intestine

Sound: *haaaaaw*

Emotions: negative—arrogance, harshness, cruelty, hatred

positive—joy, honor, respect, love, happiness

Color: red
Season: summer
Direction: south

HEART IS THE CHI OF THE LI (FIRE) HEXAGRAM

Position: Begin with the hands facing upward on the thighs. Smile to your heart, and be aware of any arrogance, haughtiness, hatred, giddiness, cruelty, or hastiness in it. Slowly begin to inhale a deep breath as you extend your arms up from the sides with your palms up. Raise your palms over your head. Interlace your fingers together and turn your clasped hands over to face the sky, palms up. Push out through the heels of the palms and extend the arms up,

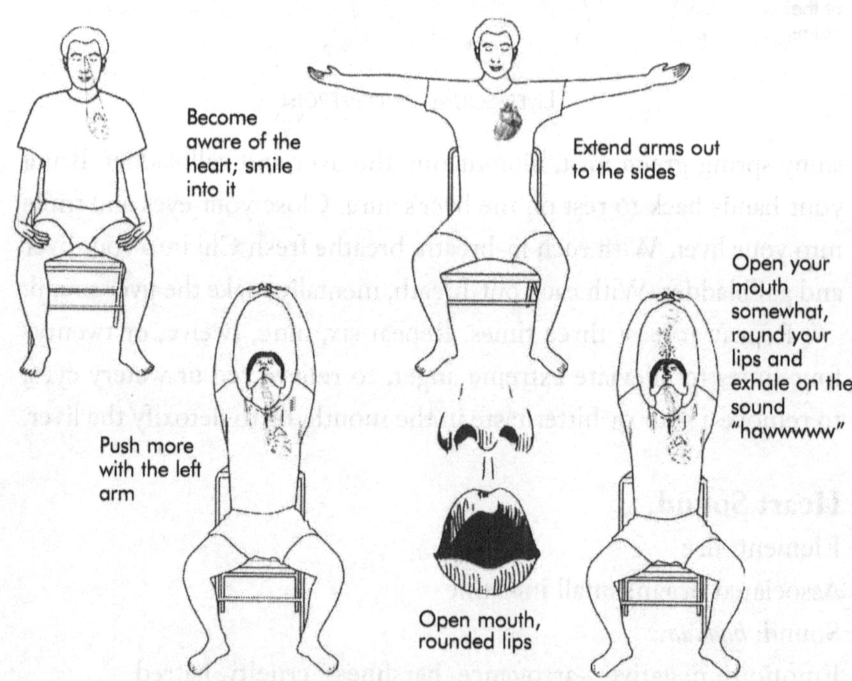

HEART SOUND AND EXERCISE

keeping the shoulders relaxed. Bend a little to the right and stretch your left arm slightly to open the area of your heart.

Sound: Keeping your eyes soft and relaxed, look up through your hands. Slowly exhale, making the sound *haaaaaw* subvocally. Feel that you are releasing any trapped heat, negative emotions, illness, or imbalance from your heart and that these are riding out of the body on your breath.

Resting posture: Once you have fully exhaled, close your eyes, separate your hands, turn the palms down, and slowly lower your arms to the sides, leading with the heels of the hands. As you move, inhale a bright red mist into the heart and small intestine. Bring your hands back to rest on your heart's aura. Smile into your heart. With each in-breath, breathe fresh Chi into your heart. With each out-breath, mentally repeat the heart sound.

Repeat at least three times. Repeat six, nine, twelve, or twenty-four times to alleviate extreme impatience, hastiness, arrogance, nervousness, moodiness, jumpiness, irritability, tongue ulcers, palpitations, sore throat, heart disease, or insomnia and to detoxify the heart.

SPLEEN IS THE CHI OF THE KEN (MOUNTAIN) HEXAGRAM

Spleen Sound

Element: earth
Associated organ: pancreas, stomach
Sound: *whooooo* (gutturally from the throat)
Emotions: negative—worry, excess sympathy, overthinking
  positive—fairness, balance, equanimity, justice, openness
Color: yellow
Season: indian summer
Direction: center (where you stand, looking out to the six directions)

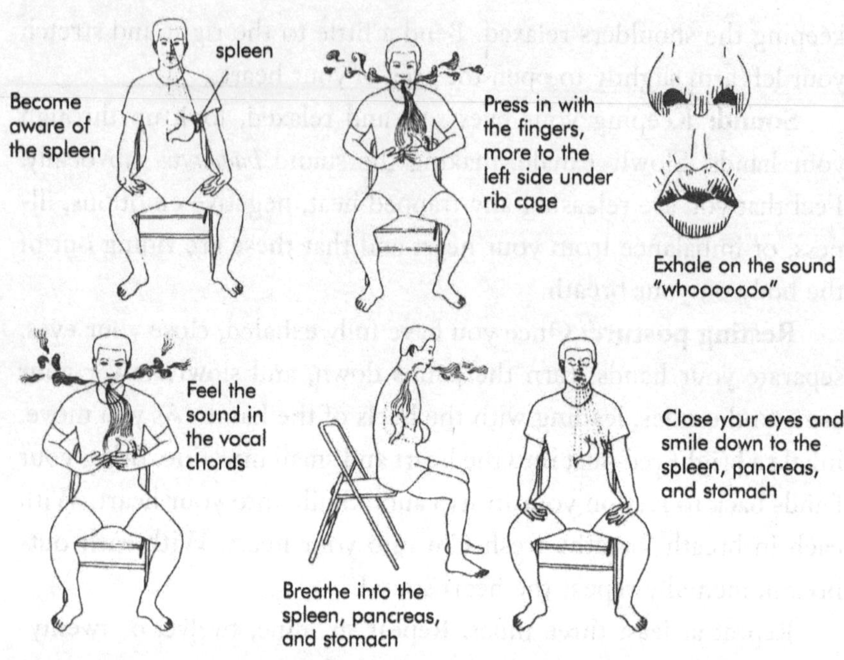

SPLEEN SOUND AND EXERCISE

Position: Be aware of your spleen, and smile sincerely into it. Place your hands on the body so that they cover the spleen, pancreas, and stomach area. Inhale deeply as you move your arms outward in an embrace, and aim the fingers up under the left rib cage. Place the fingers of both hands just beneath the sternum and rib cage on the left side.

Sound: Look out, lean into your fingers, and gently push your fingertips in. Exhale slowly and make the sound *whooooo* from the depths of your throat. Feel yourself releasing any trapped heat, worry, mental fixations, or excess sympathy.

Resting posture: Once you have fully exhaled, close your eyes, slowly release the hands, and extend your arms out, embracing the earth. Return your hands to the resting position on the spleen's aura. Smile to your spleen, pancreas, and stomach. With each in-breath, inhale fresh Chi to your spleen, pancreas, and stomach as a brilliant luminous yellow healing mist that cleanses and refreshes your organs. With each out-breath, mentally make the spleen sound.

Repeat at least three times. Repeat six, nine, twelve, or twenty-four times to alleviate extreme indigestion, heat or cold in the stomach or spleen, worry, nausea, hemorrhoids, fatigue, organ prolapse, or loose stools.

Triple Warmer Sound

"Triple warmer" refers to the upper, middle, and lower torso and to the distinct metabolic transformations that occur within each area. The upper warmer is the area above the diaphragm, where the heart and lungs are located. This area tends to become hot and is responsible for respiration and cardiovascular circulation. The middle warmer, the area between the diaphragm and the navel, becomes warm and is where the digestive organs are located. The lower warmer, the area below the navel, is responsible for reproduction and elimination and is cool in temperature. The sound *heeeee* balances the temperatures of the three levels by bringing hot energy down to the lower center and cold energy up to the higher centers.

Position: Lie on your back with your arms resting at your sides, palms up. Keep your eyes closed. Smile. With a single inhalation, breath first into the upper part of your lungs to expand the upper warmer, then into the middle of the lungs to expand the middle warmer, and finally into the lower lungs to fill the lower warmer. Breathing in this way creates more space inside the torso for each organ, helping to release and circulate any internal heat or cold.

Sound: Exhale while making the sound *heeeee* subvocally, flattening first your chest, then your solar plexus, and finally your lower abdomen. Feel the dark and cloudy color and the cold energy exit from the tips of the fingers.

Resting posture: Once you have fully exhaled, do not to focus on any emotions or purification process. Instead, just let go and relax your body and mind completely.

Repeat at least three times. Repeat six, nine, twelve, or twenty-four times to alleviate insomnia and stress.

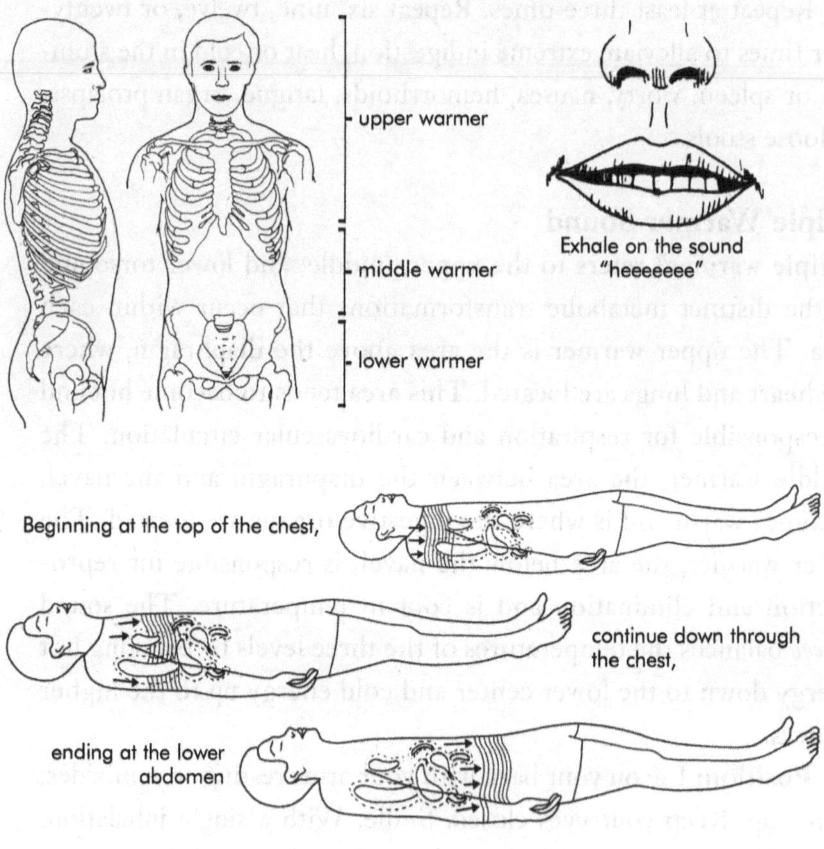

TRIPLE WARMER SOUND AND EXERCISE

When you have completed the Six Healing Sounds practice, smile softly and rest. Remain still and deeply relaxed for several minutes.

In is interesting to note that in the chakra system, the Indian system of energy vortexes in the body, the first five sounds connect to the first five chakras, from the sexual center the throat center; the sixth sound is connected to the third eye, and is an inner sound. Only when the first five sounds are completely integrated and reach a perfect silence can the sixth sound arise; it cannot manifest by itself.

Also, the first five sounds are related to the five animal kingdoms, or the five senses within humans. The human sound, which is the spleen sound, connects the four animal deities—green dragon, red phoenix, white tiger, and black tortoise—through the lower Tan Tien. The spleen is the largest node of the lymphatic system, and technically not an organ, but due to its importance in the immune system and, energetically, in Chinese medicine, it is regarded as a vital organ. As the triple-warmer is activated, the three Tan Tiens are connected: the upper conscious, the middle emotional, and lower physical.

The sounds are always performed in the creative cycle of energy relationships among the five elemental energies (which correlate to the characteristic energies of the organs). The supportive relationship between the primary vital organs and their associated organs is maintained. Since the kidneys (bladder) support the liver (gall bladder) in this creative cycle sequence, the relationship between the bladder and the gallbladder meridians is activated. In the Universal Tao teaching, the triple warmer sound is included as the sixth sound to provide the harmonizing and unifying benefit in the three Tan Tiens. Thus, the sequence for performing the Healing Sounds in the Universal Tao System is as follows: lungs, kidneys, liver, heart, spleen, and triple warmer.

The Frolics of the Five Animals

One of the oldest and most popular holistic exercises, the Frolics of the Five Animals (daiyin) has been utilized by meditators, healers, and martial arts practitioners for thousands of years. Hua Tuo, a famous Chinese physician of the Han Dyansty, developed this practice based on his observations of animals and their special attributes. Hua Tuo taught that by imitating the movements of the tiger, bear, deer, monkey, and bird, we can relax the body, eliminate bad Chi, strengthen physical power, and heal disease. The ancient sages could stretch their bodies and bend their necks like a bird, allowing the energy to circulate outside the skin and inside the body so that the sinews and joints remained smooth and flexible. This system has survived as one of the oldest methods of Chi Kung used for health and healing purposes.

With practice, the essence of the five animals will become alive in you; the energy of these animals will soar through your being, your energy channels, and your whole body.

For all five animal postures, begin standing with the feet parallel and shoulder width apart. Let your arms rest at your sides. All the nine points of the feet should be firmly rooted in the earth. Keep the chest diaphragm down and the chest relaxed. Then move into each animal posture.

Tiger's Game

Drop to the ground with both palms and feet flat on the floor; rock forward and draw backward three times. Then stretch the back upward and forward as high as possible without allowing the palms and feet to leave the ground. Then raise the head up toward the sky, and walk forward and backward seven times with both hands and feet on the floor.

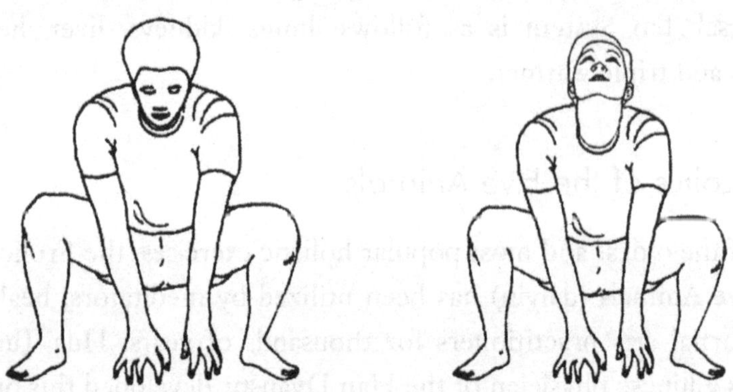

TIGER FORM

Bear's Game

Lie down on your back holding the knees with both hands. Raise the head and chest, rolling up, and lean over to the left side. Return the original position. Then raise the head and chest, rolling up, and lean over the right side. Alternate back and forth, seven times on each side. Then squat on the ground with hands pushing down on the ground.

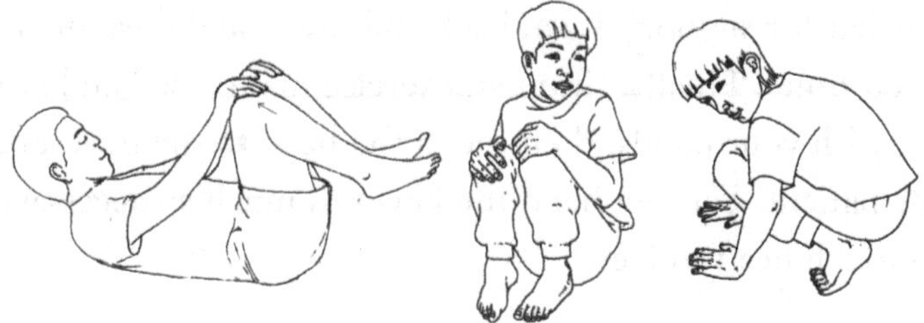

BEAR FORM

Deer's Game

Stand on all fours, with both hands and feet on the ground. Stretch the neck up, and turn the head to the left. While turning the head to the left, stretch the right leg out straight behind you. Return the starting position. Then turn the head to the right. While turning the head to the right, stretch the left leg out straight behind you. Repeat on each side three times. Following this, tuck the head and neck in and down three times.

DEER FORM

Monkey's Game

First, lie on a sturdy exercise mat or twin bed, holding onto the sides for support. Raise and lower the legs and buttocks, swinging legs over torso, seven times. Then, sit on a solid and strong structure such as an exercise device found in most gyms on which you can sit and hook the feet behind a padded support bar under the seat. An alternative would be to sit on a very strong railing that has an upper bar and a lower bar where you can hook your feet behind the lower bar for support. Lean back and lower and raise the upper body seven times. Finally, sit on an exercise mat or bed and hold both feet with your hands, then touch the head to the toes seven times. Be patient. You can bend the knees as much as necessary in order to touch head to feet.

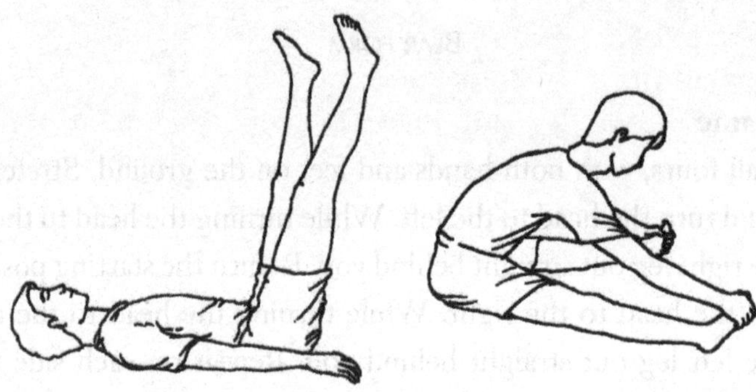

MONKEY FORM

Bird's Game

While standing, raise and stretch one leg out behind you and stretch both arms out to the sides while raising the eyebrows fourteen times. Return to center, then do the same with the other leg. Then sit, stretch out the legs, hold the feet with hands, and move each foot forward and backward seven times.

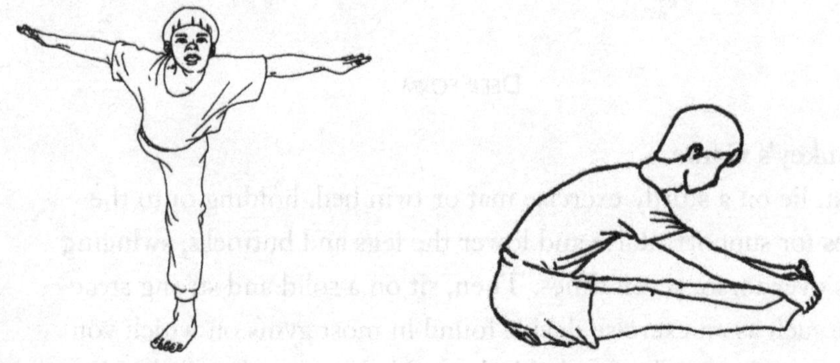

BIRD FORM

The Five Healing Colors

The Taoist path cultivates physical, emotional, mental, and spiritual health, self-awareness, and self-trust. In our stress-inducing society, emotional health is particularly important.

The changing emotional "weather" conditions of our life are often influenced by changes in our environment—seasonal changes, sensory inputs, and all kinds of stimuli from the outside world.

According to Chinese medicine, there is no single headquarters in the brain that regulates mood and emotion. Rather, the receptors and transmitters that relate to mood and emotion are dispersed throughout the body and brain. The energetic meridians in the body are multidimensional and create a functional interaction between the body/mind/emotions and the universe. These energetic patterns affect not only the body but the personality, character, mood, and emotional attributes.

The Chinese understanding of mood and emotion is organic and holistic. For Taoists, stress arises as a reaction resulting from desire. If there is no desire, the mood is stable. If the desire is strong and consistent, there will be a strong emotional reaction. Persistent negative emotions alter the bodily condition, as the organs can no longer regulate and balance each other. Somatic disorders and psychosomatic symptoms appear as stressful characteristics in the body/mind.

The "Five Healing Colors" exercise can purify and heal the mental-emotional-physical energy pathways in the body. In this exercise, we draw into the body the universal energetic color forces through visualization. The negative, imbalanced, or disharmonized Chi will be either exhaled or transformed, and the positive energetic forces are then restored. The emotional energies in the organs become harmonized and purified.

1. Sit upright in a chair. Be at ease and alert. Physically relax, letting go of muscular and emotional tensions, and turn on a very special, subtle, gentle, loving smile.
2. Focus your awareness on the mid-eyebrow. Close your eyes and imagine that you are in one of your favorite places in the world, a place where you feel safe, relaxed, and happy. Recall the sights you

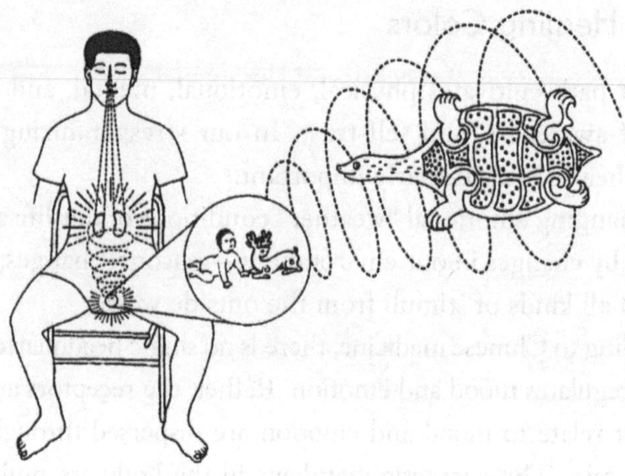

BLUE HEALING COLOR OF THE KIDNEYS

saw there, the sounds you heard, and the scents, sensations, and flavors you associate with that place.

3. Imagine that one of your favorite people is standing in front of you, smiling to you with loving, happy, radiant, shining eyes. Smile to your own face, slightly lifting up the corners of your mouth.
4. Feel yourself responding to that special person's smile with a smile of your own. Feel your eyes smiling and relaxing.
5. Now bring your attention to your kidneys. Aim your attention at these organs; picture them before your inner eye, and smile to them. Smile until you feel them smiling back to you. Picture the kidneys as a blue rose, slowly opening. See them radiate the blue healing light of gentleness.
6. Retaining the blue light and the feeling of gentleness, exhale, expelling feelings of fear or stress and the cloudy or negative energy. Repeat until the blue light of gentleness starts to radiate out from your kidneys.
7. Visualize a young child and see the child breathe out the blue color as a deer. Then visualize the water element taking shape as a big, dark blue turtle. The turtle will capture the deer. Visualize the turtle on the back of your body as a protective animal.
8. Now bring your attention to your heart. Aim your attention at this organ; picture it before your inner eye, and smile to it. Smile until

you feel it smiling back to you. Picture the heart as a red rose, slowly opening. This will activate the love and warmth of compassion in the heart. See it radiate the red healing light of love and compassion.

9. Retaining the red light and the feeling of love, exhale, expelling feelings of anger or stress and the cloudy or negative energy. Repeat until the red light of compassion starts to radiate out from your heart.

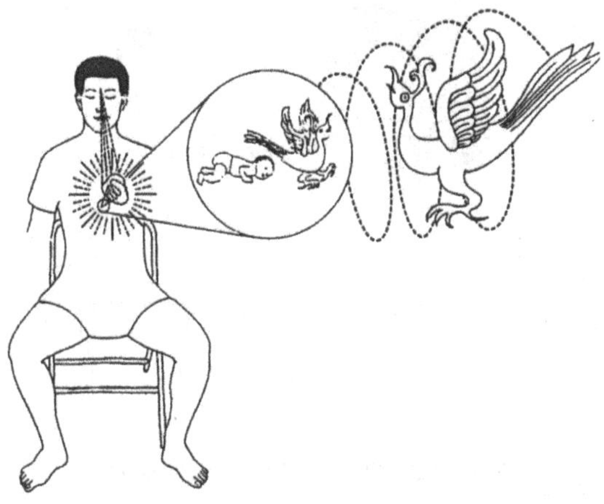

RED HEALING COLOR OF THE HEART

10. Visualize a young child and see the child breathe out the red color as a red pheasant. Then visualize the fire element taking shape as another big, red pheasant. The big, red pheasant will embrace the smaller pheasant. Visualize the pheasant on the back of your body as a protective animal.
11. Now bring your attention to your liver. Aim your attention at this organ; picture it before your inner eye, and smile to it. Smile until you feel it smiling back to you. Picture the liver as a green rose, slowly opening. This will activate the kindness of the liver. See the liver radiating the green healing light of kindness.
12. Retaining the green light and the feeling of kindness, exhale, expelling feelings of stress and the cloudy or negative energy. Repeat until the green light of kindness starts to radiate out from your liver.

13. Visualize a young child and see the child breathe out the green color as a green dragon. Then visualize the wood element taking shape as another big, green dragon. The big, green dragon will embrace the smaller dragon. Visualize the dragon on the back of your body as a protective animal.

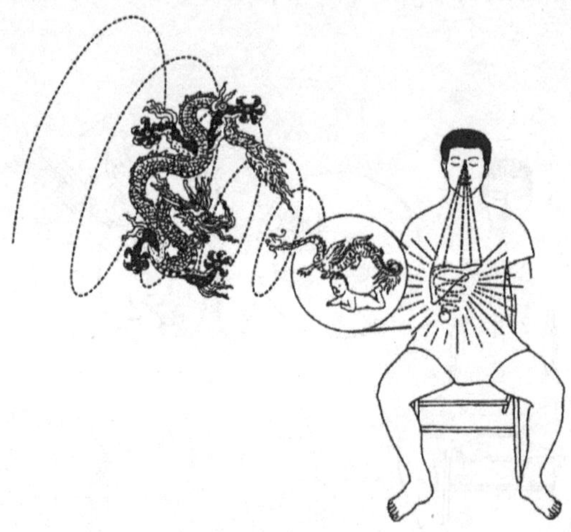

GREEN HEALING COLOR OF THE LIVER

14. Now bring your attention to your lungs. Aim your attention at these organs; picture them before your inner eye, and smile to them. Smile until you feel them smiling back to you. Picture the lungs as a white rose, slowly opening. This will activate the warmth of courage in the heart. See the lungs radiating the white healing light of courage and encouragement.
15. Retaining the white light and the feeling of courage, exhale, expelling feelings of fear or stress and the cloudy or negative energy. Repeat until the white light of courage starts to radiate out from your lungs.
16. Visualize a young child and see the child breathe out the white color as a white tiger. Then visualize the universal creative force taking shape as another big, white, tiger. The big, white tiger will embrace the smaller tiger. Visualize the tiger on the back of your body as a protective animal.

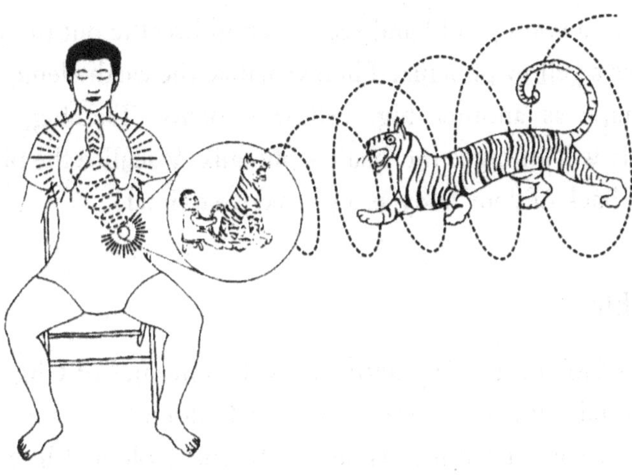

WHITE HEALING COLOR OF THE LUNGS

17. Now bring your attention to your spleen. Aim your attention at this organ; picture it before your inner eye, and smile to it. Smile until you feel it smiling back to you. Picture the spleen as a yellow rose, slowly opening. This will activate the fairness, openness, and equanimity of the spleen. See it radiate the yellow healing light of equanimity.
18. Retaining the yellow light and the feeling of openness and equanimity, exhale, expelling feelings of worry or stress and the cloudy or negative energy. Repeat until the yellow light of equanimity starts to radiate out from your spleen.

YELLOW HEALING COLOR OF THE SPLEEN

19. Visualize a young child and see the child breathe out the yellow color as a yellow phoenix. Then visualize the earth element taking shape as another big, yellow phoenix. The big, yellow phoenix will embrace the smaller phoenix. Visualize the phoenix on the back of your body as a protective animal.

Golden Elixir

The Taoist Golden Elixir practice uses the energies of Chi, saliva, and hormonal fluids to create the potent Golden Elixir for health, healing, and spiritual transformation. In the Golden Elixir practices, one cultivates and collects energies in the saliva, which are then swallowed. Swallowing the saliva after one has collected the energies in the proper way causes the energy to descend to the lower Tan Tien, the primary energy center.

The Chi energy of the saliva is much more powerful than the normal Chi energies gathered through breathing and eating, for the saliva carries an energy that is whole. It is a perfect balance of yin and yang and the five elements or phases of energy.

Taoist masters understood that it is possible to replenish the body's prenatal Chi, which is considered the most precious and powerful form of Chi. If preserved and nurtured, prenatal Chi can keep you young and healthy.

Prenatal Chi is stored in the kidneys and powers the entire body. Women can lose part of this Chi, which is actually a gift from the parents, during ovulation and childbirth; men lose theirs as a result of excessive ejaculation of sperm. When one loses too much, it means death is near. But there is a way to replenish this shrinking reservoir.

The ancient Taoist masters knew that anyone could replenish the prenatal Chi by swallowing lots of saliva. The saliva, when fortified with hormonal fluids and aroused orgasm energy and yin and yang energies drawn from the earth and heavens, is identical to the prenatal Chi.

It is important to understand that saliva is an important "medium" for collecting and unifying the various important energies. Saliva works in the same manner when you are eating food. It helps you collect, swallow, and predigest food. We also use the saliva to help digest ethereal energies. The more you practice the Golden Elixir exercises, the more you can turn your saliva into an elixir and greatly extend your life.

Basic Elixir Practice

We will start with a variation of the Inner Smile to help activate the saliva. We will mix the saliva with nature essence, universe essence, the aroused sexual energy, and the hormonal essence of all the glands. We will "knock the teeth" to activate the bones and bone marrow. Finally, we will swallow the saliva and its accumulated Chi down to the lower Tan Tien.

1. Stand, or sit in a comfortable position on your "sitting bones," with the back straight. Sit on the edge of the chair, so the sexual organs hang free and can breathe. If standing, stand with the feet shoulder-width apart, placing all nine points of the feet on the ground and gently rocking between the soles and the heels.
2. Begin by relaxing the upper, analytical mind and dropping your center of awareness down to the lower abdomen. Allow your sensing and conscious awareness to sink from the head to the navel area. This is called "sinking the upper mind down to the lower mind."
3. Close your eyes and imagine that you are in one of your favorite places in the world, a place where you feel safe, relaxed, and happy. Imagine that one of your favorite people is standing in front of you, smiling to you with loving, happy, radiant, shining eyes. Feel yourself responding to that special person's smile with a smile of your own. Feel your eyes smiling and relaxing.
4. Touch the mid-eyebrow and gently rub in a circle. Smile to it, feel it relax and open, and feel light enter this point. Use the index and middle finger to very gently rub the eyebrows from

the middle outward. Visualize them growing very long out to the sides. Your forehead will feel very relaxed.

5. Gently rub your eyeballs with the eyes closed. Smile and relax the eyeballs and feel them sink down and down to the navel area. When the eyes relax, the monkey mind will start to calm down and the eyeball energy will easily sink to the navel.
6. Smile and lightly turn up the corners of the mouth. Feel the chin bones on both sides rise up and reach to the ears, and feel the ears getting longer and longer, growing up and down and reaching the kidneys.
7. Smile to the jaw. Massage both sides of the jaws, to release tension and anger. Lightly open the mouth, drop the jaw, continuing to smile to the jaw. Feel it relax and the saliva start to flow out.
8. Once you feel a lot of saliva flowing out, gently close the mouth. Bring the smiling energy down into the organs and throughout the whole body.
9. Bring your attention back to your face; smile and lightly lift up the corners of your mouth. Place the tip of your tongue behind the upper teeth. Now press your tongue against the palate, moving it about to find a sensitive spot, the "heavenly pool," which is a depression or hole behind the teeth where the tongue likes to be.
10. Smile to the palate; smile until you feel the palate open, like a hole opening into heaven. Feel nectar flowing down from heaven.
11. Be aware of the mouth, the nose, and the eyes. Close the mouth slightly, inhale very slowly, and continue to lightly press the tip of the tongue to the palate. Feel that you are drawing in the smiling energy and the essence of the air into the eyes, nose, and mouth. When you exhale feel that you are condensing the essence of these energies in the mouth. Do this nine to eighteen times until you feel the tongue and the palate connected.
12. Sense a subtle electric vibration in the tongue, palate, salivary glands, and the glands of the brain. This will be the natural way of stimulating and strengthening the glands. Be aware of and picture the pituitary gland. Feel the vibration reach to all the glands of the

brain. Be aware of and picture the thalamus, hypothalamus, and pineal glands, and feel the electric vibration stimulate the glands.

13. Feel the saliva flowing out even more and the vibration going deeper and deeper into the brain. The palate seems to become very porous, and the hormonal secretion will drip down into the mouth. Sweep the tongue around to gather the nectar. It tastes differently from the saliva; it is thicker, sweet, and fragrant.
14. You know that you have gathered enough saliva when the mouth is full. Now, chew the saliva loudly, like you are eating delicious food, thirty-six times. This will mix the saliva with air and Chi. Move the saliva back and forth with the tongue, left and right, up and down, mixing it with all the essences and hormones. This oxygenates the mixture, blending air into the nectar. Do this thirty-six times. Move your tongue to massage the gums on the outside of the teeth. This helps strengthen the gums and will produce more saliva. Do this thirty times. Do not swallow yet; hold the saliva in your mouth.
15. Now, bring your attention to the nature force. Visualize a beautiful mountain, a river, an ocean, and a beautiful flower garden. Extend your hands out to the universe. Open your palms and feel your arms and the palms grow very large and long as they reach to nature and the universe.
16. Next, practice the dragon breath. The dragon breath is a special way to inhale, drawing or sucking Chi energy into your body. To do the dragon breath, lightly contract and pull up on the anus, perineum, and sexual organs. (See Mantak Chia's *Tan Tien Chi Kung* for a detailed discussion of perineum power exercises that work with contraction of the anus, perineum, and sexual organs.) Inhale using the dragon sound. The dragon sound is a high-pitched *Hummmmm*. Feel a pressure, like that of a vacuum cleaner, in the abdominal area and the throat. This vacuum/sucking sensation is a sucking in of nature and universal Chi.
17. Eventually the suction will manifest in the mid-eyebrow, the crown, the palms, the soles of the feet, and the sacrum.

18. Now, exhale with the tiger breath, a special way of exhaling that builds Chi pressure in the lower abdomen. To do the tiger breath, exhale with the tiger sound, which is a low-pitched, growling sound, *Hummmmm*. Push the energy that you have drawn in through the dragon breath down to the lower abdominal area. Practice the dragon and tiger breaths nine to thirty-six times.
19. Expand your awareness to nature and the universe. Once again, draw the Chi into the mouth and chew and mix the saliva a few times.
20. When the Elixir is ready, prepare to swallow. First, lightly press your chin to the back, so the crown of the head is lifted upward. When the chin is tucked back you will feel the neck lightly tighten around the throat muscle; this will make it hard to swallow. Use your tongue curled like a bridge to press up to the palate, creating a force to help push the saliva down.
21. Now, swallow the saliva. Be aware of the lower Tan Tien and the navel area. Divide the saliva into three parts. Swallow the first part, directing it to the center of navel; swallow the second part, directing it to the left side of the navel; and swallow the third part, directing it to the right side of the navel. You may hear the gulping sound, and the throat or the Adam's apple will move. This will also help activate the thyroid, parathyroid, and thymus glands.
22. Next, practice "turning the wheel." See a ball of Chi turning counterclockwise in your palms, and see and feel the saliva and Chi turning in a counterclockwise direction in the lower Tan Tien. Feel the saliva turn into Chi. Taoist sages with long years of practice discovered that the saliva has ten times more power to absorb Chi than water.
23. This Elixir can transform immediately into Chi and be used by the body to increase moisture, lubricate the organs and the joints, boost the immune and defense systems, and increase Chi flow so that the blood will flow more easily. Taoists say that when the Chi flows, the blood will circulate faster throughout

the entire body and health will be improved. So we do not need to depend only on the heart to pump blood to increase circulation. Using the mind to circulate the Chi will also increase circulation, and reduce stress on the heart.

24. Cover your navel and feel it warm; divide this warm energy into two and let it flow down the front of the legs to the big toes, and down the back of the legs to the soles of the feet. Then let the Chi rise, up the inside of the legs. Lightly pull up the anus and the perineum. Draw the sexual organs back towards the coccyx and the sacrum, and guide the Chi flow up the spine to the neck. Here the Chi divides, flowing down the outside of the arms to the middle fingers. Then it continues into the palms, up to the armpits, joining in the neck to flow to the crown, mid-eyebrow, and down to the mouth. Visualize this three to six cycles of this energy circulation. During the Elixir practice, Chi flows like electricity through the palate and the tongue, this vibration goes deep into the brain and down into the chest, and this activates and strengthens the glands. After completing the cycles of energy circulation, rest and feel you have been recharged and filled with energy.
25. This process can be enhanced immensely by practicing the Microcosmic Orbit energy circulation exercise, discussed previously in this chapter. The practice of Microcosmic Orbit energy circulation awakens, circulates, and directs Chi through two important energy routes in the body: the Governor Channel, which ascends from the base of the spine up to the head, and the Functional Channel, which runs from the tip of the tongue down the middle of the torso to the perineum. The Microcosmic Orbit practice allows the palms, the soles of the feet, the mid-eyebrow point, and the crown to open. These specific locations are the major points where energy can be absorbed, condensed, and transformed into fresh new life force.

Belt Channel Energy Circulation

An important step in Taoist healing practice is to reopen and rejuvenate the "eight extraordinary meridians" through which Chi flows in the body. We have already discussed the Microcosmic Orbit energy circulation exercise, which works with the Functional Channel and the Governor Channel. Here we will discuss practices that work with the Belt Channel.

1. Stand with feet shoulder-width apart. Inhale and exhale deeply several times, relaxing the body. Place both palms over the navel.
2. Visualize a small white dot in the middle of abdominal area. Mentally roll this small white dot forward and down, then backward and up with the rhythm of the breath. As you inhale, visualize this dot moving forward and down; as you exhale visualize it moving backward and up to form the minutest circle.

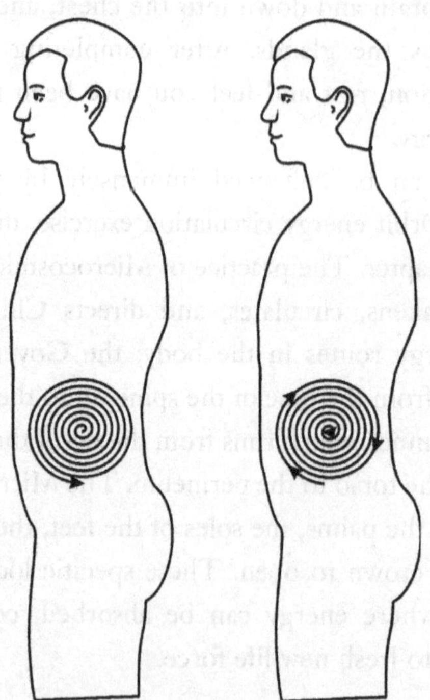

CIRCULATING THE CHI

Continue this practice, allowing the circle to become a bit larger each time. It will draw the Chi from the testes and ovaries Chi up to the chest when the count reaches forty-nine.

3. Rest for a few minutes, and experience the warmth and heat you have generated in the abdominal and chest areas.
4. Now, reverse the previous steps, retracing the expanding energy circles you have just visualized, contracting back to the dot in the abdomen. As you inhale, visualize the energy moving downward; as you exhale, visualize it moving up. After forty-nine circulations, it returns to the original white dot.
5. Feel the energetic change occurring in the body. Now, inhale, pressing the hands flat against the front part of the abdominal area. Feel an energetic connection between the front and back of the body at your midsection.

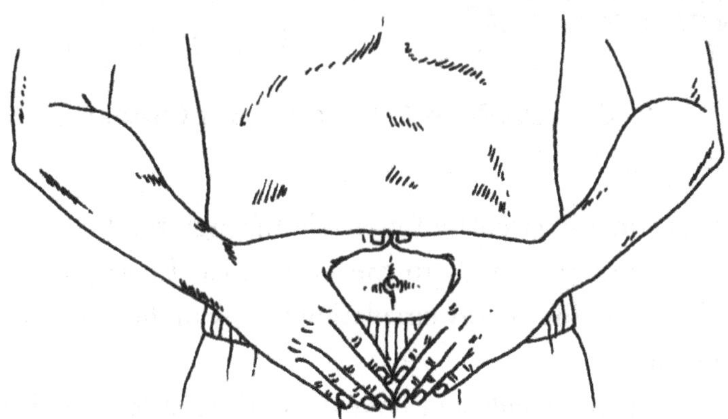

PRESS THE HANDS FLAT AGAINST THE ABDOMEN.

6. Inhale deeply and the hold the breath. Feel the intensity of the air pressure or heat or warmth or whatever sensation appears.
7. When you can no longer hold the breath, exhale and let the pressure inside the abdomen escape.
8. Practice steps 5–7, pressing hands flat against the abdomen, inhaling deeply, holding the breath, and exhaling, until you can feel Chi energy building up in the body. You may experience it as a sensation of heat and steam in the body.

9. Now open the hands. Inhale, gently moving the Chi through the Belt Channel, which flows around the waist. Exhale and place the thumbs touching the tip of the pelvic bones on either side. Then place the palms and four fingers on either side of the lower back, with thumbs in front.

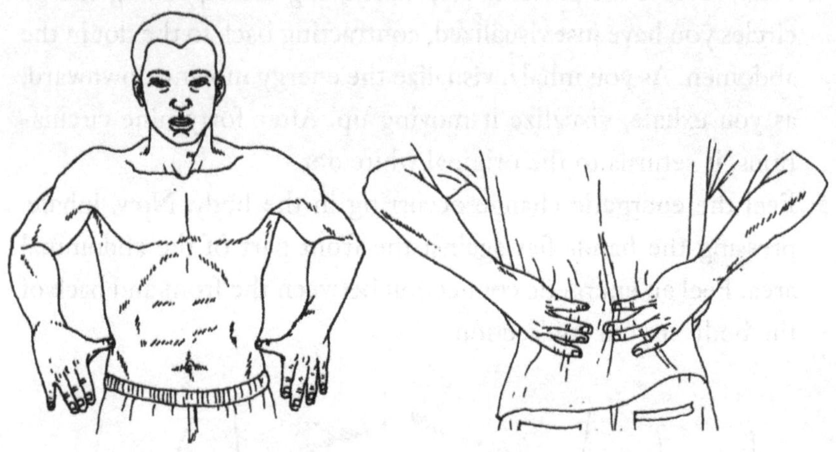

CIRCULATING THE CHI THROUGH BELT CHANNEL

10. Feel the energy circulate for awhile through the Belt Channel. Then return the hands to the navel area. Repeat steps 5–10 until you feel the energy circulating evenly in the entire abdominal area.
11. Now open the hands and hold them at waist level with palms facing the ground. Send the Chi from the palms down to the feet. Inhale, and gather the energy up and into the Belt Channel area. Exhale, and feel the circulation within.
12. When you have sufficient energy surging across the Belt Channel, it will naturally move up to the chest and brain area. As you feel the energy rising, move your hands gradually upward from waist level to chest level to eye level.
13. You will feel the Chi energy and heat increasing throughout the whole body. When you feel the body is filled with Chi, place the palms facing up to the sky. This will cool everything down.

CHI IN THE BELT CHANNEL RISES TO THE CHEST AND HEAD

14. Rest. Cover the navel with the palms. Visualize a warm, bright ball of energy in your abdomen. Then visualize the ball of energy forming a spiral. Visualize the energy spiraling in a clockwise direction. Then visualize the energy spiraling in a counterclockwise direction. This will store the Chi safely in the navel area.

Embracing Oneness

HARMONIZING HUN AND PO, HEAVEN AND EARTH

For Taoists, human beings have two souls. The *hun*, or heavenly soul, and the *po*, or earthly soul.

The *hun* is the ethereal soul. At the time of physical death, it leaves the body and ascends to heaven to return to subtle realms. The *hun* is more subtle, and is yang in nature.

The *po* is the corporeal soul. It is closely related to the physical world and descends into the earth at the time of physical death. The *po* is more physical, and is yin in nature.

Each person has one *hun* and one *po*. The Taoist practitioner seeks to harmonize these two energies, obtaining health, inner and outer balance, and self-realization. Taoist practice involves cultivating *hun* and *po* through a refining process. When we achieve a higher-level and more refined energy state, the physical or *po* aspects of our life support the *hun* or spiritual aspects. This is referred to as "experiencing heaven on earth." When in balance, we live in harmony; when in disharmony, many negative conditions can manifest, including unhealthy emotional and physical conditions.

Chi balances the forces of Jing (sexual/generative essence) and Shen (spiritual energy) in the same way that the heart/mind (*xin*) balances the forces of *po* and *hun*.

Jing, Shen, *hun*, and *po* are four of the fundamental building blocks of Taoist philosophy and practice. Jing is the biological substance of the body, and *po* is the animated soul, fueled by Jing, within the body. In addition to these four building blocks, Chi is the power source, and *xin* is the working heart/mind.

Hun and *po* are distinct aspects of the self; they can be equated with the pure self and the egoistic self, respectively. *Hun* is the spirit of Chi while *po* is the essence of the body. Accordingly, all sensory and kinesthetic activities are animated from *po*. Conscious activities, such as intuition, insight, and awareness, are generated by *hun*.

Lao Tzu writes in chapter 10 that we don the spirit and soul and draw them into Oneness. *Hun* is the impetus of reincarnation. It arises before the body exists and departs after the body ceases to breathe. *Hun* becomes the force within us that is creative and that plans, makes choices, and exerts the will.

The center for *po* in the body is the lungs. *Po* generates the "gross" bodily activities (food, sleep, and sex). When a person is controlled by *po*, without the proper balance between *hun* and *po*, the body sickens and the mind becomes callous—egoistic, possessive, and obsessive. The *po* person is greedy, rude, and jealous.

When the two souls of *hun* and *po* are in harmony, the individual is warm, caring, kind, and equanimous. Since the ego is one's subjective consciousness of self or *I*, it surfaces through the consciousness of *hun* and the subjectivity of *po*, and manifests through the *xin* (heart/mind). The harmony of *hun* and *po* flowers in the truly whole person.

In a condition of imbalance, one is not rooted to the earth (via the *po*) and is not connected to the spiritual source (via the *hun*). In this condition of disconnection, a person's life basically revolves around eating, sleeping, mating, security, and power. These individuals may feel unhappy and empty inside. They may fear looking at this pain and emptiness, and may not notice that they have gravely suppressed their godly nature.

Once we truly take responsibility for ourselves, our health, our spiritual origin, and our life task, we can start to wake up from this numb state. Then we become aware of the fear and mechanisms we have cultivated to prevent ourselves from getting in touch with our true selves. Only when we have the courage to look beneath the surface of our ordinary consciousness will we be able to open up and walk the path to freedom and spiritual independence.

As children of the universe, we are not only created by the divine intelligence and subtle substance of the cosmos, but if we allow it, we spontaneously will cocreate its evolutionary process. We are not only children of the universe and its love that gave us life, we are also its fathers and mothers, whose love is coresponsible for the way it evolves. As an ancient expression says: "Embrace the universe as a mother embraces her firstborn child."

The New Age movement may be seen as a reaction to the relentless materialism of the modern West. However, many followers of these movements, in their disdain of mundane and earthly material pursuits, have moved to the other extreme: a spirituality without grounding "roots" in the earth. In embracing spiritual ideals and rejecting material realities, they are trapped in the same duality between heaven and earth that has characterized most of history's dominant religious and philosophical traditions.

People with poor groundings and a negative relationship with their bodies frequently face a host of problems in their daily lives regarding sex, money, health, self-esteem, and relationships. They often suffer from insecurity and have an unhealthy relationship with the practical and emotional realities of their lives. They tend to seek ways to avoid or deny these realities, including their own physical existence, and thus experience a growing disconnection between body, mind, and spirit. They do understand that they need to look for truth within themselves, as they carry the divine within. But they find this difficult because of the split that they have created within themselves—between what is "above" and what is "below," between heaven and earth. In this condition of physical disconnection, one may try to escape or transcend the complexities of embodied existence through using drugs or other avoidance techniques.

The pursuit of spiritual freedom often causes such aspirants to imprison themselves in their search. As a result they are bound to end up as imbalanced as their materialist opposites. It is the deep pain they experience that pushes them onto a spiritual path that they hope will be free from all worldly obstructions. Now the same ego is hidden behind a spiritual mask. When we turn our attention away from our body we cut the intelligence away from the "matter," and we dishonor the holiest temple on earth. The higher frequencies are not balanced and integrated in the physical body, so the vital essence will gradually leave the body or will transform into high energy frequencies that can only be partly assimilated in the physical body. Physically these individuals will start to slowly weaken and all kinds of symptoms will appear, ultimately leading to premature aging. Their heart energy may be compared with a flower that is cut off from its roots; their spiritual condition is only momentary. They live only in the upper body, as they tend to ignore or are afraid of their sexuality, and they lack a connection with the belly, their energy center. And as love and sex are not connected, their relationships tend to be emotionally unstable and superficial.

Let us be true to ourselves: we were not given our bodies to deny them. Taoist self-healing practices can significantly help people in this condition of physical disconnection by teaching them how to get in touch with the true nature of their bodies, to care for them, and to make them healthy and strong. This is essential for the growth of a healthy energy body.

We can all contribute to the quality of life on this planet by dissolving the denseness and separation in our mind and our social mentality. The problem is not only in the body, but also in the absence and denial of an understanding of the infinite and unfathomable true spirit and universal mind. Taoist masters realize that truth lies in a spiritual life that includes the physical body. By consciously fusing the spirit with the core of physical existence, a new quality of life arises.

The initial focus of Taoist practice is creating a healthy and strong physical body, well rooted in the source of life, the energy of our "mother" earth. At the same time Taoist practice acknowledges that the origin of our spirit is in heaven. Our soul has chosen to incarnate on earth and seeks opportunities to grow and evolve by learning from the universe. Since everything finds its nature in Tao, the human body, soul, and spirit can be seen as different densities of the same substance. In view of our unawakened, unconscious state, most of us tend to get trapped in one of the two poles, either by focusing on an earthly life at the expense of heaven or the other way around. Like a tree, healthy men and women are rooted in the earth below and connected to the universe above.

When a Taoist student has achieved a strong navel center and enjoys a firm connection to heaven and earth within, then he or she can freely move "upward" and "downward" without getting lost. (See the first volume of *Taoist Cosmic Healing* or *Chi Nei Tsang, Chinese Abdominal Chi Massage*, by Mantak Chia, for teachings about the navel center.) The relationship between heaven and earth may be represented by a vertical axis that goes up (heaven) and moves down (earth). Along this axis we can visualize the different centers and levels of energy and their transformations (body/soul/spirit). Because of its tradition of firm rooting, the Taoist way of energy transformation is a safe one. It has been tested for many centuries. The Universal Tao practice is a self-cultivation program that we can use and apply effectively in our daily lives. The practices lead us step by step from an initial level to the highest or "immortal" practices. The Taoist way of life teaches us to reconnect with and become aware of our true spiritual origin and bring this experience down into the lowest energy center of the physical body, the lower Tan Tien. It brings spirit into matter or light to earth. After achieving this strong rooting process between heaven and earth (vertical axis), practitioners can move freely into the materialistic world (horizontal axis) without losing their connection with the spiritual.

TRIPLE UNITY

The subtle origin of the universe and the Tao is the source of all life, all beings, all things, all energy, and all their various manifestations. In the yin/yang symbol, the outer circle represents the oneness and the yin and yang energies represent the intrinsic polarity of all forms of energy. Yin and yang represent a unity of opposites, always balancing, completing, embracing, and containing each other.

According to the Taoist view, the energy of the universe is comprised of three different realms. The interaction between yin and yang created the "three pure ones" or the three energy sources in the universe: the cosmic force, the universal force, and the earth force. Knowing that these energies contain the pure light of the Tao, we recognize the three pure ones in the three interlocking circles of the triple unity symbol. The outer circle of the yin/yang symbol can also be understood to represent the cosmic light energy while yang and yin represent the universal and the earth energy.

Cosmic Chi is born out of the original Chi of the Tao and literally carries the intelligence and essence of life. Guided by this intelligence, it spreads out into the universe and manifests in different densities and forms defined by the cosmic laws. This is how stars, planets, human cells, subatomic particles, and all other forms of life take form and are nourished.

In particular, cosmic energy descends and materializes into the human baby as it is attracted into the world by the magnetic field between the earth and the moon. Since most people have lost the ability to consciously and directly absorb the cosmic light, we can only do this in a materialized form, either by eating living substances that have absorbed cosmic light (plants) or by eating living creatures (animals) that have eaten the plants. This means that we only consume light in a more or less materialized form: cosmic dust, which in turn becomes plants and animals. Evolution is leading us to once again be able to consume from the source: cosmic light. In this way yin and yang have become one another, as the circle leads us back into light after so many years of disconnection from the source.

Taoist practice focuses on restoring this direct connection with the cosmic source (light particles) so that we regain the ability to directly live from light energy. As we develop this capacity, we become less and less dependent on eating plants and animals. Taoist legends tell us that throughout the ages, some Taoist masters have been able to live for months or even years without taking any food and without losing weight, while maintaining and even enhancing their vitality. Today, there are reports that a number of people from different backgrounds throughout the world are living only on water, tea, or fruit juice. This practice may be possible because such advanced practitioners tap into cosmic light, the original source of human life and all other forms of being.

Universal and earth energy, or Chi, also have their genesis in the original energy of the Tao. The universal Chi is the radiating force of all galaxies, stars, and planets throughout the whole universe. It is the all-pervasive force that nourishes the life energy in all the forms of nature. The earth force is the third force of nature, which includes all the energies of mother earth. This force is activated by the electromagnetic field originating in the rotation of the earth. It is also integrated into all aspects of nature on our planet. The earth energy is accessed through the soles of the feet, the perineum, and the sexual organs. Earth energy nourishes the physical body. It supplies our daily life force and is one of the principal forces used to heal ourselves.

The Threefold Nature of the Universe

Tao gives rise to one.
One gives rise to two.
Two gives rise to three.
Three gives rise to all things. (42:1)

The threefold nature of the universe manifests itself in many different ways. In the Taoist vision, everything we see and experience around us has gone through three different realms or spheres of existence.

The subtle origin is the source of everything, heaven and earth. It contains the realm of Chi and all phenomena.

1. The subtle origin or pure law of existence (Tao).
2. Chi, the subtle energy.
3. All phenomena, interactions, and transformations of Chi.

The three realms are inseparable. Once we understand this threefold nature and experience its manifestation in our bodies, we have made a major step on our spiritual journey.

We have pointed to the necessity of opening up the vertical axis and establishing a deep rooting in both heaven and earth. The three principal energy centers in our body are the three Tan Tiens, discussed previously. They are in reality the containers of the physical, soul, and spirit energy. The way we become human is through a process of materialization (the body is the material densification of energy) in which the subtle energy of the Tao, connected to our spirit, incarnates through our soul into our body. Heaven descends into the earth, and what is above and below are united.

As human beings, we are the highest manifestation of the cosmic light, which has its origin directly in the Tao, the oneness. The life we lead originates from this source. From this one, unlimited intelligence a process of densifying, materialization, and multiplication has led to our individual incarnation or manifestation in the physical realm. Taoist philosophy describes this process as "the one giving birth to the two." The interaction between the two results in the differentiation and multiplicity of the world of phenomena. To connect to the spiritualizing spiral of true intelligence that we are will strengthen the connection to the Tao. In other words, the more we understand nature and the universe, the more we understand ourselves.

As noted above, in Chinese cosmology and philosophy, the world of duality, of yin and yang, gives birth to the triple unity. This triple unity we find in the three basic energies in the universe (cosmic, universal, and earth energies) and in the interaction between man, heaven, and earth. In the human body, the interaction of heaven and earth forces (two) gives birth to the three Tan Tiens. Through the practice of the Taoist path, we once again unite the three in the One.

The quality and meaning of life is all contained in the One. As the Chinese have philosophically and poetically expressed it: one is all and all is one. We have one life to live on earth at this time, regardless of the legacy of our past or our hope for the future. If we waste it or destroy it, there is no more opportunity this life. Life is a sacred and serious matter. If we do not open ourselves to this solemn truth, we will lose our spirit-self and spiral downward to our ultimate destination: death. Lao Tzu wisely concludes: *The reason people are not serious about death is because they seek the burdens of life. This is why they are not serious about death* (77:1).

REFLECTIONS ON UNIFICATION

Body-Mind-Spirit Unification

As you begin walking the path of your pilgrimage, your body will be gradually detoxified and vitalized, and the mind will gradually become still and tranquil. The spiritual pilgrimage is purification process, a liberating experience, an inner journey, and an expressive path. As the pilgrimage continues its course, the body and mind begin their inner and ultimate marital relationship. The personal experiential journey and the awakening path progress together, promoting and refining the pilgrimage to produce the *zhenren*, the authentic and pure person. The Taoist path of cultivation is biological, emotional, mental, and spiritual in nature.

During the spiritual journey, we can best navigate the trials and challenges of life by restoring our original, childlike, free-flowing nature. It is the process of embracing the oneness of the universe. Oneness is the first and the oldest child of Tao. It is the single, pure, primary, primordial, and illuminating Chi of the universe. The activity of embracing oneness is a process of gathering energy through the concentration of mind. It is a psycho-biological-spiritual process of unifying heavenly and earthly Chi. The purpose of preserving Chi is to unify the complete self. Willpower, the best tool of the mind, is essential in this process of transformation. Through dedicated practice, we achieve a psychological unification that supports the unification of the entire body-mind-spirit.

An important part of the spiritual pilgrimage is the practice of unifying all perceptual faculties (feelings, sensations, intuition, cognition) into one total and comprehensive body/mind awareness. All aspects of a person—biological, emotional, intellectual, psychological, and spiritual—must ultimately be unified into one holistic awareness. It is a combination of original spiritual perception and actual realistic perception. Spiritual perception is the highest form of perception as well as the guiding principle of knowing and understanding. Realistic perception is sensing and perceiving the world around us, ideally in a perfectly reliable and trustworthy manner. When we can unify all our perceptual capabilities, inner and outer, we can be fully sensitive and present, and respond spontaneously and with perfect appropriateness to whatever arises in each moment.

Uniting with the Tao, Uniting with Virtuous Action

So the person who works according to Tao unites with Tao.
In the same way he unites with action.
In the same way he unites with loss.
Uniting with action, the Tao becomes action.
Uniting with loss, the Tao becomes loss. (24:4–5)

The Tao is transmitted into either virtuous action (Te) or loss. If your purpose in life is the acquisition of name, fame, or fortune, you will inevitably end up with loss. If you want to wholeheartedly unite with the virtue of the Tao, you will lose everything except the virtue of the Tao.

We can disregard our mental projections and appraisals to concentrate on making a right judgment of the reality of nature, and embracing and uniting with it. The fine line of correct discrimination is the fine line of the intention of mind guarded by soul, heart, spirit, and body/mind. If the intention is selfless, there is no cause for concern. Just be who you are and do what you must. You can save someone's life through kindness or destroy a relationship by misusing the kindness. You can save someone's life through justice or kill him by restoring the established justice. If virtuous action requires you to step with the right foot, then action with the left foot will bring trouble.

Three Unions

There are three types of unions in life experience: biophysical marriage, ideal connection, and spiritual union.

The biophysical marriage is the connection of the yin and yang Chi and Jing through sexual intercourse. Sexual climax is its peak experience, followed by the products of offspring.

The ideal connection is the mental communication between the yin *hun* and yang universal Chi. The peak experience is insight and mental clarity. The products are ideas and all manifestations of culture and society throughout evolving human civilization.

Spiritual union is the marriage of bodily pure yang force and heavenly yang force. The peak experience is bliss. The product is the *zhenren*, the pure person, or the child of God.

The first union is the earthly union of a man and a woman. Though they enjoy the process and experience oneness, the act is a simultaneous exchange between death and birth. The oneness is the union of two distinct manifestations of yin and yang, of male and female, of anima and animus.

In the ideal connection, there is a union between self and thought, *hun*'s soulful consciousness and Shen's pure consciousness, idea and reality, and reality and eternity. There is the spark and illumination of mental clarity and insight. Ideas are transformed into language, tools, machines, and all the objects of human culture. The process evolves through individuals and societies.

The final union, the spiritual union, is the fruition of the Taoist path. It is the marriage of the human and divine, of human energies and cosmic energies, to produce the fully enlightened Taoist sage.

The Harmony of the Family

All of our personal history, both from this lifetime and from the beginningless past, becomes part of, and is transformed by, our spiritual pilgrimage. All our personal, social, and ancestral relationships are vehicles facilitating our sacred journey. We learn to walk our own path within the network of our history, family, and culture.

GIA JEN (FAMILY), THE 37TH HEXAGRAM

The Gia Jen (family) hexagram represents the laws obtaining within the family. The varous lines represent the various family members and their relations to one another. Thus all the connections and relationships within the family find their appropriate expression. The fact that a strong line occupies the top position indicates that strong leadership must come from the head of the family. The family hexagram conveys that the laws that govern the household, when transferred to outside life, keep the state and the world in order. The influence that goes out from within the family is represented by the symbol of the wind created by fire. Richard

Wilhelm's renowned translation of the *I Ching* states: "The family is society in embryo; it is the native soil on which performance of moral duty is made easy through natural affection, so that within a small circle a basis of moral practice is created, and this is later widened to include human relationships in general."

The Wisdom of the Taoist Sage

WHAT IS A SAGE?

Historically, sages have been the most revered persons in the human community. They possess profound wisdom, vast compassion, and deep moral responsibility. The sage is often a lonely figure, standing apart from the conventions and comforts of family life. The sage upholds truth and holiness. The sage is commonly pictured as a male figure, although there have been numerous influential female sages throughout history. The sage is concerned only with sustaining purity and the completion of yang Chi, or celestial energy. We view the sage as the culmination of wisdom and immortality. Through the sage's embodiment of wisdom and purity, we are made aware, in our earthly existence, of the defining line between heavenly spirits and earthly souls. With the aid of the example and inspiration provided by the sage, we can rise above our circumstances in this human life.

In Chinese culture, the sage is regarded as a link between heaven and earth, and as an ideal for human beings to emulate. Taoist inner alchemy cannot teach us "what" a Taoist sage is, but opens the mind to many "ways" in which we can strive to become a Taoist sage, as transmitted to us by the sages themselves. The sage speaks with God's exalted tone, acts on behalf of God's will, and represents God's most favored child.

Taoism is a philosophy and faith that offers an ideal connection between man and heaven and a profound understanding of the relationship between the power of ego and the freedom of mind.

In the Tao Te Ching, the term *sage* is the most frequently used, appearing in twenty-one chapters. In those chapters, Lao Tzu depicts the sage walking through his human life within sagehood. He places a greater emphasis on the importance of being a sage than he does on the meaning of *hearing of Tao*. A sage is a meditator who has mastered the cultivation practice of body/mind into that of a newborn baby. He is a carrier of kindness whose moral goodness nurtures people's hearts and souls, but is not clearly understood in their minds. He is a light in the world whose conduct imparts a state of being, whose position is lowly, and whose method is utter simplicity.

The sage knows that the intellect possesses the wisdom of simplicity when there is no desire in the mind; when captured by demands, it becomes crafty. The sage knows that action is kind when there is no competition; while searching for perfection, it becomes possessive. When Lao Tzu describes a sage, he employs the qualities of "wise" and "kind."

Lao Tzu calls himself a sage. He writes that *the sage wears shabby cloth but holds a treasure within* (72:4) and *The sage holds Oneness as the shepherd of the world* (23:2). The sage carries a great burden of responsibility, and potentially has a great deal of influence in this world. The sage understands and fully embraces this responsibility, with a lightness of being.

Therefore the sage says:
When I am inactive, people transform themselves.
When I abide in stillness, people organize themselves lawfully.
When I am disengaged, people enrich themselves.
When I choose non-desire, people remain simple. (57:4)

To be a sage and to live a sage's life is neither easy nor impossible. It is a life devoid of desire, ambition, name, competition, wealth, and possessions. The sage carries the aura of immortality, a quality that cannot be defined socially and culturally. To reach immortality is to become self-effacing. The sage exercises only the right conduct of speech and action, doing no more and no less than what is required. It is acting at the right time with the right person within the right space, expressing no self-explanation and no self-aggrandizement. The sage demonstrates dispassionate compassion. Tao is transformed into the virtuous Te of kindness. While the Tao can be construed as obscure, abstract, or removed, the sage's behavior illuminates the Tao as alive, active, and achievable.

The Body of the Sage

Relaxing the body, the body comes to the fore.
Beyond the body, the body comes to the fore.
Beyond the body, the body exists of itself.
Not even relying on selflessness
Enables the self to be fulfilled. (7:3–4)

The sage is the individual and universal persona in which the Tao, the meaning of virtuous action (Te), and the role of human being are embodied and characterized.

Through extensive cultivation of the Taoist transformational path, the sage's body becomes an androgynous Chi body. The sage's body is in unity with the mind, and the body and mind are no longer in tension or a mutual burden. Because of this total harmony, a sage's body is a friend of life, not an object to be displayed. With its unique ability to rejuvenate, a sage's body is a womb for producing the *zhenren*, the pure person.

The idea of relaxation in the verse above is comparable to the Buddhist idea of readiness: no sickness, no frustration, no restraint, and no expectation. It is the overall meaning of presence. *[Coming] to the fore* is permitting the body to bypass mental calculation and expectation, being free to move with its own rhythm, at its own pace, measured with its own strength, and in its own time. Thus, the mind reaches *beyond the body*, yet the stillness within holds it at bay.

Lao Tzu says that *In the world, the sage inhales* (49:3). This sentence characterizes the manner in which the sage lives his life. In order to live in the world, the sage gathers Chi through inhalation, through physical and cosmic breath. This inhalation is not the shallow and surface breathing done through the nostrils. It is the embryonic and total body breathing learned by Taoist practitioners. This breath of life is the nutrition, energy, information, and wisdom that sustain the body and mind.

The sage knows the world without stepping out of the door (the gate of life), knows the Tao without peering through the window (eyes) (47:1), and smiles like a child (49:4). This is called unifying the world of in and out. The world of in is the source and the world of out is the mechanism. They exist as matter and energy, structure and motion, process and outcome. Source is the breath of life, the nutrition of vitality, and the energy of light. Breath is the state of vapor, vitality is the state of fluid, and light is the state of solid. Light is the central focal point, vitality is the generating force, and air is the inclusive space. By inhaling in this embryonic way, the vast space and cosmic presence are instilled in the flesh, the awareness, and interaction of the body. The world is known, the self is charged, and action is pure and simple in itself.

Action in its profundity is like a newborn baby.
Poisonous insects and venomous snakes do not sting it.
Predatory birds and ferocious animals do not seize it.
Its bones are soft and its sinews supple, yet its grasp is firm;
Without knowing the union of male and female, its organs become aroused.
Its vital essence comes to the point;
Crying all day, its voice never becomes hoarse.
Its harmony comes to the point. (55:1–2)

When the body *comes to the fore* on its own, *poisonous insects and venomous snakes do not sting it. Its bones are soft and its sinews supple, yet its grasp is firm.* The central and essential action occurs in the right environment at the right time; this is engaging in right bodily conduct. This is why the mind must be relaxed. The arousal of organs supplies the power for voice, for response, for harmonious organic vibration. Softness creates the space of firmness.

Why to "value the trouble as you do the body"?
It is only because I have a body that I have trouble.
If I did not have a body, where would the trouble be?
So, if you value the world as you do the body,
You can be entrusted with the world;
If you love the body as you love the beauty of the world,
You can be responsible for the world. (13:3–4)

Because the sage values the world as he does the body, he can be entrusted with the world. Because he loves his body as he loves the beauty of the world, he can be responsible for the world. As strength, will, and harmony are achieved, the value of body is displayed, its treasure as a sacred vessel is realized. The sage is free to be fully in the world and fully responsible for the world.

WU WEI: THE ACTION OF THE SAGE

Therefore the sage lives in actionless engagement,
And preaches wordless doctrine. (2:3)

Begetting but not possessing,
Enhancing but not dominating.
This is Mysterious Action. (10:2–3)

Eminent action is inaction,
For that reason it is active.
Inferior action never stops acting,
For that reason it is inactive.
Eminent action is disengaged,
Yet nothing is left unfulfilled;
Eminent humanness engages,
Yet nothing is left unfulfilled; . . . (38:1–2)

The sage embodies the principle of Wu Wei, which means "actionless action" or "nondoing." Wu Wei refers to action or response that arises spontaneously and effortlessly from a deep sense of nonseparation between oneself and one's environment. It is not inertia or mere passivity. Rather, it is the experience of going with the grain or swimming with the current. Wu Wei refers to behavior occurring in perfect response to the flow of the Tao.

If we are to understand the principle of Wu Wei, we must consciously experience ourselves as part of the unity of life that is the Tao. Lao Tzu teaches that we must be quiet and watchful, learning to listen to both our own inner voices and to the voices of our environment in a noninterfering, receptive manner. In this way we also learn to rely on more than just our intellect and logical mind to gather and assess information. We develop and trust our intuition as our direct connection to the Tao. We heed the intelligence of our whole body, not only our brain. And we learn through our own experience. All of this allows us to respond readily to the needs of the environment, which of course includes ourselves. And just as the Tao functions in a manner to promote harmony and balance, our own actions, performed in the spirit of Wu Wei, produce the same result.

The spontaneous, natural, and effortless actions that are the expression of Wu Wei flow forth from the sage. These actions are virtuous action, Te; they are right action, appropriate to the time, place, and circumstance, and serving the needs of the harmony and balance of the Tao.

Through *living in actionless engagement and preaching wordless doctrine*, Lao Tzu discovered that *the myriad creatures act without inquiring, nourish without possessing, accomplish without claiming credit.* In ordinary life, we are educated and trained to project a possible outcome before taking action, to foresee a planned result through ego-guided action. We expect acknowledgment or reward for our efforts. But when the ego is in remission, the mind *does nondoing, engages in non-affairs, and savors non-flavor.* The essence of Wu Wei is "not to act with desire," "not to engage egoistically," and "not to become possessive."

Not even relying on selflessness
Enables the self to be fulfilled. (7:4)

Success is consequent to all affairs.
It does not proclaim its own existence.
All things return.
Yet there is no claim of ownership,
So it is forever desireless.
This can be called small.
All things return.
Yet there is no claim of ownership,
This can be called great.
The sage accomplishes greatness in not acting great.
Thus can he accomplish what is great. (34:2-3)

Not even relying on selflessness enables the self to be fulfilled. There is no thought of self, there is no thought of selflessness.

Success is consequent to all affairs. It does not proclaim its own existence. All things return, yet there is no claim of ownership, so it is forever desireless. For the sage, there is no self-consciousness, there is no self-assertion, there is no desire, and there is no aversion.

This can be called small. This is because the tranquil mind can *seek what is difficult with ease and effect what is great while it is small.* From natural observation Lao Tzu realized that *the most difficult things in the world are done while they are easy. The greatest things in the world are done while they are small, since what is easy necessarily entails difficulty. Thus the sage, through extreme trials, ends up with no difficulty.*

The myriad creatures
Act without beginning,
Nourish without possessing,
Accomplish without claiming credit.
It is accomplishment without claiming credit that makes the outcome self-sustaining. (2:4–5)

The sage responds spontaneously to what the Tao, to what the situation, calls for. There is no thought of oneself accomplishing something or claiming credit for accomplishing something.

The sage never plans to do a great thing.
Thus, he accomplishes what is great. (63:5)

The sage accomplishes greatness in not planning a great thing and not acting great; as it turns out, he accomplishes what is great. Through non-acting action, the sage does not fail. Not clinging, he does not lose.

Lao Tzu explains that when the self is inactive, the body transforms itself; when the self abides in stillness, the body organizes itself; when the self is disengaged, the body enriches itself; when the self chooses nondesire, the body remains simple. Because he has rid his mind of murkiness, the sage regains self-awareness, self-clarity, and self-expressiveness, and desire and demand disappear naturally.

THE CHARACTER OF THE SAGE

In addition to Wu Wei, several other important qualities characterize the sage: Wu Zheng (noncompetition), Shan (kindness), and Xian (wisdom). We will discuss each quality in tern.

Wu Zheng, Noncompetition

Wu Zheng means far more than noncompetitiveness. It suggests not competing and not striving as demanded from the ego. It further represents mental confusion and unease through disputing or arguing. The essential meaning of Wu Zheng is "not to strive for what is beyond self and not to pursue what does not belong to self."

People tend to have a negative attitude toward the literal meaning of noncompetition. The term *noncompetition* may connote a person who is too magnanimous, overly generous, too accommodating, too capitulating. Another negative image is of a person who is lacking confidence and self-respect, and who has no ability to protect or defend him- or herself.

This is not the ideal of the Taoist path. The nature of Wu Zheng is like the nature of water: it is yielding and fluid but infinitely strong. In Wu Zheng, there is no assertion of ego, with its false and forced needs and reactions. But there is a natural expression of being. In the complete expression of Wu Zheng, there is neither giving in nor giving up. Everything receives its due naturally, without manipulation.

The sacred mechanism of the world cannot be manipulated.
Those who manipulate it will fail,
Those who hold on to it will lose it. (29:2)

The sage trusts the way of the Tao, and thus feels no need to manipulate anything. The sage feels no need to hold on to or resist anything.

So the sage abandons extremes, extravagance, multiplicity.
[He] desires not to desire and does not value goods that are hard to get.
(29:4; 64:8)

As one continues on the path of Taoist cultivation and lets go of all attachments, there is no negativity remaining as the desires and fears of the mind are transformed into subtle awareness. The final competition will not be about gains, success, name, and possessions, but the death of them all. Whoever overcomes death overcomes life, whoever lives beyond death lives beyond life.

The sage does not collect.
As soon as he exists for others, he has more.
As soon as he gives to others, he has more.
So the Tao of heaven benefits and does not harm.
The Tao of humankind exists and does not compete. (68:2–3)

The sage realizes that when he exists for others, when he gives to others, he has abundance. At this level, the sage is able to manage the loss that causes all losses; he uses all negative influence as the treasure of teaching. Thus:

Being a good warrior does not entail power.
A good fighter is not angry.
One who is good at overcoming the enemy does not contact him.
One who is good at leading people acts humbly.
This is called the Action of noncompetition.
This is called leading people.
This is called the Ultimate as old as heaven. (70:1–2)

Shan, Kindness

> *[The sage] is kind to those who are kind.*
> *He is also kind to those who are not kind.*
> *It is the kindness of Action itself.* (49:2)

Shan refers to kindness, goodness, or compassion. Lao Tzu emphasizes that kindness is the virtue of action: *The sage is kind to those who are kind. He is also kind to those who are not kind. It is the kindness of Action itself.* It is a dispassionate compassion. In this regard, *the kindness of Action* is not judged by the *hun*'s conscious activity, nor is it grasped at or repelled by *po*'s egoism. In the expression of kindness there should be no hope for personal gain. Nor should kindness be withdrawn if personal or social recognition is not forthcoming.

By employing kindness the sage has the ability to further the good of all. No one is left out and no talent is wasted. Those who are slow or weak are encouraged and supported by kindness. At the same time, those who show talent and are quick-thinking will unfold and explore their full potential through kindness. Lao Tzu calls this *being in the tow of enlightenment . . . For everything that is good is the teacher of the good person. Everything that is bad becomes a resource for the good person. No need to honor the teachers. No need to love the resources* (27:2–3). This is because both yin and yang are emerging from and being generated by the action of kindness. The body and mind, the inner consciousness and outer behavior, mirror each other.

Eminent goodness is like water.

> *Water is good at benefiting all things,*
> *It retires to undesirable places.*
> *Thus it is near to Tao.*
> *Dwelling in good places,*
> *Drawing from good sources,*
> *Supplying from good nature,*
> *Speaking with good trust,*

Governing with good rules,
Conducting with good ability,
And acting within good time.
For this reason,
There is no competition,
There is no concern. (8:2–4)

By employing kindness, the sage acts with compassion. The sage does exactly what must be done in response to each situation, no more and no less, out of the compassion that arises from knowing the unity and interconnectedness of all of life.

Lao Tzu says that if a sage must fight, he has nothing to fear, no concern. He must make a careful and complete judgment of his surroundings when confronted with danger. He must defend himself and others; there is no miscalculation, nothing is neglected. All that should be protected is secured.

Xian, Wisdom

To know others is to be knowledgeable,
To know oneself is enlightenment;
To master others is to have strength,
To master oneself is to be powerful. (33:1)

Only those who are not slaves to life are wise to the value of life. (77:2)

It is thus, without desire, that the wise see. (79:4)

The nature of Xian in the Tao Te Ching concerns wisdom. The sage possesses deep wisdom. He or she may or may not demonstrate intellectual prowess in a wide variety of subjects; this is not necessarily the fruit of wisdom. To be wise is to see clearly, without the distortion of false desires, attachments, and fears. *Only those who are not slaves to life are wise to the value of life* defines the true power of wisdom. Only those who are not slaves to life have the inner freedom to see things as they truly are. *It is thus, without desire, that the wise see.*

> *Through discrimination, I have the knowledge*
> *to walk in the great Tao.* (53:1)

To be wise is to know the way of all things, to know the Tao. The wise are able to discriminate clearly and express and demonstrate that clarity in response to all the changing circumstances of life. It is thus that the sage *exists without ownership, accomplishes without holding on.*

The Chinese term *Xian* is equivalent to the word "sage" in English. The Chinese ideograph for Xian is a clear visual description of the life of the sage. It is composed with strokes of "human" (*ren*) and "mountain" (*shan*). In early forms of written Chinese language, the human stroke appears at the top and the mountain stroke at the bottom. It could be translated as "the human who stands on the top of a mountain." The mountain is the ideal location for the wise man; nothing on earth is higher. Only the wind, clouds, and the standing tower of a human form can loom above the mountain peak. When the character was later rearranged, the "human" stroke was placed at the left side, and the "mountain" stroke was set at the right side. Perhaps the change was made because the mountain symbolized such a cold, windswept, and lonely form. Or perhaps the emperor resented a human form other than his own occupying the highest position on earth. He ordered the linguists to reconstruct the character, placing a prone sage sleeping side by side with the mountain. In this position there was no one standing at the top to threaten his image; his prestige and unequaled power were restored.

The soul seeker, the wandering pilgrim, anyone on the spiritual quest prefers to dwell in a mountain cave rather than a warm house or grand palace. Mountains are the symbols of life on earth. The generating, developing, and transforming power of earth lies in the vastness of mountains. In contrast, valleys are a resting ground, echoing place, and rejuvenating resource. The contrasting images of mountain and valley parallel the dualities of life and death, male and female, heaven and earth, being and nonbeing. Mountains generate the forces of winds and clouds, rain and snow, plateau and plain. They are the most sacred places on earth. In their nurturing atmosphere consciousness is expanded and sickness is detoxified. Walking the Taoist way becomes a returning journey; the external search becomes internal embracing. The sage embraces the wisdom and holiness, the Xian, of the mountains.

THE PATH OF THE SAGE

Knowing the Tao

Pursuing the Tao is an act of spiritual cultivation. Without the Tao, it is impossible to walk the spiritual path. Without the Tao, cultivation has no source, no root, no power, and no meaning.

To pursue the Tao is to become centered in one's speech and conduct, to be grounded with a foundation, to be connected with nature, and to be harmoniously balanced between subjective inner experience and worldly affairs.

When eminent persons hear of Tao,
They practice it faithfully;
When average persons hear of Tao,
It seems that they practice it, and it seems they do not;
When inferior persons hear of Tao,
They ridicule it.
Without such ridicule, it would not be Tao.
Thus, the aphorism that suggests the way is:
Knowing the Tao seems costly.
Entering Tao seems like retreating.
Becoming equal with Tao gives birth to paradoxes. (40:1–3)

When one truly recognizes the Tao, one recognizes its inestimable value and is compelled to align oneself and one's life with it:

When eminent persons hear of Tao, they practice it faithfully. This practice brings a big loss: *knowing the Tao seems costly, entering Tao seems like returning, and becoming equal with Tao gives birth to paradoxes.* It takes living life to know the Tao. Entering the Tao is consuming the life force you have been given; becoming equal with the Tao stands with two legs, grabs with two hands, views with two eyes, grounds with two feet, dances with two hearts, and sleeps with two worlds. All of this is the paradoxical nature of body and mind.

> *Gusty winds do not last all morning,*
> *Cloudbursts do not last all day.*
> *What makes this so?*
> *Heaven and earth will not last forever,*
> *How could a human being last!*
> *So the person who works according to Tao unites with Tao.*
> *In the same way he unites with action.*
> *In the same way he unites with loss.*
> *Uniting with action, the Tao becomes action.*
> *Uniting with loss, the Tao becomes loss.* (24:2–5)

Heaven is eternal, and earth is long lasting. But *gusty winds do not last all morning, cloudbursts do not last all day.* Existing with the eternal Tao of the self and the temporary breathing of the Tao within us is the true duality, the true paradox. With each breath the sound and meaning of the Tao is exercised, thus one hears the Tao. By hearing and entering the Tao through its returning process, the thirst for knowledge is quenched by the light emitted through the gate of heaven. This ensures the complete knowing suggested by Lao Tzu.

Knowing the Tao is different from worldly knowing. Worldly knowing is driven by a self that wants to become rich with what the world offers. When one no longer feels compelled to be a knower in this way, the sickness is over; enlightenment is achieved.

Knowing the Tao is a spontaneous interaction between the self and the environment. It cannot be taught, repeated, or recorded.

There is no need to attempt to explain the inexplicable and to search for the invisible. This is why Lao Tzu concludes simply that *to know oneself is enlightenment.*

Knowledge that is shared, taught, repeated, and recorded is no longer that of self-knowing. It is simply a learning process; it is not the alive, present, spontaneously interconnected experience of self-knowing. *To know others is to be knowledgeable,* albeit limited, bounded, restrained. Our limited knowledge is never sufficient to explore the comprehension and understanding of others. Shared knowledge merely promotes further searching, reaching out to grasp the power of mastering and endless control. In this manner, pursuing knowledge becomes a consuming desire, a fixation, and a possessive action. It is upon this mental persuasion that Lao Tzu kindly advises that *to know what is sufficient is to be rich.* He also distinguishes the actual knowledge the mind has acquired from the mental appraisal of ourselves as knowledgeable. He states that *knowing that you don't know (everything) is superior and not knowing that you don't know (everything) is a sickness.* Only hearing and entering the Tao can be known.

Embracing Simplicity

> *[J]ust let things be.*
> *Observe the plain and embrace the simple.*
> *Do not think much and do not desire much.*
> *Get rid of learning and worry will disappear.* (19:2–3)

This is the way of hearing and entering the Tao. When we observe the plain and embrace the simple, we can be simply present; we are at peace, at rest, undistracted by worries and complexities.

Plain is the foundation of diversity, complexity, uncertainty, and unpredictability. *Simplicity* is the initial stage for growth, expansion, development, and completion. The anticipating and planning mind and the desire for results are cast out when these two are embraced. Learning will be simplified with total, mindful engagement. Lao Tzu clarifies this as: *It is easy to sustain what is at rest. It is easy to plan for that of which there is not even a sign* (64:1). Knowing this, Lao Tzu asserts that *though simplicity is small, the world cannot treat it as subservient. If lords and rulers can hold on to it, everything becomes self-sufficient* (32:2).

Also, simplicity supports efficiency. Lao Tzu advises that we *[s]eek what is difficult with ease and effect what is great while it is small*, since *the most difficult things in the world are done while they are easy. The greatest things in the world are done while they are small.* Because of this, *the sage never plans to do a great thing. Thus, he accomplishes what is great* (63:3-5).

Lao Tzu says that *the sage keeps the mind simple and is always without his own mind* (49:1,3). Simplicity of mind rather than complexity of mind is the heart of kindness. Simple mind is what Zen Buddhism calls "no-mind"—the largest expansion of mind—and the highest clarity of mind. No-mind means no ego-mind. It is a boundless expanse of awareness that allows spacious room for all that arises and resists nothing.

Living with simplicity is the practical side of cultivation. The sage lives for the world and not for himself. How? First of all, the sage keeps the mind simple: there is no distraction of attention, no waste of energy, and no confusion of mind. He is not restlessly struggling and striving for the things of the world. He is free from self-concern.

Secondly, the sage the sage engages with others simply, and he does not impose himself on others.

[S]ince the sage wants to elevate the people, his speech is down to earth.
Since the sage wants to advance the people, he positions himself at the back,
So that when he is at the front, people do not harm him.
When he stands above, people do not feel pressure.
The whole world supports him untiringly.
Since he does not rely on competition, the world has nothing
with which to compete. (66:2–4)

Thirdly, the sage is open, flexible, and not attached to specific outcomes. He is sensitive to others. The hope of people is his encouragement and their sorrow is his misfortune. When people want him, the sage is already there, waiting; when people need him, the sage is the pillar that braces them.

The Virtue of Frugality

When we embrace the plain and the simple, frugality becomes an important value. Frugality involves calculating the most direct and effective use of energy. As a result, waste is eliminated, and there is no debt, no regret, and no punishment. This is why the idea of *loss* is important in Lao Tzu's teaching. When the cost of ego is reduced to zero and when bodily metabolism functions at its optimal state, energy is consumed for the benefit and good of others. Frugality ensures a simple way of life that supports the good of all.

Frugality has no connection to the selfish strategy of meanness or greed. Meanness and greed have their source in fear and obsession; the entire world becomes solely a source to satisfy the ego's insatiable wants, lusts, and perceived needs. When gripped by greed, people constantly fear loss and lack. This has infinite worldly manifestations. True frugality is entirely different. There is no energy waste resulting from selfishness, fear, grasping, self-concern.

When frugality is the measure of daily life, one neither indulges in extravagance, nor allows selfishness to control. There should be no pollution in energy consumption; no ego anticipation in action; no contamination of heart; no confusion of mind; and no negativity arising through action.

Lao Tzu applies this to society by saying this:

> *For governing people . . . nothing is better than frugality. Only frugality enables the preemptive measures. Preemptive measures mean a great accumulation of Action. A great accumulation of Action leaves nothing to be conquered. When nothing needs to be conquered, no-boundary is known. When no-boundary is known, it allows the country to exist. The country, existing from its source, can endure. This is the Tao of having a deep root, a strong stem, a long life and an enduring vision.* (59:1–3)

In this way, neither the individual nor society need be concerned with, or consumed by, self-concern or self-protection. There is trust in life, trust in the Tao.

When frugality is maintained at home, one is perfectly grounded, and one quietly preserves the tranquility that masters the restless life. The virtue of frugality is the peace of not wanting. One is steadfastly *reaching the ultimate emptiness*, and resolute in *concentrating on the central stillness* (16:1). It is only through such qualities that all things work together. There is no bad luck, no backfire, no punishment, because one has no expectations, has done nothing wrong, and wasted nothing. One has no need to gain anything or fear losing anything. The harmony of the world becomes a true friend.

Nondualistic Mentality

In the world,
Everyone recognizes beauty as beauty,
Since the ugly is also there.
Everyone recognizes goodness as goodness,
Since evil is also there.
Since being and nonbeing give birth to each other,
Difficulty and ease complete each other,
Long and short measure each other,
High and low overflow into each other,
Voice and sound harmonize with each other,
And before and after follow each other. (2:1–2)

Emerging through the "door" of the mysterious is the duality of creation and destruction. These are mutually dependent and mutually necessary processes. All of the dualities of life are mutually dependent and mutually necessary.

When one searches only for beauty, one stigmatizes the ugly. When people see beauty as pure beauty, they view the ugly disparagingly. In valuing the good as purely good, their judgment is based upon their idea of bad. But the universal manifests through the division of two from one, each depends on its opposite. The interaction of the many dualities that emerge from oneness is what makes one truly individual. This in turn makes an individual a non-individual. Beautiful or ugly is but two sides of the same coin. *How much difference is there between beautiful and ugly?* (20:1) It is a fine line.

Based on these paradoxes, Lao Tzu proposed that *being and non-being give birth to each other, difficulty and ease complete each other, long and short measure each other, high and low overflow into each other, voice and sound harmonize with each other, and before and after follow each other* (2:2). Yet, individual character is a middle ground between individuality and totality. We still discriminate, we still make choices.

The net of heaven is broad and loose, yet nothing slips through (75:5). *Large or small, many or few, reward or punishment, are all done through Action* (63:2). This is the measure of virtue and right judgment. Because of virtue, internal conscious intention and external physical performance are integrated, and nothing is left behind. *A good traveler leaves no tracks. A good speaker is without flaw. A good planner does not calculate. A good doorkeeper does not lock the door, yet it cannot be opened* (27:1). What this means is that we need to know how to interact without imposing ourselves or being locked in by our mental projection. There should be no mental imprinting, no residue of any kind, left behind; thus, no sickness results. This differs from the commonsense approach of doing something and then letting it go. It is a matter of clearing off the steps before one slips and falls. In order to reach this state of being we can only be what we are, and know—be aware of—what is around us. This is all that we can do:

Since *hanging on to it will cause overflow; better to let go. Forced consent does not endure* (9:1). *Those who boast of themselves lose their stance. He who displays himself is not seen. He who justifies himself is not understood. He who lashes out does not succeed. He who builds himself up does not endure* (22:1). The natural outcome is: *He who does not display himself is seen. He who does not justify himself is understood. He who does not lash out succeeds. He who does not build himself up endures. Therefore, only the spirit of noncompetition makes things noncompetitive. So the old saying goes: "Yield, and retain integrity"* (23:3-5).

The Wisdom of the Sage: Childlike and Ancient

The ancient sages of Tao are subtle and mysteriously penetrating.
Their depth is beyond the power of will.
Because it is beyond the power of will,
The most we can do is describe it:
Thus, full of care, as one crossing the wintry stream,
Attentive, as one cautious of the total environment,
Reserved, as one who is a guest,
Spread open, as when confronting a marsh,
Simple, like uncarved wood, opaque, like mud,
Magnificent, like a valley.
From within the murky comes the stillness.
The feminine enlivens with her milk.
Keeping such a Tao, excess is undesirable.
Desiring no excess, work is completed without exhaustion. (15:1–5)

Lao Tzu vividly illustrates the psychospiritual quality and biological balance that the sage retains. Even though the sage returns to a childlike spiritual tranquility and lives within a refreshed bodily condition, he is not literally like a young child. There are important similarities between the body/mind state of the child and that of the sage—that is why sagehood is often compared to childhood. Yet there are important differences. The sage has the wisdom of experience that a young child does not have. In *Memories, Dreams, Reflections*, Jung writes that

> Lao Tzu is the example of a man with superior insight who has seen and experienced worth and worthlessness, and who at the end of his life desires to return into his own being, into the eternal unknown meaning. The archetype of the old man who has seen enough is eternally true. At every level of intelligence this type appears, and its lineaments are always the same, whether it be an old peasant or a great philosopher like Lao Tzu. This is old age, and a limitation.

The word "old" in this context refers to the nearly completed state of biological manifestation, and to its expanse of personal and social experience. It is the rich quality of a long life's journey. It is also the last stage before death. Jung portrays the stage of life ahead as a "limitation" because it represents death, mentally and spiritually. Yet for the sage, there is no fear. He has seen all, and is ready to "return into his own being."

The sage retains the innocence, freshness, and lack of prejudice of the child, yet at the same time possesses the wisdom of life experience. The sage can be seen as an "ancient child." The ancient child begins to withdraw from the world at the end of life not because he is sickened by the world, but because he is drawn into the heart. What attracts the eyes outward toward the world and the changing manifestations of form; what attracts the heart inwardly is the formless, changeless, and unfathomable eternity.

The main difference between the sage and the child is the life experience. *Being cautious while crossing the winter stream* describes a measured conscious awareness that comes through experience. Being attentive means being aware and focused; being reserved means being humble and acknowledging. *Spreading open* is the unrestrained mental space, *simplicity* is the ability to remain refreshed and energized, opaque is the quality of being Oneness within and without, and *magnificent* is the ability of retaining and rejuvenating the oneness within.

The wisdom of the sage is old and new, experienced and fresh, knowledgeable and humble, ready to die and ready to fly. He has a memory of life but is not restrained by memory; he has the richness of life experience but is unbounded by the meaning of life experience. He is a teacher and friend, guide and companion, destroyer of the old and protector of the new, a battery for generating and recharging everything. He is a body of soul and a heart of spirit, an upholder of justice, a voice for the nation, and a symbol for the human race.

The Nature of Te

In some translations of the Tao Te Ching, the sections on the Tao and Te are presented separately. *Te* is a difficult word to translate; it refers to action, virtue, morality, beauty, and gracious behavior. Te is the manifestation of the Tao within all things. Thus, to express the fullness of Te means to be in perfect harmony with the original nature of self and all things.

From the Taoist point of view, Tao and Te cannot truly be understood as separate. They differ only in terms of the order in which they are approached first: that of meditation or cultivation. Tao is based on meditation; Te is rooted in cultivation. To meditate is to gather and circulate Chi; to cultivate is to abandon the ego and to purify the consciousness.

In Taoist inner alchemy, Tao and Te are equally important. Yet to manage both simultaneously is a challenge, rendering the practice unrealistic. The practice of distilling the mind can appear daunting when the body is truly hungry. It would be equally unmanageable to purify the body if the mind was not fully prepared to offer the proper environment.

Once the seed of Tao is germinated, the action of Te takes place. Tao is invisible and Te is visible; Tao is intangible and Te is tangible; Tao is impersonal and Te is personal; Tao is motionless and Te is lovable; Tao inhales and Te smiles. Because of this esoteric transformation, matter is visible, form is tangible, substance is manageable, and trust is reliable. They are all the virtuous expression of Te resulting from the emerging power of the Tao.

The exhalation of Te is the sum of all human activities that have been conducted with moral judgment and supervised by the spirit. When in concert with the kind action of Te, all are inspired, encouraged, and uplifted; every action is honorable, respectable, and appropriate.

In the last exhalation in life, the purified Shen gathers the elixir or remaining energies lingering in the body and, guided by an enlightened master or an angel, exhales this through the top of the head instead of the mouth or nose. This transpires only after kind action or Te has been completed and all debts have been paid. Unless these conditions are met, the person will die as either a hungry ghost or wandering ghost.

This task can be endeavored by cultivation as well as meditation. The meditation of love can be transformed into the cultivation of virtuous action, qualified by kindness, goodness, harmony, impartiality, integrity, and holiness. Love will no longer be a mental projection but a true and honest expression of empathy, care, and concern born from nonseparation between self and other. As the power of meditation and the outcome of cultivation generate virtuous action, the sage embraces and integrates the animal, human, and divine aspects of the self.

VIRTUOUS ACTION

From the Taoist point of view, Te is what Tao "drops." Lao Tzu writes that *When Tao is lost, it becomes Action* (38:3). The word "lost" represents the complete transformation or evolution from one state of being into the next. When the infinite and unmanifest Tao is surrendered into active Te, it becomes visible. Te represents the highest state of the transformation of Tao into matter and substance, retaining the highest essence of the Tao. It is a descent of the unmanifest into the manifest.

This descending process is quite similar to the supernatural power or influence exerted by a divine being. Lao Tzu also describes Te as *mystic action.* Yet Taoism doesn't create a sharp distinction between natural and supernatural.

> *[T]he person who works according to Tao unites with Tao.*
> *In the same way he unites with action.*
> *In the same way he unites with loss.*
> *Uniting with action, the Tao becomes action.*
> *Uniting with loss, the Tao becomes loss.* (24:4–5)

Lao Tzu explains that *the person who works according to Tao unites with Tao. In the same way he unites with action (Te). In the same way he unites with loss.* The power of Tao becomes the seed of life, emerging as the elixir of virtue or evaporating into nothing. Thus Tao saves the spirit or loses the earthly life. Returning home with virtue is saving the spirit; marching forward toward the grave is loss.

The original meaning of *Te* in Chinese involved the idea of "ascending" or "elevating," indicating the uplifting of the human spirit rising from the earthly carnal body into pure spiritual action. This is consonant with the English understanding of virtue, which implies moral practice and action, conformity to the standard of right, moral excellence, integrity of character, upright conduct, and rectitude.

Yet virtue cannot be understood simplistically, according to prescriptions or rules. Te, or virtuous action, is a spontaneous and interactive engagement between body and mind, perception and response; it is the judgment of good and bad, and the conduct of divine and ordinary. Nature acts, humans perform; nature presents, humans exhibit; nature reveals, humans display; nature manifests, humans conduct; nature shows, humans behave; nature embraces, humans value; nature integrates, humans dissolve; nature unifies, humans separate.

Virtue, to the ordinary mind, is something remote, pure, and out of reach. It is a moral quality suited only to a divine being. Virtue is something that we can think about and strive for, but cannot perform. We can visualize it but cannot perceive it; we can comprehend it mentally but cannot engage it physically.

Xiaochu and Dachu

The inner alchemy called forth by walking the path of Tao and Te is addressed in the *I Ching* hexagrams Xiaochu and Dachu, which we discussed briefly in Chapter 4. In the *I Ching* there are two mystical energy fields, the small mystical field (Xiaochu) of the ninth hexagram and the larger mystical field (Dachu) of the twenty-sixth hexagram. Xiaochu deals with the animal body and its spirit, while Dachu refers to the human body and its spirit. The Taoist path involves integrating these two fields within ourselves. We need to be in harmony with the energy field of mother earth and be able to transform the energies of the earth. Yet we also need to be in harmony with the energy field of the human realm, so we can walk the way of beauty, compassion, values, and justice—the virtuous action of Te.

SMALL MYSTICAL FIELD (XIAOCHU) OF THE 9TH HEXAGRAM

LARGER MYSTICAL FIELD (DACHU) OF THE 26TH HEXAGRAM

The small mystic field deals with the small mind, the selfish, egoistic, and culturally conditioned mind. The large mystic field houses the selfless and cosmic mind. Energetically, the small mystic field deals with the biologically driven, instinctive actions of self-preservation and survival. It has no concern for the world other than what it can provide the seeking acquisitive eye and the craving hungry stomach. In the large mystic field there is no self-preoccupation, self-protection, or self-concern of the small, egoic self. There is instead a sense of self/mind that is vast and unlimited by the needs of the ego and animal nature.

The ninth and twenty-sixth hexagrams, Xiaochu and Dachu, both have the same lower trigram: the creative power of the cosmos and the invisible light of heaven. In Xiaochu, the upper trigram is wind, representing the heavenly order, conscious awareness, and instinctive behavior. As a whole, the characteristics of Xiaochu are mobility, agitation, unsteadiness, and unreliability. Cloudiness, murkiness, rigidity, and scattering are its tendencies. Mind is windy with no clear mental picture. There are clouds but no rain, wandering but no awakening, only confusion with no self-understanding. There is no awakening of the inner character.

In contrast, Dachu's upper trigram is replaced by mountain, agitation by stillness, mobility by self-action, unsteadiness by steadfastness, unreliability by trust. When the mountain grounds the spirit and nourishes the soul, the mind is clarified, the body is purified, the attitude made flexible.

The self is never lost, the energy is never exhausted, and spirit is never dead. The sage is not bounded. He sustains himself from the mother resource and does not rely upon family in order to continue his existence. He is everywhere in the world and has no need to be protected and comforted. He is clothed with light, breathes the vital force, and settles down in the universe.

Dachu points to light and clarity and to the daily renewal of character. Dachu points to walking the way of the Tao and manifesting in the world as Te.

The Te Ideograph

In the construction of the Chinese ideograph Te, the right side of the character is composed of four characters, "hand," "vessel," "one," and "heart." This part of the character can be expressed as "The single heart supports and directs the vessel of the body carried by the hand." Truly, the body is the most sacred vessel, and the hands are the most powerful and useful tools. Yet, without heart there is no foundation; without the single-minded heart, there is no transformation. This part of the ideograph depicts a meditative state in which hands are unified with the bodily vessel and guided by the single devoted heart.

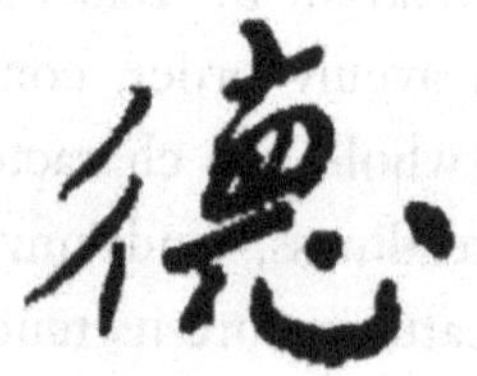

CHINESE CHARACTER TE

This action is accompanied by the careful steps of walking, represented by the left side of the character. The activity of the hands is freed from concern with the bodily vessel. Chi sustains the vessel and satisfies the heart. The hands are held together as in a meditative state. The world is in its perfect order and the body/mind is in its perfect harmony.

There is one remaining aspect of the Chinese character that expresses the meaning of Te. It implies that perception is grounded in the heart, the heart is grounded in spiritual consciousness, and spiritual consciousness is grounded in the character of nature. Everything is there and nothing is there. All the lines, angles, joints, and points of the ideography of Te are penetrated, purified, and transformed by the fire of light. This is the magic play of a sage who dwells in the Tao and moves in Te.

KIND ACTION

While the forces of nature are impersonal and impartial, even inhumane, human souls are called to empathy, kindness, and compassion. Te refers equally to virtue and kindness. When the small ego no longer rules one's life, one's action is kindness itself. In practicing kind action, love is no longer a conscious game played by ego. It no longer functions as an obsessive mental longing or uncontrolled emotional outburst. Sympathy becomes mutual encouragement. Pity becomes the fearless act of loving. Negative emotions do not hurt people and positive emotions cannot drag them down. All these emotional attributes are purified into compassion.

He is kind to those who are kind.
He is also kind to those who are not kind.
It is the kindness of Action itself.
He is trustworthy to those who are trustworthy.
He is also trustworthy to those who are not trustworthy.
It is the trust of Action itself. (49:2)

When selflessness is restored through the meditation of love, action is kind and trustworthy. When the universal loving energy is gathered within, biological and psychological needs are fulfilled, thereby leaving no room within the body and mind for desire and demand created by ego. Self-trust is established and conscious fear is relinquished. One's energy is then free and fully available.

When the sage uses the universal loving energy, his action is both kind and trustworthy. He is kind and trustworthy to all—to those who are kind and trustworthy, and to those who are not kind and trustworthy. Through kind action, both kind and unkind people are unified. Those who are kind transform those who are not kind. There is no separation between what a kind person is and the kindness itself. Those who are not kind benefit from those who are kind, and kindness itself is then underway. Those who are trustworthy improve themselves and know there is more trust in the future. Those who are not trustworthy disprove themselves, yet trust welcomes them along the way.

Through love, kind action becomes endless, inexhaustible, and unfathomable. Kind action is the very nature of a mother's power of creative nourishment, a combination of selfless love and self-sacrifice.

Te Is Smallness

The way of Te is smallness, simplicity, integrity, peace, noncompetition, and nonaction. Being small allows for growth, expansion, and development. It is the most effective way to conserve energy since the small consumes minimal energy. Once the humbleness of the honest heart steps in, the opportunism of the egoistic mind is cast out, and the desire for achievement and recognition becomes illusory.

Simplicity is the way to direct your life. There is no confusion to deal with, no mind juggling, and no disguise. With no attachment, each minute detail and quality of smallness will manifest. Just as with a newborn baby, smallness requires your full attention, the finest care, and the highest precautionary measures. Any slight of mindfulness or unintentional carelessness could cause immediate difficulty.

Realizing this, everything manifests by itself, naturally; even the method of simplicity is absent. Any intervening thought, calculation, or effort is eliminated. In smallness there is peace. Through peace, one observes that *vast action seems yielding* (40:3).

In smallness and simplicity, one's ego is out of the way, therefore there is room for all. ***Such is called mystic Action. For that reason, all things worship Tao and exalt Action. The worship of Tao and exaltation of Action are not conferred, but always arise naturally*** (51:1-2,5).

Humility and Humiliation

Humiliation is one of the most devastating emotions one can face. Lao Tzu says that "Favor and disgrace surprise the most." The word disgrace is synonymous with humiliation, a reaction no one wishes to experience. When humiliation occurs, the conscious mind is completely darkened and filled with despair, placing the recipient into a despicable state with no opportunity to hide or escape. It renders one valueless, seemingly nonexistent. On the other hand, it evolves into the most valuable time to examine oneself objectively, to face the situation with grace and understanding, to become like a child, and glorify God once again. The recipient owes thanks to the person invoking the humiliation. This experience can support the cultivation of humility, where one is not attached to one's self-image, to self-importance, or to position.

The essence of getting in touch with humiliation is to purify oneself from distortion, conceit, and pride, and to discover the impersonality of life, which will endlessly run its course. The following is a liberating meditation that works with humiliation.

1. Mentally picture the scene that precipitated your humiliation. Feel the presence of the thoughts and feelings involved.
2. Stay with the pain and suffering, and hold this experience for awhile. Then release all the energies, thoughts, and feelings associated with the humiliating experience. Let it all go, at once, and be liberated.
3. Do not be angry and frustrated about your humiliation. Look into it objectively. What does this humiliation mean? What was its purpose? What did you learn about your attachments and self-image?
4. Handle the humiliation just as you do the blowing wind or daily, mundane events of life. It is not personal and should not be pondered as anything special. This does not suggest that blowing wind and daily events are nothing, but that all things existing in life are normal and impersonal, and nothing about them is special.
5. You will find that in being humiliated there is attachment to expectations, and a certain lack of self-esteem and freedom. Destroy any rigidity you feel within you that prevents to from being open to new and unexpected things.

6. Allow your humiliation and your mind to be painstakingly purified in the same way that your body could be objectively examined and the source of its illness surgically removed. The full realization of this humiliation process is having your identity, position, esteem, and self-worth purified.
7. Decide if you will allow your body/mind to heal itself. Do you prefer to cling to the pain for reasons you may not be fully aware of?
8. The lesson is how you can free yourself from burdensome feelings and situations. Be aware that further humiliations may be in store, but now you are better prepared to deal with it should it arise.

True Dignity and False Dignity

Dignity is the quality of being worthy, honored, or esteemed. There is the essential dignity of the simple, unselfconscious expression of virtuous action. This is the dignity of Te. There is also the self-concern of the ego with its self-image. This is driven by insecurity and fear, and is not true dignity. With genuine self-esteem, cultivated through living in accord with Tao and Te, comes true self-dignity.

Self-dignity is totally opposite to ego-dignity. The conscious center of self-dignity is none other than conscious awareness. It is a state of openness, centeredness, and responsiveness.

It is not surprising that true self-dignity releases us from imprisonment in self-concern and self-image. True self-dignity has greater power than ego-dignity. Ego-dignity, which is an insatiable need for affirmation, is driven by selfishness, ethnic and other limited identities, and unconscious belief patterns. When controlled by ego dignity, forgiveness, acceptance, generosity, kindness, and compassion are lost.

In a world of "me first," above all others, how can we begin to contemplate Te, virtuous and kind action? With selfishness at the helm, people think moral action is the purview of only rare humans and divine beings. This denies the reality that unconditional, selfless, and universal love is the foundation of Being.

Love, compassion, and generosity are the expression of true self-dignity. These qualities are the natural expression of one who is released from self-concern.

TE CULTIVATION

Ji Te

Ji Te refers to the spiritual work of transforming the biophysical body into the loving Chi body used to express beauty, virtue, and compassion of Te in the world. The word *ji* means "accumulate." Ji Te is accumulating Te, the most challenging homework in all spiritual practice, more demanding than meditation and more difficult than sharing and giving. It is a constant purification process. Te is an objective energy but not a concrete object to be identified and possessed. Ji Te is the cultivation of kindness, loving energy, and self-sacrifice. The Taoist practices that accumulate and transform sexual and emotional energies are part of the path of Ji Te.

Ji Te is the process of establishing the quality of Te character. Without an accumulation of Te, there is no objective quality to be perceived by others. It is this accumulative practice, day after day, event following event, and trial after trial, that dissolves the ego, purifies the body, and distills the mind.

In our society there are many meditation techniques to learn, many skills to master, many opportunities for status seekers. Ji Te can be taught but cannot be learned intellectually. You cannot process Ji Te with the mind; you simply sacrifice your life to its practice. It is more painful than any sickness, more degrading than humiliation. It entails suffering. One must overcome any number of blockages.

No one can give someone else Te, even though they may be the recipient of its loving kindness and hospitable generosity. Any student desiring to cultivate the character of Te will quickly learn that it cannot be mastered by learning from others. It must be a process of self-mastering. Je is the manifestation of cosmic kindness, the mystic Tao in kind action. Ji Te is cultivating our capacity to be Te and express Te. It is the heart of the spiritual path.

The Mind as a Servant

From the perspective of the mind, spiritual cultivation begins in the self and ends with no-self. It is the transformation from mental engagement to full, mindful awareness. The Taoist's perspective is that spiritual cultivation begins with no-self and culminates in universal self. This is the path that culminates in the seamless expression of Tao and Te. *No-self* refers to the pure self that is not colored by the rational and intellectual mind, nor distracted by the craving and egoistic heart. No-self is the power of wisdom mind as well as the space of pure heart.

In the spontaneous expression of Te, there is no calculating mind. There is no conceptual mind standing back from the situation and observing, judging, commenting, claiming. Knowledge, to Lao Tzu, is mental information acquired by conscious desire or egoistic persuasion. Knowledge is something that can at times be useful, but the intellectual mind must serve its proper role, as a servant, not a master.

To obtain knowledge is necessary, but to apply it in accordance with Tao and Te requires great skill. The mind can become a slave to knowledge. Trying to obtain it can be an obsession. When the nature of knowledge is understood, it use is transformed, and it can serve and support virtuous action. True virtuous and kind action does not conform to the habits of mind. It does not serve the demands of the ego. It can be fully experienced but can never be thoroughly explained; completely envisioned but never absolutely understood; mindfully anticipated but never analyzed with detail. Spontaneous, natural, right action is no-minded.

When intelligence arises, there is great deal of manipulation (18:1). The obsessive intellectual proliferation of the ordinary mind makes people unhappy and society chaotic. C. G. Jung corroborates Lao

Tzu's assertion when he writes, in *Memories, Dreams, and Reflections,* that "in my experience, therefore, the most difficult as well as the most ungrateful patients, apart from being habitual liars, are the so-called intellectuals. With them, one hand never knows what the other hand is doing. They cultivate a 'compartment psychology.' Anything can be settled by an intellect that is not subject to the control of feeling—and yet the intellectual still suffers from a neurosis if feeling is undeveloped." The intellectuals can never bring in harmony what they think with what they feel. They cannot harmonize their inner experience with the virtuous action of Te. They walk through the narrow tunnel—constant logical calculation and intellectualization—that plagues modern Western civilization.

It is only when the intellectual capacity becomes still and quiet that the desires and cravings of the heart also become quiet. Only when the egoistic mind is dispelled can the true self take its rightful place. When the mind is peaceful and tranquil, the mind's natural illumination, originality, and wisdom can come forth. This is a intelligence that is far beyond anything that can be taught. It is linked with every individual's pure and uncarved innate ability. When this ability connects to its source, it becomes the universal-self.

In order to achieve this, one must master the self, the seed of the Tao. *Cultivate the self, and the action is pure. Treat the self by the standard of self.* We focus on awareness, listen to the heart, speak through the mouth, project through mentality, and battle with non-self and false-selves. We do all of this with authenticity and intention, and strive to unify and align all the many parts of the self with the Tao. When all these bits and pieces of the self are unified and crystallized through the nature of Tao, there is no longer any compartmentalization, and there is no difference between oneself and others. Then our life energy is no longer drained or dispersed through division, ambivalence, or distraction. There is an inner freedom in which we are truly present and truly available; we can respond fully in Te, kind and virtuous action.

True Te and the Veneer of Te

One of the most important distinctions Lao Tzu makes in the Tao Te Ching is that between no-minded, egoless, spontaneous action, and self-conscious, ego-centered, planned action. This is the distinction between Wu Wei, which means "actionless action" or "nondoing," and the unnatural, ego-based, forced doing that consumes so much energy in the world. Wu Wei refers to action or response that arises spontaneously and effortlessly from a deep sense of nonseparation between oneself and one's environment. Wu Wei is behavior occurring in perfect response to the flow of the Tao.

Eminent action is inaction,
For that action it is active.
Inferior action never stops acting,
For that reason it is inactive.
Eminent action is disengaged,
Yet nothing is left unfulfilled;
Eminent humanness engages,
Yet nothing is left unfulfilled; . . . (38:1–2)

When eminent action descends into inferior action, spontaneous action devolves into self-conscious action. Ego-based self-righteousness arises, and judgment steps into the picture, and *reduces the results of engagements.* Once righteousness is dispersed, *eminent justice engages but does not respond adequately to situations. For that reason it is frustrated* (38:2).

When Tao is lost,
It becomes Action;
When Action is lost,
It becomes benevolence;
When benevolence is lost,
It becomes justice.
When justice is lost,

It becomes propriety.
Propriety is the veneer of faith and loyalty,
And the forefront of troubles.
Foresight is the vain display of Tao,
And the forefront of foolishness.
Therefore, the man of substance
Dwells in wholeness rather than veneer,
Dwells in the essence rather than the vain display.
He rejects the latter, and accepts the former. (38:3–7)

A truly good man is not aware of his goodness; this is the nature of his goodness. He is not aware of himself as good. He is not aware of doing good. He just responds to life spontaneously, the response not separate from perceiving the situation, himself not separate from the situation.

Justice, as Lao Tzu describes it, is what arises when kindness is lost. Tao devolves into goodness. Goodness devolves into kindness. Kindness devolves into justice. Justice devolves into ritual.

The kind of justice that Lao Tzu refers to here indulges in self-justification and self-protection. It bears no resemblance to Te. It is based upon aggression and the counteraction of that aggression. Fairness, in the practice of justice, is not true fairness. Before the strong arm of justice, the fearless are in jeopardy and may lose their lives, but later, the karma of reaction surfaces. In the face of justice, the fearful can survive before final judgment is pronounced. Their physical bodies are temporarily protected, but their hearts cry out. As justice employs more and more procedures, society becomes more chaotic and disordered. That is not the nature of Tao; that is not kind action.

There is a clear-cut difference between moral discipline and social justice. Moral discipline consists of conscientious and virtuous deeds carried out through love and kindness. When love and kindness are remiss, the mind reacts unconsciously. Killing, stealing, lying, and all manner of "wrongful" behaviors arise. They serve the purpose of taking advantage of others (and ultimately harming oneself) in a failed effort to compensate for the deficiency of love and kindness.

From this comes righteousness, the standard judgment of moral conduct. When righteousness is lost in ego's dominance and aggression, religious and political rules flourish, shaping social behavior by its own standard of righteousness. Rather than Te, spontaneously kind and virtuous action, society is shaped by dogmatic rules and procedures. It is the veneer of Te, not Te itself. Moral conduct is replaced by collective activities and expectations. A selective group is approved to positions of authority by the collective mind. Moral discipline becomes mechanical and superficial. Unconditional and selfless love descends into the conditional demands of selfish love. Kindness then becomes a tool for personal benefit and compassion becomes a guise for ego gratification. True kindness and virtue are lost in a maze of crude, dehumanizing, and rationalized rules that are defended by the ego. This is propriety, merely the veneer of virtuous action.

Not Possessing

When the self is unified it is able to enter into the mystical space of Wu Wei, or actionless action. The action of Wu Wei, though mysterious, is rather plain and simple.

Begetting but not possessing,
Enhancing but not dominating.
This is Mysterious Action. (10:2–3)

Tao enlivens and nourishes, develops and cultivates, integrates and completes, raises and sustains.
It enlivens without possessing.
It acts without relying.
It develops without controlling.
Such is called mystic Action. (51:3–5)

The actionless action that expresses Te begets but does not possess. It enhances, enlivens, and nourishes, but does not dominate. It does not claim ownership. There is just the action, just the Wu Wei. There is no self—no "I"—doing something. There is no subject (self) in relation to an object (other). There is no self in relation to an action. There is just doing. This is the purity of Te, of virtuous and kind action.

Governing Self and Nation

LIVING SIMPLY

> *There is no crime greater than fostering desire.*
> *There is no disaster greater than not knowing when there is enough.*
> *There is no fault greater than wanting to possess.*
> *Knowing that sufficiency is enough always suffices.* (46:2–3)

Lao Tzu teaches that craving for fame and wealth often results in depravity and destruction. As Lao Tzu warns, *Extreme fondness is necessarily very costly. The more you cling to, the more you lose*. The individual and the human community live in harmony through living simply. Selfish craving and extravagance cause us to lose our grounding, our sense of balance, and our connection with all of life.

Taoists believe that simplicity of the mind cannot be separated from simplicity of the lifestyle. We can and should live a simple, spontaneous way of life by freeing ourselves from greed and craving for more than we need. The Tao Te Ching emphasizes the harmfulness of greed as it can impoverish people morally and spiritually.

Contentment arises from nonattachment. In Taoism the energy that drives our wants and desires can be transformed so that gratification or repression is no longer necessary. This is true freedom and true contentment.

For Taoists, the cycle of life and death is as natural as the cycle of day and night. Fortune and misfortune embrace each other. Through understanding this, contentment is possible even under extreme adversity. Death is merely an extension of life, with each complementing the other. When the negative and the positive are seen as an integrated whole in harmony, life has no problem at all. All problems are created when we are out of touch with the Way of nature. The Taoist seeks to surrender to the Tao, and not struggle, strive, or impose one's narrow desires and will upon the Way of nature.

The teaching on surrender is very important in spiritual cultivation, for what can spiritual liberation mean if not the liberation from our egoic impulse to strive to be different from what we are, or from the mechanism of grasping and rejecting?

The contentment taught by Taoism has many implications for modern society. Luxury and extravagant consumption are wasteful and harmful to the health and mental well-being of the individual and the society. Craving for wealth and material possessions impoverishes us morally and spiritually, and freedom from such craving enriches us by enhancing our capacity for love, mental serenity, health, and happiness. Understanding that fortune and misfortune contain each other can help us avoid mental frustrations when misfortune strikes. The same insight applies to other dualities such as success and failure, health and illness, and praise and blame.

The impulse of striving to be different from what we are causes tension and stress. Learning the art of Wu Wei, or actionless action, has enormous benefits for the individual and for society.

Part of the meaning of Wu Wei is not imposing our subjective thinking and beliefs on others. According to Taoism, dictatorship is doomed to failure because it violates this principle of not imposing and causes disharmony.

Taoism teaches that Tao, the great Way of nature, has no selfish motives, that Nature gives and nourishes without claiming anything in return. This is the ultimate guidance about contentment. The Taoist message of contentment does not imply a passive resignation to fate, but rather a selfless devotion and commitment to the well-being of all humanity.

Right Balance

As we have seen repeatedly, Lao Tzu advocates a simple, natural, and peaceful way of life. Serenity is found by returning to the eternal source by emptying oneself of all desires, and by flowing like water. The universe has two complementary principles, the male or active principle (yang) and the female or receptive principle (yin). Harmony results from the natural balance of the active and receptive qualities. Those who are too aggressive inappropriately meddle and interfere in the natural course of affairs and cause unnecessary problems. Those who are too passive lose their center, their grounding and authenticity, and likewise fail to maintain a natural order. To maintain the correct balance, Lao Tzu emphasizes Wu Wei, actionless action. By being receptive to the Tao, one knows intuitively how much to do and when to stop. The primary responsibility of each person is to understand and master oneself.

To know others is to be knowledgeable,
To know oneself is enlightenment;
To master others is to have strength,
To master oneself is to be powerful.
To know what is sufficient is to be rich. (33:1–2)

The way of spiritual power never interferes or inflicts, yet through it everything that needs to be accomplished is accomplished. It responds naturally to what is. All we need to do is to follow the way things are, and the world will be reformed of its own accord. The conflict of personal desires is what obscures the way, but when we free ourselves of desire then we find peace. By understanding our own nature, we can understand the nature of all things, and we can follow the natural dynamic rhythm of life, neither imposing nor hesitating. We are still and centered within, and can act appropriately, without reluctance or force.

> *All things under heaven flourish in their vitality,*
> *Yet each returns to its own root.*
> *This is stillness.*
> *Stillness means returning to its destiny.*
> *Returning to its destiny is steadfastness.*
> *To know steadfastness means enlightenment.*
> *Not to know steadfastness is to act forcefully.*
> *Acting forcefully brings disaster.*
> *Knowing the steadfast implies acceptance.* (16:3)

THE SAGE AND THE PEOPLE

Achieving without Force

Lao Tzu uses the word "country" with a double meaning. It of course can refer to an independent nation, its lands and citizens, and its ruler. It can also refer to the human body, its bones and flesh, governed by the mind. "Taking control of a country" can indicate taking control of one's self—all the many unruly aspects body, mind, and emotions—and unifying the territory of the self under the direction of a higher guidance.

A country, in the sense of "nation," is defined by its people. The people are the caretakers of the land. As a society, the people are a collective body/mind defined of customs, habits, attitudes, values, and rules.

Lao Tzu recommended following the Tao in both personal life and political life. He teaches that violence opposes the nature of life, the way of life. Whatever opposes life will soon perish. The use of force tends to rebound, causing destruction for all parties. When armies march the countryside is laid to waste. Whenever a large army is raised, scarcity and want follow. The more weapons the state has, the more trouble there will be. It is better to withdraw than to attack. One should not underestimate one's enemy. It is possible to confront them and win them over without fighting them. When there is a battle, those who are kind truly win. A good leader is not violent; a good fighter does not get angry; a good winner is not vengeful; a good employer is humble. This is the Taoist way of dealing with people.

Using the Tao as the rule for governing the people,
Do not employ the army as the power of the world.
For this is likely to backfire.
Where the army has marched, thorns and briars grow.
Being good has its own consequence,
Which cannot be seized by power.
Achieving without arrogance,
Achieving without bragging,
Achieving without damage,
Achieving without taking ownership.
This is called achieving without force. (30:1–4)

There is a saying on using military force:
I dare not be the host, but rather a guest.
I dare not advance an inch, but rather retreat a foot.
This is called performing without performing, rolling up one's sleeves without showing the arms.
By not holding on to an enemy, there is no enemy. (71:1–2)

Mercy brings courage and victory; economy brings abundance and generosity; humility brings natural leadership. Heaven gives loving mercy to those it would not see destroyed. Whoever knows how to preserve life with these qualities will not be harmed, because there is no death in him. The one who is brave in fighting will be killed, but the one who is brave in not fighting will live. How can we judge who is evil and to be killed? There is a master executioner who regulates death, and if someone attempts to undertake His work he rarely escapes without injuring himself. Living things are tender and flexible, but dead things are stiff and rigid; thus an inflexible government will be defeated. A large country is like the lower part of a river where the waters converge; it can win over small countries by placing itself below them, and a small country can win over a large country by serving it.

The deeper the sage is connected to the source, the more mindful are people's actions. As they become more mindful they also become more faithful and loving toward their source. The sage has faith in himself and in the people; as a result, the people have trust.

The reason why rivers and seas have the capacity for kingship over all the valleys is that they excel in lowliness.
That is why they have the capacity for kingship over all valleys.
Thus, since the sage wants to elevate the people, his speech is down to earth.
Since the sage wants to advance the people, he positions himself at the back,
So that when he is at the front, people do not harm him.
When he stands above, people do not feel pressure.
The whole world supports him untiringly.
Since he does not rely on competition, the world has nothing with which to compete. (66:1–4)

The sage is simple and humble. He does not put himself above others. He is not separate from others; he empathizes with their experiences, needs, aspirations, and fears. The people therefore do not resist but embrace his example and guidance.

The sage is neither a political nor religious leader, but a combination of both. He has the least ego but balances the emperor's enormous ego. This is especially important in the history of Chinese political structures and religious practices.

During the Chou Dynasty (1122-221 B.C.E.), the Chou emperors developed a powerful idea to legitimize their power. The Chou kings, whose chief deity was heaven, called themselves "sons of heaven," and their success in overcoming the prior dynasty was seen as the "mandate of heaven." From this time on, Chinese rulers were called "sons of heaven" and the Chinese empire was called the "celestial empire." The transfer of power from one dynasty to the next was based on the mandate of heaven.

This concept is still an integral aspect of Chinese theories of authority. The Chou defined the kingship as an intermediary position between heaven and earth; the relationship between heaven and earth is mediated by the emperor. Heaven desires that human needs be provided for, and the emperor is appointed by heaven to see to the welfare of the people. This is the "decree" or "mandate" of heaven. If the emperor or king, having fallen into selfishness and corruption, fails to see to the welfare of the people, heaven withdraws its mandate and invests it in another. The only way to know that the mandate has passed is the overthrow of the king or emperor. If usurpation succeeds, then the mandate has passed to another, but if it fails, then the mandate still resides with the king.

The mandate of heaven is an important social and political concept in Chinese culture, and asserts that government that is based on the selfless dedication of the ruler to the benefit of the general population. The emperor was seen an agent of heaven and a force that regulates the moral universe. The emperor is supposed to "act on behalf of the Tao of Heaven (*ti-tian-xing-dao*)." The emperor was seen as both a human being and a heavenly deity. His ego was fueled enormously by his religious persona and autocratic monarchy. The result was often authoritarian and capricious use of power. Thus, the simplicity, humility, and down-to-earth quality of the sage were extremely important as a counterbalance.

Serving the People

To love and serve the people is to be unselfish and have a nonminded (unselfconscious) awareness, intention, attention, and engagement. When the ego-self and its selfishness are expunged from the mind, the heart is open, and love is all-pervasive. To love the people is to act with faith and kindness. When there is adequate faith, people live happily and die peacefully. Faith allows the sage's mind to be as pure and clean as that of a child, and the people's minds to be clear and simple as an uncarved log. The sage's smile is the hope within people's hearts.

> *Those who practiced Tao in olden times did not enlighten people,*
> *Rather they made them simple.*
> *What makes it the hardest to govern the people is what they already know.*
> *It becomes most difficult to govern people because of their knowledge.*
> *So, using knowledge to govern the country, knowledge itself becomes*
> *the thief of the country.*
> *Not using knowledge to govern the country, knowledge*
> *itself is the Action of the country.* (65:1–3)

According to Lao Tzu, *Those who practiced Tao in olden times did not enlighten people, rather they made them simple.* No one can bestow enlightenment upon another. Enlightenment must be an individual journey over universal land. When people live a simple life, they become enlightened along their own God-given journeys. The sage does not impose knowledge, fixed ideas, or rules upon the people. The sage trusts the innate wisdom of each individual.

Lao Tzu goes on to say that *What makes it the hardest to govern the people is what they already know. It becomes most difficult to govern the people because of their knowledge.* He is referring here to cleverness. Knowledge is a mental product, a seed of mind, usually claimed by the ego. The intellect tends toward complexity rather than toward simplicity. Yet to know what one knows is a gift. To be able to know is a human skill; to obtain knowledge is to obtain an ego possession; and to transfer the knowledge is to transfer the ego obsession.

The best way to deal with knowledge is to abandon it; the best way to deal with the knower is to become grounded with the stillness of the unknown. *Using knowledge to govern the country, knowledge itself becomes the thief of the country. Not using knowledge to govern the country, knowledge itself is the action of the country.* When we are not attached to knowledge or to being the one who knows, knowledge can serve the good of the country.

> *Always realize that these two are the model for ruling.*
> *Always be aware that this model is the mystic Action.*
> *Mystic Action is deep and far-reaching.*
> *It is the opposite of matter.*
> *Only thus does it approach the Great Harmony.* (65:4–5)

The model for ruling that Lao Tzu is referring to here is the knowledge that he who tries to govern a state by his knowledge or cleverness is a scourge to it, while he who does not rule by knowledge and cleverness is a blessing.

No Claim of Ownership

> *Success is consequent to all affairs.*
> *It does not proclaim its own existence.*
> *All things return.*
> *Yet there is no claim of ownership,*
> *So it is forever desireless.*
> *This can be called small.*
> *All things return.*
> *Yet there is no claim of ownership,*
> *This can be called great.*
> *The sage accomplishes greatness in not acting great.*
> *Thus can be accomplished what is great.* (34:2–3)

Worldly success is determined by the society's acknowledgment of one's accomplishments in worldly affairs. To act in the world because one is motivated by a desire for social recognition is to be small-minded and small-hearted. To follow the Tao is to respond spontaneously in each moment through right action, without attachment to the outcome. This is the power and greatness of right action. Attachment to recognition and reward obscures one's vision and inhibits one's ability to perform right action: *The sage accomplishes greatness in not acting great. Thus can he accomplish what is great.* Lao Tzu says that *Success is consequent to all affairs. It does not proclaim its own existence* (34:2). Why cleave to it?

In Taoism, real success is about personal liberation and transformation. There is no concern for social acknowledgment or recognition. For many people, their *engagement in affairs fails prior to success* (64:6). They are either lost within themselves or they exhaust themselves before they reach success. But *the sage desires not to desire* (64:8). For the sage, *there is no claim of ownership* (34:2). The sage is therefore free to respond with Te, kind and virtuous action. *He is able to support the nature of all things* (64:8). This is the key to real "success" for the ordinary individual, the sage, or the leader of a nation.

THE ROLE OF GOVERNMENT

A Light Touch

Lao Tzu writes that *governing a large country is like cooking a small fish* (60:1). A leader should not stir it too often, or it will come apart. The best government does not make its presence felt.

Lao Tzu suggests that the best way to govern a nation is to govern in accordance with the nature of things and to be simple and sparing. A good government does not disturb the people unnecessarily; it is not engaged in many activities that interfere with the life of the people. A good government does not make many policies or issue many orders; it runs the country in such a way that when its work is done, people will say: "All this happened naturally."

> *The reason people are starving is because the government taxes too much.*
> *This is the reason for starvation.*
> *The reason people are hard to govern is because their leaders are actively engaged. This is why they are hard to govern.* (77:1)

> *The more prohibitions there are in the world, the poorer people will be.*
> *The more destructive weapons people have, the more chaotic the nation will become.*
> *The more know-how people have, the more bizarre things will appear.*
> *The more rules and demands that flourish, the more thefts there will be.*
>
> (57:3)

Lao Tzu advises that too many taxes starve the people; too many rules and regulations make the land ungovernable. The more prohibitions there are, the poorer the people will become. The more laws are passed, the more thieves there will be. The more luxuries that are invented, the more avaricious people will become. However, *when the government is silent, people are sincere* (58:1).

Governing a country can be as complex as healing physical illness. When the body is in harmony with the mind and environment, the resulting state is that of health. Yet when this harmony is lacking, there is imbalance and illness. When dealing with illness, the mind must take responsibility for seeking its own cure. Working through sickness allows for further growth and transformation. Living with sickness allows one to understand the meaning and value of life. The body must live and die; the soul must be drawn into the eternal marriage of love and peace.

All problems within a society are created by the confusion and conflict of the mind. It is critical to know that the mind exhausts the bodily energy in the same manner that the government exhausts people's energy. Governments flourish from the actions of their people. Without people, the government is an empty ego form and its administrative office becomes an empty funeral chapel. Government is the powerhouse of involved people seeking to meet their collective needs.

The role of a government is to integrate the diverse elements of a society into a grand harmony. A great nation *is the mother of the world and the integration of the world* (61:1). Government is an invisible mind with kindness and a visible body with subtle yet strong force. It should be a beautiful harmony of simplicity, not a proliferation of complexity. This is right lawfulness.

A wise leader regards the needs of the people as his own. Whoever truly understands the people's needs knows how a government should govern.

Harmonious Relations

A great nation flows downwardly; it is the mother of the world, and the integration of the world.
The mother is always tranquil and overcomes the male by her tranquility; so she benefits the world.
A great nation relies on a low position to take over a small nation.
A small nation, being in a low position, is taken over by a great nation.
So being lower allows taking over or being taken over.
Being a great nation only desires to unify the people.
Being a small nation only seeks people's business.
They both get what they want, but the greater is being lower.

(61:1–6)

A small nation lacks the wealth and diversity of resources that a great nation has. Her most important and only business is her people. Yet for all nations, large and small, the sole concern should be the welfare of the people.

Nations are defined by, and distinguished from other nations, by their cultures, religions, mythic traditions, ethnicities, and histories. How can one understand modern Western culture without understanding the role of science? How can one understand Indian history without first knowing the tradition of Yoga? How can one understand the Chinese mind with no knowledge of Taoist philosophy?

Harmonious relations between nations depends on embracing these differences. If the mind is open, the lines that define and divide nations become visible but permeable. The space surrounding all becomes vibrant. Everyone can walk across the lines. This is mutual and neutral coexistence. Harmonious and mutually supportive coexistence is the nature of the communicative heart of human beings.

CONFLICT

Softness Is the Strongest Force

War is the final result of mental conflict, ego confrontation, distorted justice, absent conscience, and assertion of power. When there is a conflict or confrontation due to misunderstanding and mistrust, the tension and heat may accelerate to the degree that antagonism and contention are the only reality. Coercive, exploitative, suppressive, and abusive actions may culminate in war.

When people are born, they are soft and gentle.
When they die, they are stiff and callous.
When myriad things, grasses and trees, are born, they are soft and tender.
When they die, they are withered.
So stiffness and callousness are the company of death.
Softness and suppleness are the company of life.
The powerful army will not win.
A stiff tree will break.
So stiffness and power stay below.
Softness and suppleness stay above. (78:1–5)

Lao Tzu teaches that ultimately, the weak and oppressed overcome the power holders: *When opposing armies clash, those who cry win!*(71:4). Softness and suppleness, in the end, is the strongest force. Because it yields, it does not break.

By its very nature, war is self-destructive. If there were no blockage, no misunderstanding, no ego obsession, no holding-on, there would be no war. War is the conflagration of individual and civilizational conflict. To understand the nature of war is to understand the nature of human inner conflict—the conflict between spiritual conscience and insatiable ego, between submission to the power of body and the full display of the power of mind.

In one sense, war can be seen as an evolutionary process. Humans are called to discover another strategy for conflict resolution beyond passive reaction and aggressive control. War evolves from the destructive character of egoist aggression, whereas peace arrives through the constructive nature of human spirit. The old habits and systems held firmly for generations must be severed to allow the new to exist. The process of change is extremely difficult. It may take a war to forcefully demand the transition, ensure the change, and announce the new order.

The inner dynamics of war can be recognized as twofold, with both positive and negative dimensions. As the boundaries of attachment are broken in order to enter into the freedom of unknown, the future is uncertain and unpredictable. It can likened to the decaying process of any material substance. Yet war is too painful and shattering for anyone to be required to experience its ravaging consequences. It is devastating to be at death's door in the prime of life, witnessing fallen comrades cross its threshold. Within the war zone, there is no inner space and tranquility, there is only gunfire, the sound of explosions causing untold destruction, the crying of hearts, the burning of flesh.

The underlying fuse for this erupting conflict was ignited by the power of ego, the power of mind gone mad. Since war has no conscience, it disregards social justice. The person who launches war justifies himself to protect his ego.

Nothing matters in war except who is defeated and who is victorious. To the victor goes the power to define justice, to the defeated go the smoldering embers of future revenge.

When the inner conscience is alive in everybody's heart, there will be no war. However, when war is necessary, the side with inner conscience stands the greater chance of victory. This is not to say that the lack of inner conscience will necessarily precipitate loss. The outcome depends on who is granted the power by the turn of nature. Nobody can change this or influence this immutable fact. Call it the power of God or the justice of God; this turn of nature is beyond man's manipulation.

This is the truth of the animal world, of which we are an

element. The stronger, quicker, and more intelligent hold the seat of power. The weaker, slower, and less intelligent form the masses. They are relegated to carry out the more menial tasks, to be subservient. The financially poor, the mentally retarded, the uneducated live out their natural lifespan as best they can. The richer, stronger, and smarter take charge of their submissive partners lest they lose their position. In world history, Rome, Persia, China, Mongolia, France, and England, all enjoyed their time of glory. America is now having its time. Can it last? On this subject Lao Tzu warns:

Using the Tao as the rule for governing the people,
Do not employ the army as the power of the world.
For this is likely to backfire.
Where the army has marched, thorns and briars grow.
Being good has its own consequence,
Which cannot be seized by power.
Achieving without arrogance,
Achieving without bragging,
Achieving without damage,
Achieving without taking ownership.
This is called achieving without force. (30:1–4)

War Is the Last Resort

Lao Tzu has takes a humanistic stance on war, asserting that war is the last resort and that armies are the mechanism of bad luck. For Lao Tzu, weapons are the instruments of fear; they are not the tools of the sage. The wise use weapons only when they have no choice, for peace is dear to their hearts. The wise do not rejoice at victory in war, because to rejoice in this victory is to delight in war. By its very nature, winning a war is based upon the death and surrender of others. Victory should be observed with the gravity of a funeral service. All who die should be mourned with sorrow.

The army is the mechanism of bad luck.
The elements of the world may oppose.
So those who have ambitions cannot rest. (31:1)

So the army is not the nobleman's weapon.
As a mechanism of bad luck,
He uses it only as the last resort.
Then the best way is to use it quickly and destructively.
Do not enjoy this.
To take delight in it is to enjoy killing people.
Those who enjoy killing people do not attract the favor of the world. . . .
Speaking in an image of sadness,
After killing the people, every one stands in mourning.
Victory is celebrated as a funeral service. (31:3,6)

Patriotism is an extension of narrow, selfish love. It rejects impartiality, compassion, and justice. War is the extreme expression of competition. There is ultimately no winner. The destruction and damage of war deeply touches all parties. A sense of fear and uncertainty about the future lurks for the victorious side, a passion for vengeance and retaliation arises on the losing side.

It is far better for individuals and nations to remain simple and noncompetitive. To remain content, and to live in peace with their neighbors.

Let people return to:
Use the technique of knotting the rope,
Enjoying the food,
Appreciating the cloth,
Delighting in customs,
Settling into their living conditions.
The neighboring countries are in sight.
The sounds of dogs and chickens are heard.
People grow old and die without interference from each other.
(67:2–3)

How beautiful such a picture of the people and nation is: simple government and plain citizens. If all people mind their own way, they are mindful only of their own business and are content with themselves. Then everyone's mind is at peace, and the whole world flows harmoniously at the pace of a peaceful state.

9 Longevity and Immortality

Immortality is commonly understood to be the ultimate goal of Taoist practice. It takes many, many years of conscious cultivation to achieve the Taoist goal of physical/spiritual immortality, and it is a very rare attainment. However, anyone can improve his or her everyday life in a practical sense by learning the basic Taoist practices. Just believing and having faith in spiritual/immortal reality is useful for focusing one's commitment to the spiritual path, but that alone does not get the job done. If people choose, they can also cultivate their experience to the higher levels of spiritual attainment. We begin by learning to be present in this life, and by transforming stress into vitality and developing compassion through love. We then recycle that special quality of energy to keep the body healthy and in harmony with mind and spirit—and learn to cultivate true nature as spirit. Then we become open to develop possibilities beyond the cycles of life and death.

Taoists value health and longevity for their benefits in enabling a better quality of life. In addition, health and longevity are valued because they provide the strength and time necessary for sustaining the prolonged effort necessary to achieve spiritual immortality. Does longevity make one a sage or immortal? The renowned Taoist master White Cloud (Mantak Chia's teacher) explained that his teacher lived to be well over a hundred years old. The Grand Master had gone to a cave in the high mountains for prolonged meditation involving out-of-body travel in the higher planes and returning to the source. For that kind of practice, he had put wax in his nose and other orifices to keep out insects and dust. White Cloud had to make sure that his teacher's body was not eaten while his teacher's spirit was away traveling to source. There are many stories like this, where a faithful disciple or other attendant looks after an advanced meditator's body.

If a Taoist practitioner lives to be very old and has seriously applied him- or herself in cultivating and transforming energy into spirit, it is very likely that he or she could become a sage. It depends on the individual's level of practice. The same applies for immortality. If one hasn't finished transforming one's energy, one could become a partial spiritual immortal or partial physical/spiritual immortal.

Immortality does not mean keeping the same body forever. Nor does it mean that you have awareness of your spirit in different incarnations. Meditators do often report an awareness of past lives—and this may be useful and interesting—but this is not what Taoists mean when they refer to "attaining immortality." One's soul-spirit has not been liberated when it is being cycled through various incarnations. It is still in need of purification until it achieves the evolved state of spiritual liberation.

There is a difference between spiritual immortality and physical/spiritual immortality. It depends on the degree of practice one has mastered. The distinction is easy to grasp. For spiritual immortality, one has achieved the ability to withdraw one's purified spirit energy from the body and traverse the inner regions independently—and merge in oneness with the eternal source—the Tao or Wu Chi or God. In this state, the liberated spirit can manifest on the inner planes, but the physical body has returned to dust, and the spirit cannot return in the physical form.

In contrast, one who has attained physical/spiritual immortality has been able to complete the more tedious and time-consuming process of transforming all of one's physical, soul, and spirit energy into the spirit body during the time of life in the physical body. Thus, one gains all the powers of spiritual liberation, plus the ability to manifest at will in the physical form. In other words, when one has achieved physical/spiritual immortality, one has mastered the ability to dematerialize and rematerialize the human body. This is a rare and extraordinary attainment.

THE PSYCHOLOGY OF IMMORTALITY

The philosophy of physical immortality strips the mind of all kinds of fears and miseries. It permits love and divine energy to express themselves more fully in your personality. Therefore, even if you don't realize physical immortality, the philosophy is a wholesome group of ideas to work with. In fact, the philosophy of physical immortality produces a more positive life even if it does not achieve the ultimate goal. The belief that death is inevitable will kill you if nothing else does. But the truth is that your spirit is already eternal; you only have to move your mind and body into harmony with your eternal spirit. The philosophy of physical immortality gives your body a chance.

According to the psychology of physical immortality, one of the biggest differences between one person and another is the quality of their thoughts. Thoughts of everlasting life produce health. Psychosomatic science has proven that our beliefs influence our health. Even if you survive old age, illness, and accidents, and practice Taoist techniques for health and healing, your own belief in death will get you in the end—unless you change it. Seriously questioning the idea that death is inevitable is good and practical for both mental and physical health.

Put simply, the cause of death is pollution in the body: physical pollution and energy pollution. Spiritual purification involves getting rid of physical and energy pollution faster than we take it in. The more we are able to purify this pollution faster than we accumulate it, the more we can live in the spirit, and the more control we have over our lives. When we do not purify this pollution, we move toward aging and death.

To practice the psychology of immortality, reduce negativity in your thoughts and feelings. Learn to breathe with deep, cleansing, abdominal breaths. Practice the Taoist exercises for sensing Chi (vital energy or life force) and Jing (generative energy/sexual essence). Learn to cultivate these energies, conserve them, and refine them into Shen (spiritual energy). Use the Shen to enter the Wu Chi, to return to the Tao, and to attain immortality. Develop a personal philosophy of physical immortality: eternal life of spirit, mind, and body.

From Gaui to Cui

GATHERING TOGETHER (CUI) OF THE 45TH HEXAGRAM

In the *I Ching*, the idea of cultivating, conserving, refining, and transforming vital life energies is illustrated in the forty-fifth hexagram, Cui, which means "gathering together." The sage gathers together, purifies, and transforms all the energies of the body, mind, emotions, and spirit. The Cui hexagram depicts a temple that is built to pay tribute to ancestors. In this temple, which can also be seen as the temple of the human body, all spirits are united. All wounded souls and cloudy minds—and all aspects and energies of the body/mind—are purified.

This transformation is the transition from the forty-third hexagram, Guai, which means "breakthrough," to the Cui hexagram. The Guai hexagram signifies a breakthrough after a long accumulation of tension, as a swollen river breaks through its dikes, or in the manner of a cloudburst. The energies that "break through" are "gathered together" and transformed.

In this transformation, the spiritual mind is elevated to follow a higher spiritual path. One's needs are diminished, and instinctive behavior is abandoned in order to embrace the power of Te. When Te unifies all the spirits within the family, the lost souls are recovered and unified. Spiritual flowers and fruits are produced, longevity is ensured and immortality results.

This can be also envisioned as the transition from order to work, from discipline to obedience, and from self-realization to self-actualization. Longevity is the order, the discipline, and the self-realization. Immortality is the work, the obedience, and the self-actualization. Longevity is a wish and immortality is the result of the wish.

Live Fully

In the history of mankind, longevity has been the most common desire. And there is no greater wish than to attain spiritual immortality. The pursuit of physical and spiritual immortality is a powerful and extremely positive spiritual practice. Yet only a small minority of people can predict their physical life journey. The masters of meditation can do so. A good doctor can predict the final outcome of a patient's life based on pathological evidence. A clear-minded person may get a small glimpse or foresight. Ultimately, however, the spiritual life is independent from the physical life.

The mind plays an important role in death and dying. If a person has made up his or her mind to commit suicide, no one can prevent it. The decision comes from within. The proper approach is to live life fully without fighting against the nature of life and death. This can be illustrated from the life stories of Buddha or Jesus, both of whom were religious founders as well as superior masters of meditation. Buddha once ate poisoned meat to hasten his last breath; Jesus was crucified after his last meal. They each knew what awaited them: death through mastering the spirit's way.

A life span of several hundred years was not uncommon for ancient Taoist sages. For example, Guang Chengzi, the Yellow

Emperor's guru, is reported to have lived over twelve hundred years. Yet longevity cannot replace immortality. One needn't live a long physical life in order to achieve immortality. Wang Chunyang, the founder of the Complete Reality School of Taoism, lived only to the age of fifty-eight.

CHANGE AND CHANGLESSNESS

When the ego retreats completely, the body is able to live its fullest physical life journey. When the mind disappears completely, the immortality or the native spiritual essence becomes fully present. Longevity is the process of changing within unchanging, while immortality is the character of the sameness of unchanging within the changing. Changing from and toward unchanging can never be predicted by the ego.

Understanding the white and holding on to the black
Enables the formation of the world.
Being the formation of the world, ongoing action does not stray.
When ongoing action does not stray, it returns to the infinite.
This simplicity takes shape as a mechanism.
The sage makes it the head ruler.
Great ruling never divides. (28:3–4)

The formation of the world is constructed within the mechanism; great ruling is what governs it. This is the mechanism of life and death, birth and rebirth. From sunrise to sunset, from night to day, it is a sleepless resting continuity of free changing process. From male to female, white to black, fire to water, it is the power of penetration. From female to male, black to white, water to fire, it is the power of receptiveness. Penetrating and receiving continues with no sign of beginning or end. The two never stray apart from each other: the Oneness within, the formation of the world. This action comes from nowhere, yet is present and exists everywhere.

As our mind begins to work, we understand the workability of the world. When our mind starts changing direction, we make sense of the change in our changing world. When our mind ceases to change, we conclude that changing is unchanging. The unchanging reality beyond the movement of the mind is the nature of the Tao and the birth of universe.

Eternity

Heaven is eternal, and earth is long lasting.
What makes heaven and earth eternal and long lasting is that they do not give birth to themselves.
It is this that makes them eternal and long lasting. (67:1–2)

Eternal changelessness, beyond birth and death, is the immortality of the Tao. Longevity deals with form, both transforming and deforming. It exists between birth and death, growth and retirement, moving forward and turning back. Immortality reveals the presence of everlasting eternity. Lao Tzu further explains:

Reaching the ultimate emptiness,
Concentrating on the central stillness,
All things work together.
From this I observe their returning.
All things under heaven flourish in their vitality,
Yet each returns to its own root.
This is stillness.
Stillness means returning to its destiny.
Returning to its destiny is steadfastness.
To know steadfastness means enlightenment. (16:1–3)

Here Lao Tzu is examining the Tao through returning to the eternal stillness. He finds that destiny moves along its steadfast course without being troubled by the mind; that is the realization of enlightenment. Knowing this is the mind's acceptance of impartiality and equanimity. This impartiality is being with the body of the Tao, a process of returning, nonbeing, and nothingness.

The body and mind can handle the changes and cycles of life just as it does the motion of the sun and the waning and waxing of the moon. Time takes care of itself. There is no need to remember everything and there is no need to hold onto everything. Renewal and change is the child of the Tao. This is the process of acceptance; this is the quality of inner steadfastness; this is the regal mind and the body of the Tao.

All that we experience is change. From the moment of our conception to the development of our independent life path, from the flash of an idea to its expression in the world, we are constantly participating in a process of evolutionary change.

Each movement is an enlightened journey. If the mind is not present and the body is not ready, repetition and continuation must take place until the mind is free. This is the glory and grace of enlightening reality. Live fully, die completely. Then move on without looking back just as though nothing has happened. This is the true paradox of Lao Tzu's teaching. To practice this requires purity, innocence, and humility. It also requires the inner flexibility of the tender reed.

When people are born, they are soft and gentle.
When they die, they are stiff and callous.
When myriad things, grasses and trees, are born, they are soft and tender.
When they die, they are withered.
So stiffness and callousness are the company of death.
Softness and suppleness are the company of life. (78:1–3)

Lao Tzu understood from his own experience and his observation of the natural world that fluidity, flexibility, softness, and suppleness are the conduits of life. With this fluidity, one does not resist change and time, and thus is not ravaged by it. *Softness and suppleness are the company of life.*

The Presence of Spirit

How to suffuse one's mental content with presence is the major issue of cultivation, or the application of Wu Wei, or inactive action, non-minded action. To suffuse one's mental content with presence is to allow fully the presence of spirit. It is to engage with the constant, moment-by-moment unification of biophysiological action and psychospiritual awareness. A total mental awareness is needed with no inquiry into the meaning and result of each activity. No hypothesis is necessary prior to the activity, and no control is exerted toward the outcome of the activity. To love and to be loved is the effective practice of being fully present. When the reality of presence is absent or blocked, an energy imbalance and deficiency is created. The mind manifests with wishes and longings for the loss of the connected, loving presence. If the disconnection continues to exist, hope is lost, depression darkens the mind, and the richness of life dwindles away. It is like a beautiful flower withering away.

This is what Lao Tzu refers to when he says *extreme fondness is necessarily very costly*. Yet, the fondness is a feedback resulting from the energetic quality of either light or darkness. To be fond of the spiritual path will involve sacrifice of the physical life but will free the self, while to be fond of the dark force depletes all, pleasing only the materialistic and hellish world.

Instead of being fully engaged with presence, the mind tends to close off its environment as the ego advances. This is the nature of animated egoistic activity in its fear of losing the presence connection. The ego augments further pressure on the biophysiological action. Through this process, the psychospiritual richness of living, of "being with the presence," descends into obsessive ego control. The richness of life is replaced with the desire of becoming materially rich. Through obsession the ego attains satisfaction; through possession the mind avoids being lost in the reality of nature. The transcendent nature of reality becomes merely a mental configuration. The real vision of heaven becomes distant. Living is meaningless; dying seems unsatisfactory.

> *The more you cling to, the more you lose.*
> *So knowing what is sufficient averts disgrace.*
> *Knowing when to stop averts danger.*
> *This can lead to a longer life.* (44:2–3)

This refers to actual objects to which the mind clings as well as the very act of clinging. Objects represent images and are the symbols of that clinging behavior. And in this clinging, one is attached to the future, dwelling in fear and a sense of lack or impoverishment. One is no longer present, no longer allowing fully the always full and enriching presence of spirit. This is the drive that depletes the Chi or life force, ultimately leading to illness and death.

TAOIST SEXUAL PRACTICES FOR LONGEVITY AND IMMORTALITY

Tao is the harmony of yin and yang. The earliest manifestation of this harmony in human beings is the descending eternal yang Chi of heaven and the ascending and evolving yin Chi of mother earth that occurs at conception. However, this harmony or balance is almost always lost and must be regained. Most people are rarely in touch with the true nature of eternal harmony. Rarely do we experience the blissfulness of that harmonious beauty; however, it can be experienced in Taoist sexual practice.

Taoists believe that when a man and woman join together to make love, their orgasmic energy joins together as well as the sperm and egg, combining the universal, cosmic, and earthly Chi forces. (Taoists refer to this process as the reunion of heaven and earth.) The process is so powerful that it can create a new human life. Yet common sexual practices waste valuable life force. People unknowingly deplete themselves of energy in numerous ways, thereby destroying their health. By redirecting sexual energy, they can have the best sexual experience and also cultivate energy for healing and rejuvenating their bodies, and transforming lower energies into higher spiritual energies.

Generally, common orgasms are mere pulsations of the genitals which occur only in the genital region. (They are referred to as genital or outward orgasms.) For men, such orgasms are short in duration and cannot be repeated once the seminal fluid is gone. Although a woman's experience lasts longer, there is not much benefit to her body if her sexual energy is habitually left unchanneled, only to drain out during menstruation. The loss of Jing (sexual/generative essence) can negatively affect one's health and sexuality.

Taoist sexual practices cultivate and transform Jing and Chi into Shen

An internal orgasm, which leads to a total body orgasm, occurs throughout the entire body, as well as in the genitals. It can be extended in its duration and repeated for hours. By moving the pulsation of the orgasm up to the higher centers of the body, Jing can be retained and the orgasmic sensation increased tenfold. This also retains the seminal fluid in men. If one knows how to maintain orgasms for long periods of time, the universal and earthly Chi forces can be activated and combined into a higher bliss, which is a powerful healing energy.

Taoists believe that the only reason one should ejaculate or allow the loss of Jing to occur is for the purpose of having children. Unfortunately, people carelessly lose their health in their quest for genital orgasms. Ejaculation causes a brief sensation in which sexual energy is passed out of the body and lost. Women who lose energy are also deprived of true sexual pleasure and satisfaction. Internal orgasms are a healthier and longer-lasting approach to sex with no loss of stimulation to the genitals. The sensations actually travel through all of the organs, glands, and nerves, thrilling and revitalizing them with sexual energy.

Some religions attack sex, creating a great deal of fear and negativity about sexuality. Sex is a powerful yet neutral force. It should not be judged as good or bad, but it can multiply any positive or negative quality that exists within us. This same sexual energy, which can create another human being, or enhance one's spiritual growth, can also increase our negative states if we neglect to recycle it. Sex is like fire. Fire can cook your food, warm your house, and help to provide a comfortable life. If it is misused, however, it can burn down your house. The same principle applies to sexual energy, which can benefit anyone's health, vitality, and longevity. Unfortunately, some religions have condemned it while trying to prevent its misuse, thereby promoting confusion.

Through their practice of celibacy, masters, monks, nuns, and priests learn how to use sexual energy to enhance their virtues and connect with the spirit. By focusing upon divinity as a means of raising sexual energy up to the higher centers of their bodies, they transform it into virtuous energy, which enhances their spiritual growth, leading to union with God or Spirit. This can only occur when sexual energy is conserved and transferred up to the higher centers and the crown.

The purpose of celibacy is simply to avoid the loss of Jing, but celibacy alone does not move Jing up to the higher centers for transformation and reunion with the higher forces. Also, most people find celibacy to be impractical in daily life. Unfortunately misconceptions about such practices deter them from learning how to properly control and use sexual energy. (See Mantak Chia's *Taoist Secrets of Love* and *Healing Love through the Tao* for detailed discussion of the Taoist transformative sexual practices.)

When people learn to conserve their sexual energy, they begin to love, conserve, and protect nature. When they lose too much Jing through common sexual practices, or through drugs, alcohol, and smoking, humans can become progressively destructive. In their constant search for sensorial excitement through fast sex and addictive substances, some people become violent without reason and abusive to their environment.

It is interesting to note that most businesses in the world try to appeal to us by stimulating our senses with sexual titillation. Unfortunately, society and the business world follow the common misconception that sex was intended to release pent up energies and emotions. The truth is that sex is a means of building up the energies that the body needs. Sexual desire is not really a search for release, but often it is a search for new sources of energy to replenish lost Jing Chi.

When too much sexual energy is lost, the brain and sensory organs become empty. Then people unconsciously seek other sources to fulfill their desires for stimulation. They desire more orgasmic pleasures because they are so used to passing Jing out of their bodies that their need for internal energy becomes desperate. In searching to fulfill their internal needs, they actually drain themselves more by relying upon old sexual habits. Unfortunately, drugs and alcohol also offer the kinds of stimulation (like false orgasms) that further deplete the body of energy. These substances therefore become addictive as they weaken the body and mind. The more energy that is lost, the more the body must replace to achieve high levels of stimulation. When people smoke, drink, or take drugs, their desires for stimulation possess them more as their energies decrease.

The Taoists suggest that this state is like a little death, a self-destruction through overstimulation of the senses, with vital energies pouring out. Destructive attitudes gradually increase as these people try to replace lost Jing through means which further drain them. This is often the cause of violence as the search for sexual energy becomes obsessive. Once the body is in this state, the subconscious mind carries the destruction further. Its tendency is to destroy itself and everything around it.

Besides the problems of lust, anger, and violence, there are other attitudes that are related to greed and obsession. Money can stimulate you through the power it offers, but if you allow money to take up all your time and energy, it will also begin to take over your life. Such problems occur because we lose so much sexual energy in our daily lives that we have little or no control over our bodies and minds. For this reason, as noted above, many religions fear sex and warn their followers to be wary of its potential destructiveness. The problem is that they do not give their followers some means of controlling this powerful energy. Many will suggest celibacy, suppression, or restrictions, and thereby promote confusion about the bad effects of sex. Such suppression often has a reverse effect. If you withhold emotions for too long, they eventually explode outward at some unexpected moment, causing a great disturbance. Similarly, a sexually deprived person may create a great disturbance when the hold is finally lost on his or her sexual energy.

The Taoist sexual practices, when properly mastered, enable one to cultivate, purify, channel, and transform all the energies available to human beings, resulting in health, vitality, and longevity. This provides the energy for higher spiritual practices and spiritual transformation, ultimately leading to spiritual immortality.

HARMONY IS ETERNAL

Longevity and spiritual immortality are cultivated through living in harmony at all levels of existence. Spirit is yang and soul is yin. When they are embraced, oneness is preserved. We are the children of the earth mother and heavenly father. Divine yang Chi and earthly yin Chi is instilled within our body/mind.

> *Harmony is eternal.*
> *Knowing harmony is discernment.* (55:3)

Human life is enhanced through connection to the universal harmony of heaven and earth, divine and human, inner and outer. When we become simple, still, and quiet, we can become sensitive to this harmony. This is true discernment. It is knowing what is eternal and essential, and knowing what is not.

The High Is Founded upon the Low

> *Esteem is rooted in the humble.*
> *The high is founded upon the low.*
> *This is why the lords and rulers call themselves widows and orphans without support.*
> *Is this not the root of being humble?*
> *Much praise amounts to no praise.* (39:4–6)

The fifteenth *I Ching* hexagram, Chian, sheds light on this process. *Chian* means modesty. This hexagram is made up of the trigrams Ken (keeping still, mountain) and Kun (the receptive, earth).

MODESTY (CHIAN) OF THE 15TH HEXAGRAM

The mountain is the youngest son of the divinity, the representative of heaven and earth. It dispenses the blessings of heaven, the clouds and rain that gather at its summit, and shines forth radiant heavenly light. This shows what modesty is and how it functions in great and strong people. Kun, the earth, stands above. Lowliness is a quality of the earth: this is the very reason why it appears in this hexagram as exalted, by being placed above the mountain. This shows how modesty functions in lowly, simple people: they are lifted up by it.

Harmony between heaven and earth, between yang and yin, masculine and feminine, spirit and soul, creative and receptive, is acknowledged and united, unified and embraced, reserved and preserved. They can be as close as they wish, and they can be as distant as they need to be. They are the One, the Oneness, the complete, harmonized, pure self. The relationship within and in between is then expanded, no longer restrained by role playing. The relationship is transformed; self and image are no longer separately defined. All people are brothers and sisters. Love is both inner vision and passion extending to the lengths of the universe. Compassion is inhalation and exhalation. Kindness is giving and receiving. Desire is no longer stressful, wisdom is no longer staged. Renewal and refreshment in all relationships is harmoniously granted. The ego is lost into unconditional love and awareness. The mind is expanded into universal understanding. Te is the expression of life's journey.

Form and Formless

Each moment is a transformation; each moment is a death. We are composed of the form given us (physical, mental, and spiritual) and the formless form we have within. Form is composed of everything about our individual physical being, from hair to nails. Formless form is the soul and spirit granted us. Form must die, but formless form never dies. It is the very nature of energy transformation. At a subliminal level, matter and energy are inseparable. It is form because of its changing and transforming quality, it is formless because of its innate perfection and completion.

The fire never extinguishes itself, yet each fire's glow must be extinguished. The water is never dried up, yet each water molecule evaporates. We are going to die, yet we will never die. Who dies? It is the transformation of body/mind form.

We live, we die. . . .
Why so? It is the nature of life itself.
As a matter of fact, I hear of those who are good at preserving their lives;
Walking through, not avoiding rhinos and tigers.
Entering battle without wearing armaments.
The rhino has no place to dig its horns.
The tiger has no place to drag its claws.
The soldier has no place to thrust his blade.
Why is this so?
Because they have no place to die. (50:1,3–5)

At this and every moment, we are walking between birth and death. We are living in flux and change, yet in perfect stillness. Yet by not fearing death, not fearing the future—not fearing life—we embrace life fully, and we live with light hearts and minds. We live transparently, and *the rhino has no place to dig its horns.*

Hun and Po at Death

To die consciously is to have lived through the conscious awareness of *hun*, or heavenly soul. It is to be released from the morbid obsession of *po*, or earthly soul. The *hun* is the ethereal soul. The *hun* is more subtle, and is yang in nature. The *po* is the corporeal soul. It is closely related to the physical world and descends into the earth at the time of physical death. The *po* is more physical, and is yin in nature.

During the last exhalation at death, if *hun*'s mortal, conscious awareness stays with *po*, it will merge into the earthly energy pattern of a ghost. It will pass through the gateway of the mouth, nose, or even ears. This energy pattern will not ascend and associate itself with the higher energy sphere at the third eye or crown point, as it ideally would. If it is good, it becomes a wandering ghost; if it is evil, it becomes a hungry ghost.

With conscious death, the mortal conscious awareness of *hun* discharges itself from *po* by returning to its original form of Shen. By embracing the light, this individual spirit crystallizes into spiritual being, like a beam of laser light. When love is purified selflessly and completely, it is the pure self and pure love of God-self within. The spiritual body is light and spiritual motive is love. The body is formless and its action is deathless.

Immortality is beyond physical and mental. It is an ultimate integration and embrace that leaves nothing pushed aside or left behind. There is blissful satisfaction within and no fear of being alone. There is no sense of who is dead and or one who is alive; no awareness of living and dying. Soaring from life is not sadness—one has passed through the forgiveness of heart and the attachment of mind. Consciousness becomes a mirror and ego is nothing other than an old habit. This is lasering with pure light, being with pure light, returning to the complete self and God's love. This is the application of being immortal and entering immortality. Lao Tzu calls this ***the Tao of having a deep root, a strong stem, a long life, and an enduring vision*** (59:3). The root is the source and the stem is the form; life is the act and vision is the light.

Your Choice Matters

Whether you want to stick with mortality or choose immortality is entirely your own choice. The heavenly father gives you the light and consciousness. The earthly mother gives you your body and instincts. You are embraced by light. Freedom of choice is given to your heart, the freedom of action granted to your mind, and the freedom to channel the energy is there for the taking. If you follow the inclinations of your ordinary thinking mind, you will chase after ideas, rise and fall with your emotions, protect your beliefs, and sleep fitfully with nightmares.

Let the light shine through you to live with compassion. Remain untroubled with the mind's loneliness and longing; then you can live with inner peace. You can know with pure awareness, enjoy working with the changing character of nature, and be happy on your sacred path. Lao Tzu emphasizes that: *The person who works according to Tao unites with Tao* (24:4). He adds simply: *Only those who are not slaves to life are wise to the value of life* (77:2).

Trust and Faith

In the Chinese language the character *xing* means both trust and faith. From within, the person reveals their natural trust and faith in the inherent goodness of life, and speaks from the heart.

To live in this way will generate a true fellowship of trust. Others listen not only to the vibration of voice but also the emanation of the inner being. What others integrate is not merely the intellectual understanding of words, ideas, or beliefs. There is an awareness of the openness of heart and the honesty of mind, which conveys respect, energetic communication, and inner connection.

> *Trustworthy words are not beautiful.*
> *Beautiful words are not trustworthy.*
> *The knower does not know everything.*
> *The know-it-all knows nothing.*
> *Kindness is not overindulgent.*
> *Overindulgence is not kind.*
> *The sage does not collect.*
> *As soon as he exists for others, he has more.*
> *As soon as he gives to others, he has more.*
> *So the Tao of heaven benefits and does not harm.*
> *The Tao of humankind exists and does not compete.* (68:1–3)

Lao Tzu explains that appearances are not always trustworthy; beautiful speech can be beguiling and insincere.

The one who claims knowledge and takes pride in it does not truly know. There is no need to display knowledge. The know-it-all hungers insatiably for information and recognition and is not truly wise. The one who knows that he doesn't know is truly wise.

True kindness and compassion does not overindulge but supports the genuine well-being of others. Kindness is beauty that emanates honest loving and benevolent caring. Kindness is readily accepting and willingly given. It is an expression of Wu Wei, inactive acting. There is a respect, neutrality, and selfless responsibility in the harmony of action.

In this kindness and living for the good of all, the sage is full and complete. He wants for nothing.

In Wu Wei, one expects nothing in return, loses nothing, and gains nothing. There is no judgment or attachment to any outcome. There is just simplicity and generosity of response. This is the revelation of universal kindness.

So the sage, through nonaction, does not fail.
Not clinging, he does not lose. . . .
He is able to support the nature of all things and, not by daring,
to impose action. (64:5,8)

SPEAKING THE TAO

The Tao that is voiced is no longer that of eternal Tao.
The name that has been written is no longer that of eternal name.
The nameless is the beginning of the cosmic universe.
The named is the mother of the myriad creatures. (1:1–2)

We began with the wordless uttering of the Tao in the first chapter. We now discuss what it means to speak the Tao. Voice and speech are natural and instinctive actions of the human being. Pure, honest, humble, and innocent voice is the "sound of Tao."

To ask the meaning of this voice is to ask the meanings of sounds of thunder, earthquakes, rain, birdsong, or any natural vibrations that come through natural phenomena. We hear them and know them. There is no need to understand or interpret.

In the actionless action of Wu Wei, the head, voice, hands, and feet act without engaging. It is the weightless clouds and colorless spirit that execute this actionless action. When one head and two feet act harmoniously, the feet do not work independently. They are one since they must work together, and neither completes an action by itself. The quality of this unity is that it leaves no space for projection, such as conscious manipulation, personality configuration, and emotional reaction. Nor does it separate the body from the mind.

Eminent action is inaction,
For that action it is active.
Inferior action never stops acting,
For that reason it is inactive.
Eminent action is disengaged,
Yet nothing is left unfulfilled;
Eminent humanness engages,
Yet nothing is left unfulfilled; . . . (38:1–2)

The *eminent action* that we are now exploring is "speaking the Tao."

Types of Speech

There are four different ways of engaging in speech.

1. Lao Tzu states that *Those who know, do not say. Those who say, do not know.* If someone truly and absolutely knows, what purpose does it serve to talk about it? Communication is, in a sense, an attempt to clarify mentally. Speech itself serves as a vehicle moving back and forth between knowing and not-knowing. The speech expresses what one already knows, explains what one

wants to know, requests what one seeks from self and others, and defends the habitual position of merely knowing.

2. Speech is a self-promise, a way to encourage oneself, engage with oneself, and build trust within the self. The twofold purpose of speech is: a) to establish a relationship and build a mutual trust; b) to cling to fixated habits and grasp firmly the attachment to body/mind. The order of business in making a promise is to ensure engagement, to commit to the process, and to bind to the result of what has been planned. The virtue of a promise must be realized as a promise to only oneself.

   A promise can be a way to deal with insecurity; it is a powerful form of ego protection and fear suppression. The more insecure one feels, the deeper the fear one encounters. A promise is also a bargain involving trust. Much of this trust involves not just words, but giving one's word. Addressing this, Lao Tzu explains that speaking with good trust is the way of the Tao (8:3).

3. Speech is an expression of the belief system of the mind, individual and collective, personal and cultural. It is a premise or a statement to which the mind adheres. It is a technique of binding and rejecting. Individual identity, group dynamics, and social construction are all based upon the effective and powerful use of speech. In this manner the individuality and personality merge with the social and cultural environment.

4. Speech is a way of revealing inner trust and confirming the capacity for trustworthy relationships between the inner self and self-concept, and between self and others. Based on this inner trust, people's statements about their "inner voice" are universally accepted and understood. This highlights the authentic meaning of speech, a tool and vehicle for trust and trustworthiness.

Right Speech

Each of the preceding types of speech can have either a positive or a negative aspect. Numerous spiritual teachings emphasize "right speech," which is often explained in negative terms—avoiding harmful speech. Harmful speech can be defined as: lies (words spoken with the intent of misrepresenting the truth); divisive speech (spoken with the intent of creating rifts between people); harsh speech (spoken with the intent of hurting another person's feelings); and idle chatter (spoken with no purposeful intent at all).

The focus is on the intent. This is where the practice of right speech intersects with self-awareness and discipline. What are the motives for your speech? As we become more aware of ourselves and more honest with ourselves, we cultivate a natural sense of when to speak and when to remain silent.

In positive terms, right speech means speaking in ways that are trustworthy, harmonious, supportive, and authentic. When you practice these positive forms of right speech, your words become a gift to others. In response, other people will start listening more to what you say, and will be more likely to respond in kind. This gives you a sense of the power of your actions: the way you act in the present moment does shape the world of your experience.

Quality of Speech

Upon accepting the limits of speech, we must then appreciate the qualities of speech. Speech can save or destroy the lives of self and others.

First, one must know oneself very well. If one has deep self-awareness and self-honesty, one's speech is authentic and original. Second, one's intention should be sincere self-expression and spontaneous response. There should be no motivation within the speech other than honest, heartfelt vibration. Third, the purpose of speech is clear and complete within the speech itself; there is no further need for clarification and supplementation.

> *[S]ince the sage wants to elevate the people, his speech is down to earth.* (66:2)

Any experienced individual understands the result of overintellectualization in speech. This is a kind of indulgence that loses the heart and intent of the communication.

> *Being overly informed leads to exhaustion,*
> *Better to be centered.* (5:3)

Each time specific information is exchanged there is energy transmission, whether mental, emotional, or mechanical. There are countless elements that shape the meaning and quality of propagation of information; it is also colored by any inner conflicts or needs of the informant. It is not an easy task to accurately pass information from one to another—neither adding nor omitting anything in the translation.

If there is no gap in the space between speaker and listener, the information is tangible and trustworthy. There is no tension in teaching and learning, and there is no blockage between supply and demand. They are One. There is no egotism or self-consciousness, and no one is counted as better or worse. There is no rigid identity of one called "teacher" and the other named "student." The teacher is rewarded by teaching and the student is informed through learning. The older generation passes down its wisdom and is left with nothing; the recipients receive everything but also have nothing. There is no attachment to being the one who knows.

Wordless Communication

In the world, the sage inhales and *smiles like a child* (49:3,4). He realizes two things. One is that *the Tao of heaven is . . . good at responding without speaking* and *appearing without being asked* (75:4); the other is that *wordless teaching and the riches of nonaction are matched by very little in the world* (43:3).

The childlike smile of the sage is the most authentic expression of love. It is profound wordless communication. This kind of smile is bright but not dazzling, innocent, humble, and vulnerable. This smile indicates quiet happiness and joy. It conveys self-control, lack of prejudice, and respect. This smile has no defensive mechanism, no fearful protection, and no intellectual wisdom.

Who could possibly turn away from that innocent and radiant smile? This is the quality of pure love, the expression of kindness, and the ultimate communication.

The sage's smile also conveys a wordless teaching. It teaches the love of light and life. It also reveals the limits of language. Anyone who is not obsessed with mental structures can experience the power of nonverbal communication, which profoundly communicates feelings and subtle sensations between heart and mind.

THE WAY OF TRUSTWORTHINESS

On the surface most people do not appear to be trustworthy and trusting. Many people seem to be anxious and fearful, and driven by anxieties, needs, and wishes. These needs and wants obscure people's ability to trust others and to be trustworthy themselves. Yet when two people come to know each other very well, they establish trust together. It takes time, effort, and a suitable environment to build a trustworthy relationship, yet people do it all the time.

The demands and requirements for establishing self-trust, however, are much greater. Normally, people are unwilling to investigate the nature of self-trust. It requires a thorough knowledge of the self and total self-honesty. Self-examination must be objective and selfless. To be trustworthy is to place trust in oneself as well as others without preference or prejudice, and to comply fully with that trust.

. . . He is trustworthy to those who are trustworthy.
He is also trustworthy to those who are not trustworthy.
It is the trust of Action itself. (49:2)

It is not necessary to trust others before trusting oneself, nor is it necessary to act for others in order to be trusted. The nature of trustworthy action is integrity and harmony of intention, word, and deed.

The Virtue of Faith

Faith is an act of total submission to Oneness and embrace of Oneness. In this submission and embrace, there is no yesterday or tomorrow. Faith accepts that which is present and trusts whatever has been revealed. Faith is happy with the conceivable and content with manageable; faith is fulfilled with whatever is achievable and well aware of the uncontrollable. Faith is essential but has no central kernel. Faith is omnipresent, sometimes observable but without a focal point. Faith clears the path to what we can be; it reveals what love is; it expresses selfless devotion. Faith is the unfolding of all that we can manifest.

Faith is visible when the heart is open. It is as close as the breath. It lies within the devoted heart and smile of love. The rational mind cannot grasp it. God instills its bravery; the self experiences the sublime blissfulness within. Space cannot hold it; time cannot trace it. Faith nourishes our spirit.

Faith generates trust, promotes loving activity, assures kind action, ensures the meaning and quality of life, and elevates the life above and beyond its cyclical journey of birth and death.

However, in the attempt to create faith within the church, we are usually left with a constructed faith, not with a genuine, direct experience. In constructing faith with words, the linguistic interpretation becomes the main attraction. When we defend faith by raising the sword, destruction and revenge are forthcoming. Gambling our faith against life is rewarded with an exhausted corpse. Visualizing faith conjures up an empty symbol. Projecting faith with rationality constructs a self-defined delusion.

The true inner experience of faith can never be a commodity nor a possession in the mind of our ego eyes. Genuine faith cannot be capitalized on in this way.

In the modern world, we have become so fixated with our quest for material gain that we fear the face of God. We selfishly and mercilessly exploit our natural world. Life is driven by ego needs, fueled by consumerism and sensationalism. Life is no longer viewed as sacred. Most people have lost faith in life itself.

When faith is weak, there is distrust.
Especially in the worth of speech.
Results speak for themselves. (17:2–3)

Faith and trust are intimately connected. When one has faith and trust, one is trustworthy. Consequently, one's actions demonstrate this trustworthiness and beckon others to a brotherhood of faith and trust.

When we look beyond the call of ego's demands, our minds become still and calm. When the minding mind is set aside, that very mind magically becomes faithful. Then we understand that God is faithful, the world is faithful, as we are faithful.

THE TREASURE OF THE TAO

Lao Tzu is very practical in his use of few words in his teaching. He declares that

My words are easy to understand and easy to apply.
Yet no one in the world can understand them and no one could apply them.
Words have their origin, and events have their leader.
Only because of prevailing ignorance am I not understood.
The few who understand me, the more precious I am.
So the sage wears shabby cloth, but holds a treasure within.

(72:1–4)

Lao Tzu treasures the Tao and wants to offer it to others. Yet he knows that it is subtle and difficult to grasp. Because of the prevailing social, cultural, and material conditions, people's minds are obscured, and his teaching is not understood. Yet Lao Tzu has utter faith in the penetrating power of the Tao.

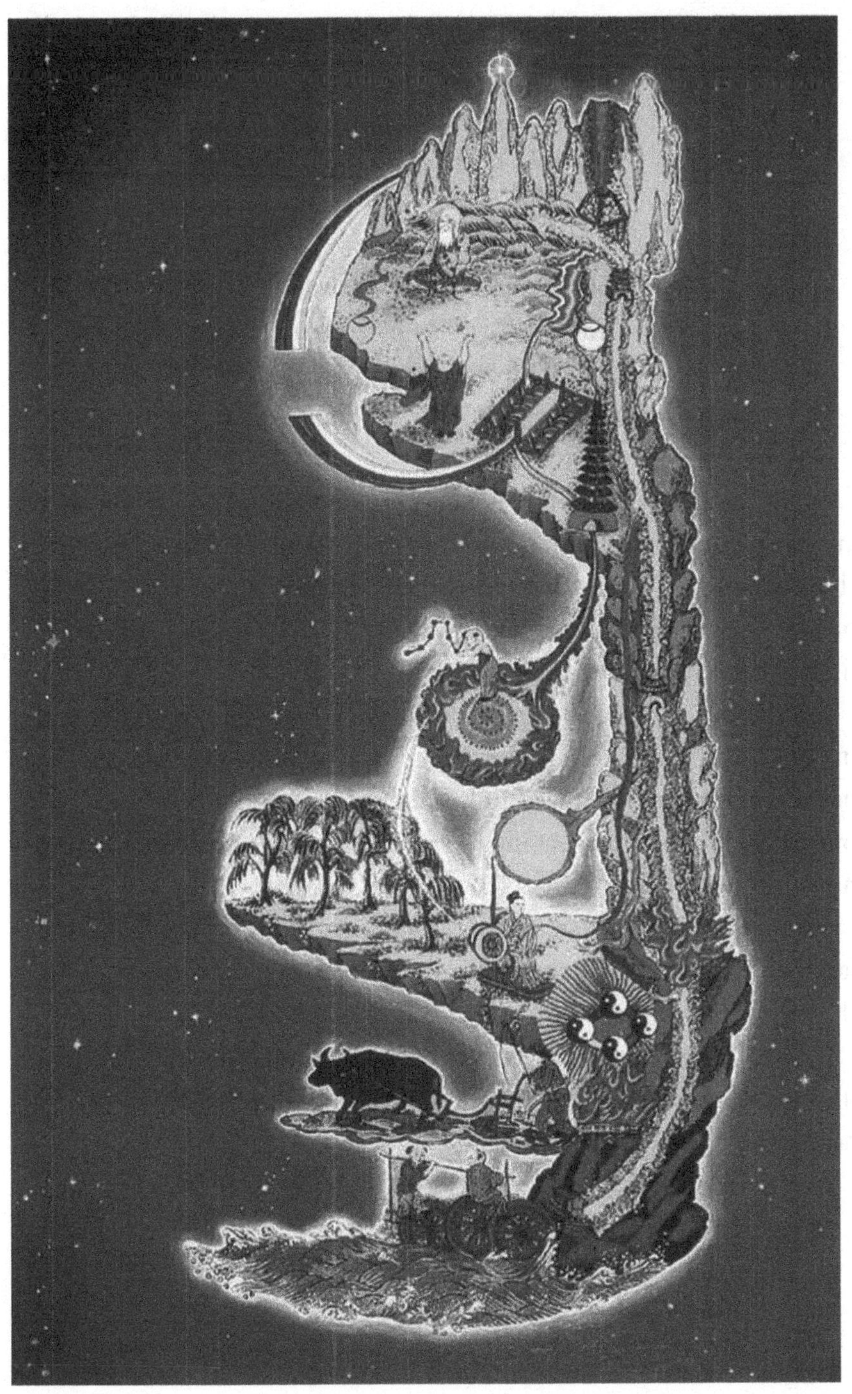

THE INNER ALCHEMY OF THE TAO

[The sage] is kind to those who are kind.
He is also kind to those who are not kind.
It is the kindness of Action itself.
He is trustworthy to those who are trustworthy.
He is also trustworthy to those who are not trustworthy.
It is the trust of Action itself.
In the world, the sage inhales.
For the world, the sage keeps the mind simple.
All people are fixated on the ears and eyes.
While the sage always smiles like a child. (49:2–4)

The sage is good to those who are good and also to those who are not good because he has faith in goodness itself. The sage trusts those who are trustworthy and also those who are not trustworthy because he has faith in trustworthiness itself. The sage has faith in life itself, in the Tao itself, in Te itself.

Those who are kind are those who have faith within, without, and in between. Faith within is the power of Tao; faith in between is the harmony between ourselves and others; faith without is living without calculation and expectation. Love needs no calculation; action needs no expectation.

Tao pervades all, Te encompasses all. Harmony is energized, and faith is suffused. This is the realization of Tao, the application of Te, the meditation of harmony, and the cultivation of faith.

The Tao is the most precious treasure. Awaken to the Tao and find something essential to do before your life is over. Recognize and hold close the treasure within.

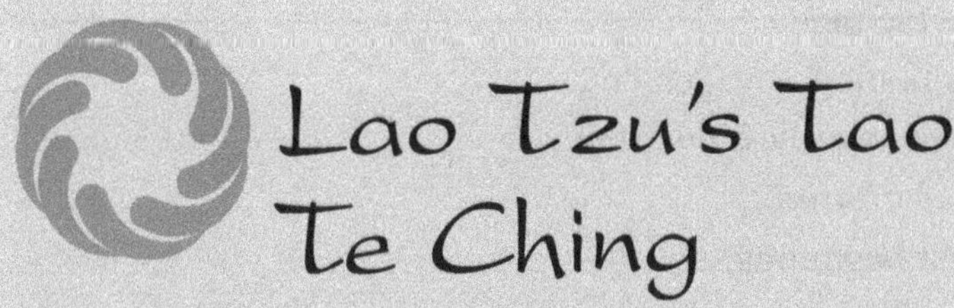

Lao Tzu's Tao Te Ching

Translated by Edward Brennan and Tao Huang

Chapter 1

1. The Tao that is voiced is no longer that of eternal Tao.
   The name that has been written is no longer that of eternal name.
2. The nameless is the beginning of the cosmic universe.
   The named is the mother of the myriad creatures.
3. Being at peace, one can see into the subtle.
   Engaging with passion, one can see into the manifest.
4. They both arise from a common source but have different names.
   Both are called the mystery within the mystery.
   They are the door to all wonders.

Chapter 2

1. In the world,
   Everyone recognizes beauty as beauty,
   Since the ugly is also there.
   Everyone recognizes goodness as goodness,
   Since evil is also there.
2. Since being and nonbeing give birth to each other,
   Difficulty and ease complete each other,
   Long and short measure each other,
   High and low overflow into each other,
   Voice and sound harmonize with each other,

And before and after follow each other,

3. Therefore the sage
   Lives in actionless engagement,
   And preaches wordless doctrine.
4. The myriad creatures
   Act without beginning,
   Nourish without possessing,
   Accomplish without claiming credit.
5. It is accomplishment without claiming credit that makes the outcome self-sustaining.

Chapter 3

1. Do not exalt intelligence and people will not compete;
   Do not value rare goods and people will not steal;
   Do not display for public view and people will not desire.
2. So the sage's governing methods are:
   Emptying the mind,
   Vitalizing the stomach,
   Softening the will,
   Strengthening the character.
3. This always makes people not know and not desire.
   This always makes the knower dare not act.
   Therefore, nothing is beyond ruling.

Chapter 4

1. Tao functions in empty harmony.
   When used, it remains full.
2. For sure, this source is the very ancestor of the myriad things.
3. Blunting the sharp edges,
   Unraveling the tangles,
   Husbanding into the light,
   Being as ordinary as the dust.
4. Ah! Limpid, it seems to exist forever.

5. I do not know whose son it is,
This who is exceeding the Heavenly Emperor.

Chapter 5

1. Nature has no benevolence,
It treats all things like strawdogs;
The sage has no benevolence,
He treats his people like strawdogs.
2. Between heaven and earth it seems like a bellows:
Empty, yet inexhaustible,
The stronger it is activated, the greater the output.
3. Being overly informed leads to exhaustion,
Better to be centered.

Chapter 6

1. Valley spirit is deathless, It is called the mystical female.
2. The gateway of the mystical female,
Is called the root of heaven and earth.
3. Hovering, it seems ever present. Put to use, it is never exhausted.

Chapter 7

1. Heaven is eternal, and earth is long lasting.
2. What makes heaven and earth eternal and long lasting is that they do not give birth to themselves.
It is this that makes them eternal and long lasting.
3. Hence the sage,
Relaxing the body, the body comes to the fore.
Beyond the body, the body comes to the fore.
Beyond the body, the body exists of itself.
4. Not even relying on selflessness
Enables the self to be fulfilled.

Chapter 8

1. Eminent goodness is like water.
2. Water is good at benefiting all things,
   Yet it actively competes.
   It retires to undesirable places.
   Thus it is near to Tao.
3. Dwelling in good places,
   Drawing from good sources,
   Supplying from good nature,
   Speaking with good trust,
   Governing with good rules,
   Conducting with good ability,
   And acting within good time.
4. For this reason,
   There is no competition,
   There is no concern.

Chapter 9

1. Hanging on to it will cause overflow; better to let go.
   Forced consent does not endure.
   Filling the house with gold and jade will not bring safety.
   Riches and royalty result in pride; they bring about their own punishment.
2. When the work is done, the body withdraws.
   This is the Tao of heaven.

Chapter 10

1. Donning the spirit and soul, and drawing them into Oneness,
   Can this come apart?
   Gathering in Qi and making the body supple,
   Is this not an infant?
   Being clear-headed and eliminating any mystic vision,
   Can even a speck exist?
   Loving the people and governing the country,

Is this not inactive?
Opening and closing the Gate of Heaven,
Is this not the female?
Comprehending the four corners of the world,
Is this not knowledge?

2. Begetting and nourishing;
Begetting but not possessing,
Enhancing but not dominating.

3. This is Mysterious Action.

Chapter 11

1. Thirty spokes join at one hub,
Yet it is the emptiness inside the hub that makes the vehicle useful;
Clay is molded into a vessel,
Yet it is the hollowness that makes the vessel useful;
Windows and doors are cut out,
Yet it is their empty space that makes the room usable.

2. So, any having makes for excess,
Any not-having makes for usefulness.

Chapter 12

1. Five colors blind the eyes.
Racing and hunting madden the heart.
Pursuing what is rare makes action deceitful.
Five flavors dull the palate.
Five tones deafen the ears.

2. So, the sage's method is for the belly, not for the eyes.
He abandons the latter and chooses the former.

Chapter 13

1. Favor and disgrace surprise the most.
Value the trouble as you do the body.

2. Why do "favor and disgrace surprise the most"?
Favor enhances only the inferior,

Receiving it is a surprise,
And losing it is also a surprise.
This is why "favor and disgrace surprise the most."

3. Why to "value the trouble as you do the body"?
It is only because I have a body that I have trouble.
If I did not have a body, where would the trouble be?
4. So, if you value the world as you do the body,
You can be entrusted with the world;
If you love the body as you love the beauty of the world,
You can be responsible for the world.

Chapter 14

1. Look for it and it can not be seen, it is called invisible;
Listen to it and it can not be heard, it is called inaudible;
Reach for it and it can not be touched, it is called intangible.
2. These three are beyond reckoning, so
When these three merge, they are One.
3. As for this One,
There is nothing above it remaining to be accounted for,
There is nothing below it that has been excluded.
Ever searching for it, it is beyond naming.
4. It returns to no-thing.
Its state is described as no state,
Its form is described as formless.
It is called the vision beyond focus.
5. Follow after it, and it proves endless.
Go before it, and no beginning can be found.
6. Employ the Tao of today in order to manage today's affairs and to know the ancient past.
7. This is called the principle of Tao.

Chapter 15

1. The ancient sages of Tao are subtle and mysteriously penetrating.
Their depth is beyond the power of will.

2. Because it is beyond the power of will,
   The most we can do is describe it:
3. Thus, full of care, as one crossing the wintry stream,
   Attentive, as one cautious of the total environment,
   Reserved, as one who is a guest,
   Spread open, as when confronting a marsh,
   Simple, like uncarved wood, opaque, like mud,
   Magnificent, like a valley.
4. From within the murky comes the stillness.
   The feminine enlivens with her milk.
5. Keeping such a Tao, excess is undesirable.
   Desiring no excess, work is completed without exhaustion.

Chapter 16

1. Reaching the ultimate emptiness,
   Concentrating on the central stillness,
   All things work together.
2. From this I observe their returning.
3. All things under heaven flourish in their vitality,
   Yet each returns to its own root.
   This is stillness.
   Stillness means returning to its destiny.
   Returning to its destiny is steadfastness.
   To know steadfastness means enlightenment.
   Not to know steadfastness is to act forcefully.
   Acting forcefully brings disaster.
   Knowing the steadfast implies acceptance.
   Acceptance is impartial.
   Impartial is regal. Regal is heaven. Heaven is Tao.
   Tao is beyond danger even when the body perishes.

Chapter 17

1. The eminent has consciousness of self.
   The next down are loved and praised.

The next down are feared,
At the bottom is the source.

2. When faith is weak, there is distrust.
   Especially in the worth of speech.
3. Results speak for themselves.
   This, people call me Nature.

Chapter 18

1. When the Great Tao is abandoned,
   There is benevolence and righteousness.
   When intelligence arises,
   There is a great deal of manipulation.
   When there is disharmony in the family,
   There comes about filial piety.
   When the country is in big trouble,
   There arises patriotism.

Chapter 19

1. Get rid of wisdom, abandon intelligence, and
   People will benefit a hundredfold.
   Get rid of benevolence, abandon justice, and
   People will return to filial piety and kindness.
   Get rid of skill, abandon profit, and
   Thieves will disappear.
2. These three are inadequate.
   So just let things be.
3. Observe the plain and embrace the simple.
   Do not think much and do not desire much,
   Get rid of learning and worry will disappear.

Chapter 20

1. How much difference is there between yea and nay?
   How much difference is there between beautiful and ugly?
2. What one fears is what he cannot help but fear.

3. One is in the wilderness without central ground.
4. Ordinary people are fulfilled,
Eating delicious food,
Reaching the climax of romance.
I am desireless and without anticipation,
Like a baby who does not yet.
Gathering energy together, entering the abyss beyond the point of no return.
5. Ordinary people have more than enough,
I am a fool at heart, as a water droplet is to the spring.
6. People of affairs are bright and intelligent.
I alone am unintelligent.
People of affairs are cunning and clever.
I alone am dull and unsophisticated,
Unnoticed in the depth of the sea,
Looked for in an endless horizon.
7. Ordinary people are productive,
I alone maintain the living essence within.
I alone stay with a unitary source, as if stubborn.
8. I want to be wholly different from everyone else,
By taking my sustenance from the mother source.

Chapter 21

1. The marks of profound action follow only from the Tao.
2. The substance of Tao is boundless and unfathomable.
Unfathomable and boundless,
In its center there is form;
Boundless and unfathomable,
In its center there is an object;
Embryonic and dark,
In its center there is essence;
The essence is very pure,
In its center there is trust.
From now to the days of old,

Its name never dies,
Because it creates all things in their beginning.
3. How do I know the source of all beginnings?
From this.

Chapter 22

1. Those who boast of themselves lose their stance.
He who displays himself is not seen.
He who justifies himself is not understood.
He who lashes out does not succeed.
He who builds himself up does not endure.
2. In the sense of Tao,
This is said to be eating too much and acting too much.
It results in disgust.
3. Those who desire will not endure.

Chapter 23

1. Yield, and retain integrity.
In the depths of whirling, there is stillness.
The hollow enables the plentiful.
The old gives way to the new.
The small allows for increase.
Excess breeds confusion.
2. Therefore the sage holds oneness as the shepherd of the world.
3. He who does not display himself is seen.
He who does not justify himself is understood.
He who does not lash out succeeds.
He who does not build himself up endures.
4. Therefore,
Only the spirit of noncompetition makes things noncompetitive.
5. So the old saying, "yield, and retain integrity," is but a few words.
But when rightly understood, integrity returns.

Chapter 24

1. Natural speech consists of few words.
2. Gusty winds do not last all morning,
   Cloudbursts do not last all day.
   What makes this so?
3. Heaven and earth will not last forever,
   How could a human being last!
4. So the person who works according to Tao unites with Tao.
   In the same way he unites with action.
   In the same way he unites with loss.
5. Uniting with action, the Tao becomes action.
   Uniting with loss, the Tao becomes loss.

Chapter 25

1. Matter is formed from chaos.
   It was born before heaven and earth.
   Silent and void.
   Standing alone, without territory,
   Able to be mother to the world.
2. I do not yet know its name,
   I call it Tao.
   With reluctance I deem it to be Great.
   Great refers to the symbol.
   The symbol refers to what is remote.
   What is remote refers to returning.
3. Tao is great.
   Heaven is great.
   Earth is great.
   Kingship is great.
   These are the four great things in the world,
   Kingship is one of them.

4. Humankind takes its origin from earth.
   Earth takes her origin from heaven.
   Heaven takes its origin from Tao.
   Tao takes its origin from Nature.

Chapter 26

1. The heavy is the root of the light.
   Tranquility is the master of the restless.
2. Thus, the noble person will travel all day without leaving his seat.
   Though the center of the highest authority,
   And surrounded by luxury,
   He remains clear-minded.
3. How could the king of myriad chariots treat his body with less care than he gives the country?
4. Being careless loses the foundation.
   Being restless loses mastery.

Chapter 27

1. A good traveler leaves no tracks.
   A good speaker is without flaw.
   A good planner does not calculate.
   A good doorkeeper does not lock, yet it cannot be opened.
   A good knotter does not use binding, yet it cannot be undone.
2. Therefore, the sage is good at his earnest demands upon people.
   So no one is left out.
   No talent is wasted.
   This is called being in the tow of enlightenment,
   And it ensures the good person.
3. For everything that is good is the teacher of the good person.
   Everything that is bad becomes a resource for the good person.
   No need to honor the teachers.
   No need to love the resources.
4. Though knowing this is a great paradox,
   It is the subtle principle.

Chapter 28

1. Understanding the male and holding onto the female
   Enables the flow of the world.
   This being the flow of the world, the eternal action abides.
   Knowing that the eternal action abides is to return to childhood.
2. Understanding the pure and holding on to the impure
   Enables the cleansing of the world.
   With the cleansing of the world, ongoing action suffices.
   When ongoing action suffices, it returns to simplicity.
3. Understanding the white and holding on to the black
   Enables the formation of the world.
   Being the formation of the world, ongoing action does not stray.
   When ongoing action does not stray, it returns to the infinite.
4. This simplicity takes shape as a mechanism.
   The sage makes it the head ruler.
   Great ruling never divides.

Chapter 29

1. I see that those who want to take over the world and manipulate it do not succeed.
2. The sacred mechanism of the world cannot be manipulated.
   Those who manipulate it will fail,
   Those who hold on to it will lose it.
3. Matter
   Either leads or follows,
   Either heats or chills,
   Either strengthens or weakens,
   Either enhances or destroys.
4. So the sage abandons extremes, extravagance, multiplicity.

Chapter 30

1. Using the Tao as the rule for governing the people,
   Do not employ the army as the power of the world.
   For this is likely to backfire.

2. Where the army has marched, thorns and briars grow.
3. Being good has its own consequence,
   Which cannot be seized by power.
4. Achieving without arrogance,
   Achieving without bragging,
   Achieving without damage,
   Achieving without taking ownership.
   This is called achieving without force.
5. Matter becomes strong, then old.
   This is called "Not-Tao."
   Dying young is "Not-Tao."

Chapter 31

1. The army is the mechanism of bad luck.
   The elements of the world may oppose.
   So those who have ambitions cannot rest.
2. Therefore the nobleman takes his place on the left side,
   And the commander on the right side.
3. So the army is not the nobleman's weapon.
   As a mechanism of bad luck,
   He uses it only as the last resort.
   Then the best way is to use it quickly and destructively.
   Do not enjoy this.
   To take delight in it is to enjoy killing people.
   Those who enjoy killing people do not attract the favor of the world.
4. The good inclines to the left,
   The bad inclines to the right.
5. Thus the intelligent officer stays on the left,
   The army commander stays on the right.
6. Speaking in an image of sadness,
   After killing the people, every one stands in mourning.
   Victory is celebrated as a funeral service.

Chapter 32

1. Tao is eternally nameless.
2. Though simplicity is small,
   The world cannot treat it as subservient.
   If lords and rulers can hold on to it,
   Everything becomes self-sufficient.
3. Heaven and earth combine and allow sweet dew.
   Without rules, people will naturally become equal.
4. At the outset, the rule must be expressed.
   Once it exists, stop speaking of it.
   The result of not speaking of it is to eliminate danger.
5. In a manner of speaking, Tao is to the world
   As the rivers are to oceans and seas.

Chapter 33

1. To know others is to be knowledgeable,
   To know oneself is enlightenment;
   To master others is to have strength,
   To master oneself is to be powerful.
2. To know what is sufficient is to be rich.
   To act with determination is to have will.
   Not to lose one's substance is to endure.
   To die, but not be forgotten, is to be immortal.

Chapter 34

1. As the Tao is all-pervading,
   It operates on both the left and the right.
2. Success is consequent to all affairs.
   It does not proclaim its own existence.
   All things return.
   Yet there is no claim of ownership,
   So it is forever desireless.
   This can be called small.
   All things return.

Yet there is no claim of ownership,
This can be called great.
3. The sage accomplishes greatness in not acting great.
Thus can he accomplished what is great.

Chapter 35

1. Holding on to the great Symbol,
The whole world carries on.
On and on without doing harm.
2. Being happy at peace,
Enjoying greatly the music and food.
Travelers stop by.
3. When the Tao is spoken forth plainly
It has no flavor at all.
4. Look, but that is not sufficient for seeing.
Listen, but that is not sufficient for hearing.
Use it, but it is not exhausted.

Chapter 36

1. When you want to constrict something,
You must first let it expand;
When you want to weaken something,
You must first enable it;
When you want to eliminate something,
You must first allow it;
When you want to conquer something,
You must first let it be.
This is called the Fine Light.
2. The weak overcomes the strong.
Fish cannot live away from the source.
The sharp weapon of the nation should never be displayed.

Chapter 37

1. Tao is eternally nameless.

If lords and rulers would abide by it,
All things would evolve of themselves.

2. What evolves desires to act.
I, then, suffuse this with nameless simplicity.
Suffusing with nameless simplicity is eliminating humiliation.
Without humiliation, peace arises.
Heaven and earth regulate themselves.

Chapter 38

1. Eminent action is inaction,
For that action it is active.
Inferior action never stops acting,
For that reason it is inactive.

2. Eminent action is disengaged,
Yet nothing is left unfulfilled;
Eminent humanness engages,
Yet nothing is left unfulfilled;
When eminent righteousness engages,
It reduces the results of engagements;
Eminent justice engages, but does not respond adequately to situations.
For that reason it is frustrated.

3. When Tao is lost,
It becomes Action;
When Action is lost,
It becomes benevolence;
When benevolence is lost,
It becomes justice.
When justice is lost,
It becomes propriety.

4. Propriety is the veneer of faith and loyalty,
And the forefront of troubles.

5. Foresight is the vain display of Tao,
And the forefront of foolishness.

6. Therefore, the man of substance
   Dwells in wholeness rather than veneer,
   Dwells in the essence rather than the vain display.
7. He rejects the latter, and accepts the former.

Chapter 39

1. Those from the past have attained Oneness.
2. By attaining Oneness, heaven is clear.
   By attaining Oneness, earth is at peace.
   By attaining Oneness, the spirit is quickened.
   By attaining Oneness, the valley is filled.
   By attaining Oneness, the king puts order in the whole world.
   All these result from Oneness.
3. Without its clarity, heaven is liable to explode.
   Without its peace, earth is liable to erupt.
   Without its quickening, the spirit is liable to die out.
   Without its fullness, valleys are liable to dry out.
   Without proper esteem, the king is liable to fall.
4. Esteem is rooted in the humble.
   The high is founded upon the low.
5. This is why the lords and rulers call themselves widows and orphans without support.
   Is this is not the root of being humble?
6. Much praise amounts to no praise.
7. Without preference, Being is as resonant as Jade and as gravelly as stone.

Chapter 40

1. When eminent persons hear of Tao,
   They practice it faithfully;
   When average persons hear of Tao,
   It seems that they practice it, and it seems they do not;
   When inferior persons hear of Tao,
   They ridicule it.

2. Without such ridicule, it would not be Tao.
3. Thus, the aphorism that suggests the way is:
   Knowing the Tao seems costly.
   Entering Tao seems like retreating.
   Becoming equal with Tao gives birth to paradoxes.
   Eminent action is like a valley.
   Complete understanding resembles being disgraced.
   Vast action seems yielding.
   Action that builds up seems remiss.
   Pure integrity seems perverse.
   The great square has no angles.
   The great talent matures late.
   The great voice sounds faint.
   The great image has no form.
   The Tao is praised but is unnameable.
4. Only Tao is good at beginning and good at completion.

Chapter 41

1. Tao moves by returning.
   Tao functions by weakness.
2. All things under heaven are born of being.
   Being is born of nonbeing.

Chapter 42

1. Tao gives rise to one.
   One gives rise to two.
   Two gives rise to three.
   Three gives rise to all things.
2. All things carry yin and embrace yang.
   Drawing Chi together into harmony.
3. What the world hates is the widow and orphan without support.
   But lords and rulers name themselves these.
4. Do not seek gain from losing, nor loss from gaining.
5. What people teach, after discussion becomes doctrine.

6. Those who excel in strength do not prevail over death.
   I would use this as the father of teaching.

Chapter 43

1. What is softest in the world penetrates what is hardest in the world.
   Nonbeing enters where there is no room.
2. From this I know the riches of nonaction.
3. Wordless teaching and the riches of nonaction is matched by very little in the world.

Chapter 44

1. Which is more cherished, the name or the body?
   Which is worth more, the body or possessions?
   Which is more beneficial, to gain or to lose?
2. Extreme fondness is necessarily very costly.
   The more you cling to, the more you lose.
3. So knowing what is sufficient averts disgrace.
   Knowing when to stop averts danger.
   This can lead to a longer life.

Chapter 45

1. Grand perfection seems lacking, yet its use is never exhausted.
   Grand fullness seems empty, yet its use never comes to an end.
   Grand straightforwardness seems bent.
   Grand skill seems clumsy.
   Grand surplus seems deficient.
2. Activity overcomes cold.
   Stillness overcomes heat.
   Peace and tranquility can be the measure of the world.

Chapter 46

1. When there is Tao in the world, work horses are used to fertilize the land.

Without Tao in the world, the war horse flourishes in the countryside.

2. There is no crime greater than fostering desire.
   There is no disaster greater than not knowing when there is enough.
   There is no fault greater than wanting to possess.
3. Knowing that sufficiency is enough always suffices.

Chapter 47

1. In order to know the world, do not step outside the door.
   In order to know the Tao of heaven, do not peer through the window.
2. The further out you go, the less you know.
3. So the sage knows without moving, identifies without seeing, accomplishes without acting.

Chapter 48

1. Having a zest for learning yields an increase day by day.
   Hearing the Tao brings a loss day by day.
   Losing more and more until inaction results.
   Inaction results, yet everything is done.
2. Managing the world always involves nonengagement.
   As soon as there is engagement, there is never enough of it to manage the world.

Chapter 49

1. The sage is always without his own mind.
   He uses people's minds as his mind.
2. He is kind to those who are kind.
   He is also kind to those who are not kind.
   It is the kindness of Action itself.
   He is trustworthy to those who are trustworthy.
   He is also trustworthy to those who are not trustworthy.
   It is the trust of Action itself.

3. In the world, the sage inhales.
   For the world, the sage keeps the mind simple.
4. All people are fixated on the ears and eyes.
   While the sage always smiles like a child.

Chapter 50

1. We live, we die.
2. The companions of life are three and ten.
   The companions of death are three and ten.
   That people live their active life necessarily leading to the ground of death is three and ten.
3. Why so? It is the nature of life itself.
4. As a matter of fact, I hear of those who are good at preserving their lives;
   Walking through, not avoiding rhinos and tigers.
   Entering battle without wearing armaments.
   The rhino has no place to dig its horns.
   The tiger has no place to drag its claws.
   The soldier has no place to thrust his blade.
5. Why is this so?
   Because they have no place to die.

Chapter 51

1. Tao enlivens.
   Action nourishes.
   Matter forms.
   Mechanism completes.
   For that reason, all things worship Tao and exalt Action.
2. The worship of Tao and exaltation of Action are not conferred, but always arise naturally.
3. Tao enlivens and nourishes, develops and cultivates, integrates and completes, raises and sustains.
4. It enlivens without possessing.
   It acts without relying.

It develops without controlling.
5. Such is called mystic Action.

Chapter 52

1. The world begins with the mother as its source.
2. When you have the mother, you know the son.
   When you know the son, return to preserve the mother.
   Although the body dies, there is no harm.
3. By closing your mouth and shutting the door, there would be no wearing down of life.
   When opening the mouth and pursuing your affairs, life cannot be preserved.
4. Seeing what is small is discernment.
   Preserving subtleness is strength.
   Using the light enables one to return to discernment.
5. Without losing the center of the body is called penetrating the eternal.

Chapter 53

1. Through discrimination, I have the knowledge to walk in the great Tao.
   The only fear is what is other than that.
2. The great Tao is quite smooth, yet people prefer a short-cut.
   The court is so busy legislating that the fields go uncultivated and granaries are all empty.
   They wear the magnificent clothing, girdle the sharp swords.
   They are gorged with food and possess many brides.
   Their bounty suffices but they continue to steal.
3. This is opposite of Tao.

Chapter 54

1. What is well-built is not pulled down.
   What is well-fastened is not separated.
   Sons and grandsons worship unceasingly.

2. Cultivate the self, and the Action is pure.
   Cultivate the family, the Action is plentiful.
   Cultivate the community, the Action endures.
   Cultivate the nation, the Action is fruitful.
   Cultivate the world, the Action is all-pervading.
3. Treat the self by the standard of self.
   Treat the family by the standard of family.
   Treat the community by the standard of community.
   Treat the nation by the standard of nation.
   Treat the world by the standard of world.
4. How do I know how the world is such?
   Thus.

Chapter 55

1. Action in its profundity is like a newborn baby.
   Poisonous insects and venomous snakes do not sting it.
   Predatory birds and ferocious animals do not seize it.
2. Its bones are soft and its sinews supple, yet its grasp is firm;
   Without knowing the union of male and female, its organs become aroused.
   Its vital essence comes to the point;
   Crying all day, its voice never becomes hoarse.
   Its harmony comes to the point.
3. Harmony is eternal.
   Knowing harmony is discernment.
   Enhancing life is equanimity.
   Generating vitality through mind is strength.
4. When things reach their climax, they are suddenly old.
5. This is "Non-Tao."
   "Non-Tao" dies young.

Chapter 56

1. Those who know, do not say.
   Those who say, do not know.
2. Close the mouth.
   Shut the door.
   Merge into light.
   As ordinary as dust.
   Blunt the sharpness.
   Unravel the entanglements.
3. This is called mysterious sameness.
4. You are not intimate by acquiring it.
   You are not distant in not acquiring it;
   You do not profit by acquiring it.
   You do not lose it by not acquiring it;
   You are not ennobled by acquiring it.
   You are not disgraced by not acquiring it.
5. This enables the nobility of the world.

Chapter 57

1. Using the right lawfulness to govern the country.
   Using unexpectancy to conduct the battle.
   Using disengagement to take over the world.
2. How do I know this is so?
   Thus.
3. The more prohibitions there are in the world, the poorer people will be.
   The more destructive weapons people have, the more chaotic the nation will become.
   The more know-how people have, the more bizarre things will appear.
   The more rules and demands that flourish, the more thefts there will be.

4. Therefore the sage says:
   When I am inactive, people transform themselves.
   When I abide in stillness, people organize themselves lawfully.
   When I am disengaged, people enrich themselves.
   When I choose nondesire, people remain simple.

Chapter 58

1. When the government is silent, people are sincere.
   When the government is intrusive, the state is decisive.
2. Disaster is what fortune depends upon,
   Fortune is what disaster subdues.
   Who knows a final outcome?
3. There is no right lawfulness.
   Justice tends towards the extreme.
   Kindness tends towards evil.
   People have been familiar with this for a long time.
4. So,
   Be rounded without cutting.
   Be compatible without puncturing.
   Be straightforward without trapping.
   Be bright without dazzling.

Chapter 59

1. For governing people and serving the heaven, nothing is better than frugality.
2. Only frugality enables the pre-empty measures.
   Pre-empty measures mean a great accumulation of Action.
   A great accumulation of Action leaves nothing to be conquered.
   When nothing needs to be conquered, No-boundary is known.
   When no-boundary is known, it allows the country to exist.
   The country, existing from its source, can endure.
3. This is the Tao of having a deep root, a strong stem, a long life, and an enduring vision.

Chapter 60

1. Governing a large country is like cooking a small fish.
2. If Tao is utilized to manage the society, its ghost will not become spirit.
   Not that ghost is not spiritual, but that the spirit harms no people;
   Not only does the spirit harm not the people, but that the sage is harmless.
3. As those two cause no harm, they are united in Action.

Chapter 61

1. A great nation flows downwardly; it is the mother of the world and the integration of the world.
2. The mother is always tranquil and overcomes the male by her tranquility; so she benefits the world.
3. A great nation relies on a low position to take over a small nation.
   A small nation, being in a low position, is taken over by a great nation.
4. So being lower allows taking over or being taken over.
5. Being a great nation only desires to unify the people.
   Being a small nation only seeks people's business.
6. They both get what they want, but the greater is being lower.

Chapter 62

1. Tao is the conductor of all things.
   The treasure of the good.
   The protector of the bad.
2. Beautiful words can advertise well.
   Noble conduct brings praise to people.
3. As for those who conduct the bad, why reject them for it?
4. Therefore, after the crowning of the emperor comes the appointing of three administrations.
   Being presented with jade in front of the team of four horses is not better than sitting and entering thus.
5. The reason why this is valued of old is,

It allows having without asking, and it allows forgiveness of wrong.
Thus, it is most valuable to the world.

Chapter 63

1. Do nondoing.
   Engage in non-affairs. Savor non-flavor.
2. Large or small, many or few, reward or punishment, are all being done through Action.
3. Seek what is difficult with ease.
   Effect what is great while it is small.
4. The most difficult things in the world are done while they are easy.
   The greatest things in the world are done while they are small.
5. The sage never plans to do a great thing.
   Thus, he accomplishes what is great.
6. Facile promises necessarily result in little trust.
   What is easy necessarily entails difficulty.
7. Thus the sage, through extreme trials, encounters no difficulty.

Chapter 64

1. It is easy to sustain what is at rest.
   It is easy to plan for that of which there is not even a sign.
   What is fragile is easily broken.
   What is minute is easily dispersed.
2. Act upon it before it exists.
   Regulate it before it becomes chaos.
3. A massive tree grows from a little sprout.
   A nine-story-building rises from a clod of earth.
   A thousand fathoms begin with a single step.
4. Those who impose action upon it will fail.
   Those who cling to it lose it.
5. So the sage, through nonaction, does not fail.
   Not clinging, he does not lose.
6. The common people's engagement in affairs fails prior to success.
7. So the saying goes, "Give as much careful attention to the end as

to the beginning; then the affairs will not fail."

8. It is on that account that the sage desires not to desire and does not value goods that are hard to get.
   He learns not to learn and restores the common people's losses.
   He is able to support the nature of all things and, not by daring, to impose action.

Chapter 65

1. Those who practiced Tao in olden times did not enlighten people, Rather they made them simple.
2. What makes it the hardest to govern the people is what they already know.
   It becomes most difficult to govern people because of their knowledge.
3. So, using knowledge to govern the country, knowledge itself becomes the thief of the country.
   Not using knowledge to govern the country, knowledge itself is the Action of the country.
4. Always realize that these two are the model for ruling.
   Always be aware that this model is the mystic Action.
5. Mystic Action is deep and far-reaching.
   It is the opposite of matter.
   Only thus does it approach the Great Harmony.

Chapter 66

1. The reason why rivers and seas have the capacity for kingship over all the valleys is that they excel in lowliness.
   That is why they have the capacity for kingship over all valleys.
2. Thus, since the sage wants to elevate the people, his speech is down to earth.
   Since the sage wants to advance the people, he positions himself at the back,
3. So that when he is at the front, people do not harm him.
   When he stands above, people do not feel pressure.

The whole world supports him untiringly.

4. Since he does not rely on competition, the world has nothing with which to compete.

Chapter 67

1. A small country has few people.
2. Weapons are far more numerous than the people, but they are not used.
   Let people be serious about death and enjoy a long journey.
   Though there are carriages and boats, they are not useful for travel.
   Let people return to:
   Use the technique of knotting the rope,
   Enjoying the food,
   Appreciating the cloth,
   Delighting in customs,
   Settling into their living conditions.
3. The neighboring countries are in sight.
   The sounds of dogs and chickens are heard.
   People grow old and die without interference from each other.

Chapter 68

1. Trustworthy words are not beautiful.
   Beautiful words are not trustworthy.
   The knower does not know everything.
   The know-it-all knows nothing.
   Kindness is not overindulgent.
   Overindulgence is not kind.
2. The sage does not collect.
   As soon as he exists for others, he has more.
   As soon as he gives to others, he has more.
3. So the Tao of heaven benefits and does not harm.
   The Tao of humankind exists and does not compete.

Chapter 69

1. Everyone in the world says I am great, great without parallel.
   Being without parallel is what enables greatness.
   If there is a long-standing parallel, it becomes small.
2. I always have three treasures:
   First is compassion.
   Second is frugality.
   Third is to not dare act in front of the world.
3. So compassion enables courage.
   Frugality enables abundance.
   Not daring to act in front of the world enables the mechanism to endure.
4. Today there is courage without compassion.
   There is abundance without frugality.
   There is appearance alone without substance.
   This means no-life.
5. Through compassion: fight and win; defend and be secure.
6. When the heaven establishes itself, it always relies upon compassion.

Chapter 70

1. Being a good warrior does not entail power.
   A good fighter is not angry.
   One who is good at overcoming the enemy does not contact him.
   One who is good at leading people acts humbly.
2. This is called the Action of noncompetition.
   This is called leading people.
   This is called the Ultimate as old as heaven.

Chapter 71

1. There is a saying on using military force:
   I dare not be the host, but rather a guest.
   I dare not advance an inch, but rather retreat a foot.

2. This is called performing without performing, rolling up one's sleeves without showing the arms.
   By not holding on to an enemy, there is no enemy.
3. There is no disaster greater than having no enemy.
   Having no enemy almost destroys my treasure.
4. When opposing armies clash, those who cry win!

Chapter 72

1. My words are easy to understand and easy to apply.
   Yet no one in the world can understand them and no one could apply them.
2. Words have their origin, and events have their leader.
3. Only because of prevailing ignorance am I not understood.
   The fewer who understand me, the more precious I am.
4. So the sage wears shabby cloth, but holds a treasure within.

Chapter 73

1. Knowing that you don't know (everything) is superior.
   Not knowing that you don't know (everything) is a sickness.
2. So the sage's being without sickness is that he knows sickness as sickness;
   Thus, he is without sickness.

Chapter 74

1. People are fearless before the power.
   If fear arises, it will be a great fear.
2. Not constraining the living environment.
   They do not get bored by life.
   Because we do not get bored, there is no boredom.
3. Therefore the sage is self-aware but not introspective.
   He has self-respect but does not price himself.
4. He rejects one and takes the other.

Chapter 75

1. Courage combined with daring promotes killing.
   Courage not combined with daring promotes life.
2. These two can be either beneficial or harmful.
3. Who knows the reason for what heaven hates?
4. The Tao of heaven is
   Good at winning without fighting,
   Good at responding without speaking,
   Appearing without being asked,
   Good at strategizing while fighting.
5. The net of heaven is broad and loose,
   Yet nothing slips through.

Chapter 76

1.` Whenever people are unafraid of death, how can killing be used as a threat?
   Whenever people are afraid of death and are acting contrary, I will catch and kill them; who else can act so?
   When people are absolutely afraid of death but perform killing, they are the best qualified to be executioners.
2. This is like doing carving for a master craftsman.
   Doing the carving for a master craftsman, how could one's hand not get cut?

Chapter 77

1. The reason people are starving is because the government taxes too much. This is the reason for starvation.
   The reason people are hard to govern is because their leaders are actively engaged. This is why they are hard to govern.
   The reason people are not serious about death is because they seek the burdens of life. This is why they are not serious about death.
2. Only those who are not slaves to life are wise to the value of life.

Chapter 78

1. When people are born, they are soft and gentle.
   When they die, they are stiff and callous.
2. When myriad things, grasses and trees, are born, they are soft and tender.
   When they die, they are withered.
3. So stiffness and callousness are the company of death.
   Softness and suppleness are the company of life.
4. The powerful army will not win.
   A stiff tree will break.
5. So stiffness and power stay below.
   Softness and suppleness stay above.

Chapter 79

1. The Tao of heaven is like drawing a bow.
   The high bends down,
   The low rises up.
   The surplus decreases.
   Insufficiency is supplied.
2. So the Tao of heaven reduces what is surplus and enhances what is insufficient.
   The human Tao reduces what is insufficient and caters to the surplus.
3. Who can use the surplus to benefit the heaven?
   Only those who possess Tao.
4. So the sage
   Exists without ownership,
   Accomplishes without holding on.
   It is thus, without desire, that the wise see.

Chapter 80

1. Nothing in the world is softer and more supple than water.
   When confronting strength and hardness nothing can overcome it.
2. Using nothing simplifies.

Using water overcomes hardness.
Using weakness overcomes strength.
There is no one in the world who does not know it, but no one can apply it.

3. So it is a saying of sages that:
Whoever can bear the disgrace of the country is the ruler of the country.
Whoever can bear the misfortune of the world is the ruler of the world.
4. Truthful speech seems paradoxical.

Chapter 81

1. Reconciling a great hatred necessarily entails unsolved hatred.
How can this be kindful?
2. So the sage honors the left-hand tally but does not blame people.
3. Before the kind Action, hold onto the tally.
Before the kindless Action, hold onto the openness.
4. The Tao of heaven is impersonal.
It enhances those who are kind.

Bibliography

Capra, Fritjof. *The Tao of Physics*, 2nd ed. Boston: Shambhala Publications, 1985.

Griffiths, Anthony J. F., et al. *Modern Genetic Analysis.* New York: W. H. Freeman and Co., 1999.

Jung, C. J. *Memories, Dreams, Reflections.* New York: Vintage Books, 1989.

Legge, James. *I Ching, Book of Changes.* New York: Gramercy Books, 1996.

Ni, Hua-Ching. *Esoteric Tao Teh Ching.* Santa Monica, Cal.: Seven Star Communications Group, 1992.

Olson, Stuart Alve. *The Jade Emperor's Mind Seal Classic.* St. Paul: Dragon Door Publications, 1993.

Schonberger, Martin. *The I Ching and the Genetic Code: The Hidden Key to Life*, 2nd ed. Santa Fe: Aurora Press, 1992.

Yan, Johnson F. *DNA and the I Ching: The Tao of Life.* Berkeley, Cal: North Atlantic Books, 1991.

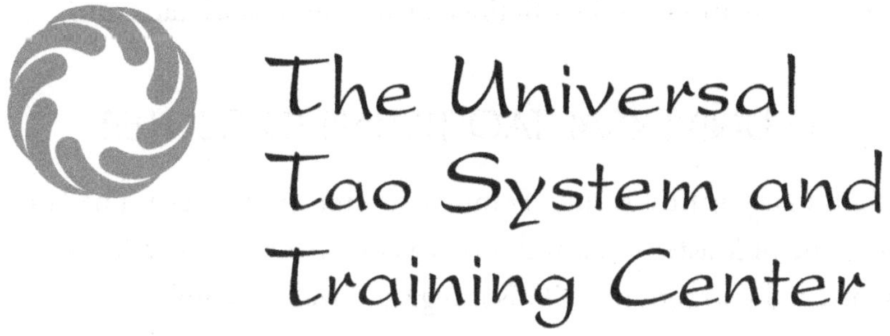

The Universal Tao System and Training Center

THE UNIVERSAL TAO SYSTEM

The ultimate goal of Taoist practice is to transcend physical boundaries through the development of the soul and the spirit within the human. That is also the guiding principle behind the Universal Tao, a practical system of self-development that enables individuals to complete the harmonious evolution of their physical, mental, and spiritual bodies. Through a series of ancient Chinese meditative and internal energy exercises, the practitioner learns to increase physical energy, release tension, improve health, practice self-defense, and gain the ability to heal oneself and others. In the process of creating a solid foundation of health and well-being in the physical body, the practitioner also creates the basis for developing his or her spiritual potential by learning to tap into the natural energies of the sun, moon, earth, stars, and other environmental forces.

The Universal Tao practices are derived from ancient techniques rooted in the processes of nature. They have been gathered and integrated into a coherent, accessible system for well-being that works directly with the life force, or Chi, that flows through the meridian system of the body.

Master Chia has spent years developing and perfecting techniques for teaching these traditional practices to students around the world through ongoing classes, workshops, private instruction, and healing sessions, as well as books and video and audio products. Further information can be obtained at www.universal-tao.com.

THE UNIVERSAL TAO TRAINING CENTER

The Tao Garden Resort and Training Center in northern Thailand is the home of Master Chia and serves as the worldwide headquarters for Universal Tao activities. This integrated wellness, holistic health, and training center is situated on eighty acres surrounded by the beautiful Himalayan foothills near the historic walled city of Chiang Mai. The serene setting includes flower and herb gardens ideal for meditation, open-air pavilions for practicing Chi Kung, and a health and fitness spa.

The Center offers classes year-round, as well as summer and winter retreats. It can accommodate two hundred students, and group leasing can be arranged.

For information worldwide on courses, books, products, and other resources, contact:

Universal Healing Tao Center
274 Moo 7, Laung Nua, Doi Saket, Chiang Mai, 50220, Thailand
Tel: (66)(53) 921-200
Email: universaltao@universal-tao.com
Website:www.universal-tao.com

For information on retreats and Health Spa, contact:

Tao Garden Health Spa & Resort
Email: reservations@tao-garden.com
Website: www.tao-garden.com

Good Chi • Good Heart • Good Intention

Index

Index of Tao Te Ching Chapters